Headscarf

The Day Turkey Stood Still

Richard Peres

Headscarf
The Day Turkey Stood Still

Published by
Garnet Publishing Limited
8 Southern Court
South Street
Reading
RG1 4QS
UK

www.garnetpublishing.co.uk
www.twitter.com/Garnetpub
www.facebook.com/Garnetpub
blog.garnetpublishing.co.uk

This book was formerly published as *The Day Turkey Stood Still* by Ithaca Press

First Paperback Edition 2013

ISBN: 9781859643181

British Library Cataloguing-in-Publication Data
A catalogue record for this book is available from the British Library

Jacket design by Garnet Publishing
Typeset by JM InfoTech INDIA
Cover photo provided courtesy of the Kavakci family

Printed and bound in Lebanon by International Press:
interpress@int-press.com

TO UMIT CIZRE
For your mind
And your love

My gratitude
Will always be
As constant as
The Marmara Sea

Contents

Preface

Our meeting was pure happenstance, a serendipitous alignment of stars.

Umit Cizre, my wife and well-known Turkish political scientist, returned home after her first day at the Woodrow Wilson Center for International Scholars in Washington (USA) and told me that her assistant, Fatima, was the daughter of a well-known person in Turkey, a woman who had entered Parliament after her election wearing a headscarf. 'We all watched her on television,' she said. 'The whole country was riveted. It was incredible. And the country has never recovered from it.'

Fatima's mother is Merve Kavakci.

I searched for her name in YouTube and found ninety videos of a headscarved woman walking into the Turkish Parliament to non-stop jeers and clamouring. At one point a moustached man appeared and shouted his speech with a scowl on his face. It was a chaotic and perplexing scene. I found out that Merve Kavakci had been elected to the Turkish Parliament but was prevented from taking her oath of office that day and subsequently forced to leave Turkey.

I thought that what happened was strange in a country where practically the whole population considered themselves to be Muslim; it would be difficult to sleep anywhere in Turkey without hearing a local mosque broadcast the call to prayer five times a day. Like most Americans, at the time, I was not well informed about Islam having only generalized views in the post-9/11 world of terrorist attacks and threats that have dominated the media and the way Americans view the world.

We found out that Merve Kavakci was teaching Political Science courses at George Washington University. After leaving Turkey she earned a master's degree from Harvard and her PhD from Howard University.

My curiosity about her grew. Who was this woman who seemed to cause so much havoc in Turkey? Weeks later Merve invited us, through her daughter, to meet for dinner in Georgetown.

As we approached the restaurant, I saw two smiling women in headscarves wave to us from inside. By the time we walked in, they were standing at the entrance to greet us, courteous and polite in the extreme. Merve Kavakci was wearing a funky big red plastic watch that I immediately noticed, and stylish jeans. Their bright eyes seemed to flash in the darkened restaurant. They greeted us with what I would discover is typically friendly Turkish hospitality.

Although they would be breaking the month-long fast of Ramadan with us, they seemed in no hurry to order. There was a rush of conversation and we stayed there for three hours; subsequent dinners and meetings would be the same. We talked and talked as I began a journey of discovery that would result in my living in Turkey and interviewing participants of what was known as the 'Merve Kavakci Affair'.

Merve had published a personal commentary in Turkish, under the title of 'Headscarfless Democracy'; some academic articles had appeared about the incident; and the bedlam in Parliament that day was cited in numerous books about modern Turkish history. Yet her story had never been accurately told to the Western world. In addition, her book had not been widely distributed in Turkey, nor did it provide the background information needed for people in the West to make sense of it. (She later had her dissertation published – *Headscarf Politics in Turkey: A Postcolonial Reading* – for a limited audience.) Merve was looking for a writer to translate her original work, or help get the story out, but to no avail. Despite all the reporting in Turkey and elsewhere, it somehow got missed by an untold number of potential authors and commentators before I embarked on this endeavour.

Thus a couple of dinners in Georgetown progressed to my interviewing Merve for hours at a time in her university office. In perfect and deliberate English, she recalled many details and her feelings. In the meantime, I began my own research, reading all the key works on Turkey and anything written about the incident in Parliament. The person depicted by these writers, most of whom had never interviewed or met Merve, described a different persona, a fictitious one, the 'agent provocateur' image labelled by the then President Suleyman Demirel, or a puppet manipulated by Islamic leader and ex-Prime Minister Necmettin Erbakan, and a vilification that was and remains in stark contrast to the reality of what happened and her true character. My own personal litmus test for gauging the polarization in Turkey was to tell an unsuspecting person about the subject I was writing. For most so-called 'white' Turks the response was shock, dismay and a look of incredulity. They included my students at Bilkent University who were children at the time of the incident in Parliament and only knew what they had read and what their parents had told them about Merve Kavakci.

Over time I began to understand the quiet, steadfast presence in this person who became the pivotal actor of a resolute notion of representative democracy and human rights in the history of Turkey. Ten years had passed, but her spirit seemed neither diluted nor mellowed. As her sister, Ravza, once told me, 'They didn't realize she would hold out this long; they didn't realize she was so strong.' The more we talked, the more I realized that inner and consistent strength.

In an earlier life I had spent several years investigating civil rights violations for the State of New Jersey and even wrote a book on the subject, *Dealing with Employment Discrimination*. I recognized in Merve the characteristics of many of the people whose cases I handled; I was well versed in civil rights law, lived through the civil rights movement in the USA, and personally investigated hundreds of discrimination cases. For these reasons, I felt comfortable telling this compelling story in a factually sound yet personal way.

Of course, the headscarf issue in Turkey, as well as France, Germany and other countries, is drenched in intense political overtones. In Turkey, it is especially a complex and volatile issue that is viewed within the context of modern Turkish history and adherence to a secularism that came in the new Republic after six hundred years of Ottoman rule closely integrated with Islam. One cannot fully understand the issue without understanding the Turkish revolution in the 1920s headed by Mustafa Kemal (Ataturk) whose picture adorns practically every building, office and store in Turkey today.

Turkey is a wonderful country, rich in culture and history, yet fractured as much as the earthquake-prone fault lines that run deep below the earth's surface in most of Anatolia. Half of Turkey thinks that Merve Kavakci had a 'hidden political agenda' directed by others, and is a threat to the Turkish state. The other half sees her as its democratic salvation and hero for all the headscarved women who are denied rights in that country. The intense feeling Merve Kavakci evokes cannot be understood without considering the fact that even the headscarved wives of Turkey's President and Prime Minister, whom Merve still communicates with, are generally not be taken to state events.

Headscarf: The Day Turkey Stood Still is foremost a human rights story, notwithstanding its historical and political context. Understanding the travails of human rights issues starts, and ends, with humans, with people, not politics. Until we dig deep into the human context we will neither understand the full story of any so-called 'conflict of civilizations', nor develop the kind of transformative empathy that enables political change and the establishment of a peaceful and just society.

Beginning on 2 May 1999, Merve Kavakci endured the wrath of a nation for all to see, but her burden of being treated differently began much earlier and is emblematic of all the millions of headscarved women in Turkey who do not enjoy their right to express and live their religion in terms of dressing in the way they believe their religion requires in the public sphere – including education, teaching, working for the state and public professions. Knowing the tight bond of family, the perspective of past events, and the nature of her religious beliefs will help the reader to understand, I hope, the personal story of Merve Kavakci, as a baby step to understanding the billion personal stories that comprise a world that defies clichés, generalizations and simple bias.

When asked why she had refused on 1 December 1955 to give up her seat to a white person, the way she had on so many other occasions, Rosa Parks, who was in fact a seamstress in Montgomery, Alabama at the time, said that she was simply 'tired of giving in' and she 'wanted to know for once and for all what rights she had as a human being and a citizen'. She left the leadership roles of the civil rights movements to others. Years later she recalled, 'When that white driver stepped back toward us, when he waved his hand and ordered us up and out of our seats, I felt a determination cover my body like a quilt on a winter night.' After reading *Headscarf: The Day Turkey Stood Still* I hope that you will have some understanding of how one headscarved woman suffered a basic violation of human dignity and respect, and can thus better appreciate the quiet but constant nature of her determination and that of others to effect change.

In addition to human rights, there is the political rights aspect of this story. As an elected Member of Parliament, Merve Kavakci also wanted to represent her constituents – in particular the women who talked to her repeatedly before the oath-taking ceremony and expected her to walk into Parliament wearing the same headscarf as they wore, and resist pressure to take it off. The night before, they called her, imploring, 'You're going to walk in, aren't you? You're going to do it, right?' This is democracy at its core, the baseline person-to-person contact between people and their representatives. Unfortunately, this core principle of political representation clashed with the tenets of Turkish nationalism and secularism, causing a harsh response and a torrent of actions that are documented in this book.

Third, this is also a story of women's rights. Prime Minister Ecevit, after all, yelled in Parliament on that fateful day, 'Put this woman in her place.' And it was a wall of secular, uncovered women deputies in Parliament who were supposed to prevent Merve from ultimately taking her oath, at least that was the initial plan, so as not to make the issue seem like one of men treating women unfairly. Part of this story's character as a women's issue also relates to religious women who endure another layer of smothering patriarchy and unfair treatment because they are women in Turkey. Millions of women in Turkey are affected by this phenomenon to this day. Turkey has the worse record of women's employment in Europe and ranks low on all scales of gender equality. Discrimination against women in employment is rampant, there is a lack of facilities for protecting battered women and honour killings persist particularly in rural areas.

This book describes, for the first time, the story of Merve Kavakci's run for Parliament, told with her cooperation and within the context of Turkish politics, historical events and characters. It presents a far more revealing and objective picture than the one presented to the Turkish people by the newspaper cartels at the time, or as described by even Western journalists and cited in academic papers. I hope that this book on one level helps readers to understand the conflicts that lie at the foundation of Turkey, a country that has the potential of setting new standards of democracy in the Middle East, and that it provides commentators, policy makers and academics with an understanding of people's democratic aspirations regardless of culture, religion and nationality.

The struggle for human, political and women's rights that underscores the wearing of headscarves by eighteen million women will undoubtedly affect the course of the twenty-first century in Turkey and beyond. The underlying political movements related to these issues may intensify. There is certainly a need for the West to better understand the Islamic world generally and issues of human rights individually. The explosion of prejudice in August 2010 regarding the building of an Islamic community centre in New York City is the latest example of the gap that exists between some Americans and an understanding of Islamic people. Meanwhile in the Middle East, a wave of revolutionary sentiment is sweeping the region in defiance of authoritarian and repressive regimes. The fault lines may be redrawn and the parties change, but the issues remain. It's my wish that *Headscarf: The Day Turkey Stood Still* adds to the general body of knowledge that derives from all these issues, that it helps our understanding of them and promotes empathy towards the universal, human need for freedom. And, of course, I hope that it benefits in some way the covered women of Turkey.

A note on terms

I have generally refrained throughout the book from using two popular terms that refer to political Islam – namely, 'Islamism' and 'Islamist' – although others using these terms may be quoted. The reason for this is that these terms are rife with negative connotations for many readers; they also actually have a wide variety of meanings and are subject to various definitions by both scholars and political actors. Thus I have tried to avoid their use.

On the other hand, I have used the term 'Islamic' to characterize those people who are devout practitioners of Islam. In Turkey today approximately 60 per cent of the population fall into this category, people who try to pray five times a day, avoid drinking alcohol and eating certain foods, and who fast during Ramadan. The point is that the political views of Islamic people are as diverse as the parties they join. The Western press in particular often refer to Islamic-friendly political parties as 'Islamist', including the current ruling AK (Justice and Development) Party in Turkey. This practice is confusing and misleading and should be avoided. We should not make assumptions regarding the political views of Islamic people and the parties they support, because they do, in fact, vary significantly.

Richard Peres
October 2011
Istanbul, Turkey

Acknowledgements

A book of this nature is not written without a great deal of assistance from others. First and foremost, Dr Merve Kavakci Islam deserves my heartfelt thanks. She granted every interview request, answered all questions, provided photographs and documentation, reviewed the manuscript and facilitated my contacting key players in this story. I appreciate not only her cooperation but also her trust in my deconstructing what happened from both historical and personal perspectives and coming to my own conclusions about the extraordinary events recorded in this book.

Dr Umit Cizre, my wife, partner and well-known scholar of Turkish politics and civil–military relations, made it possible for me to live in Turkey, carry out research and access her invaluable intellect, guidance and knowledge throughout the writing of this book. During the course of two years I quickly became one of her lucky students as she helped me figure out the black art of Turkish politics and a country not easily understood by Americans.

I am indebted to Marie Hanson and her colleagues at Garnet Publishing and Ithaca Press for recognizing the value of this work and their assistance in book preparation.

Special thanks to Susan Littauer for her honest editing, moral support and confidence in me.

My thanks to the Kavakci family for their constant cooperation, interviews and access to photographs: Yusuf and Gulhan Kavakci, Ahmet and Ayten Gungen, Orhan Gungen, Ravza Kavakci Kan, Elif Kavakci Tanriover, Fatima Kavakci and Mariam Kavakci. I am also greatly appreciative to those who granted me interviews – namely, Nazli Ilicak, Abdurrahman Dilipak, Sibel Eraslan, Temel Karamollaoglu, Recai Kutan, Kim Shively, Esra Arsan, Mustafa Kamalak, Yildiz Ramazanoglu, Saim and Nuran Altunbas, Aslan and Bahar Polat, Osman Ulusoy, Fatma Benli, Zeynep Erdim and Mehmet Silay.

I also greatly appreciate the invaluable assistance of Ozlem Cosan who provided instant translations and assistance during numerous interviews in Ankara and Istanbul. Many thanks also to Dayla Rogers for her eye-opening paper and translations. Additionally, I thank Esra Elmas for her translation work and sharing her research on Merve Kavakci.

Notwithstanding all of those whose assistance I have thanked, I take full responsibility for this book's content.

Richard Peres

1

Introduction:
The Turkish Context

On 2 May 1999, Merve Safa Kavakci,[1] newly elected Member of Parliament, entered Turkey's Grand National Assembly in Ankara to take her oath of office. She was wearing a multi-shaded blue headscarf, which matched her well-fitted, dark blue suit. The scarf was wrapped tightly around her head, covering all her hair and pinned beneath her chin – the style of a religious Islamic woman. As soon as she entered and began her walk calmly and steadily to a seat in the second row in the centre of the Turkish Parliament, accompanied by Nazli Ilicak, an uncovered woman deputy of the same party, the jeers of about one hundred Parliamentarians began, letting out a long chorus of 'get out get out get out', clapping in unison and protest, banging their hands on their desks, while millions of Turkish citizens watched on television transfixed by the spectacle.

Although many Turks believed the opposite, for Merve Kavakci her walk into Parliament was a simple act of democracy, representing the headscarved women from the first electoral district in Istanbul who had voted for her, as well as the rest of her constituents – many of whom were secular men and women not as devout in their religious practices. But it was headscarved women who had been calling her all day, encouraging her to take her rightful seat in Parliament after her election and maintain the symbol of her religious faith, something that no other woman had ever done in the history of Turkey. Merve Kavakci would be the first covered woman, as well as the youngest deputy in the history of the Republic, to take her oath of office.

However, for the pro-secular, Kemalist bloc in Turkey, her stroll down the aisle was a virtual act of war, a provocation in defiance of the loosely defined but powerful Kemalist ideology that formed the foundation of the Turkish Republic beginning in 1923, as established by Mustafa Kemal, now called Ataturk, or father of Turkey. Perhaps like no other act in the history of Turkey, it revealed a complicated fracture that splits this country – Islamic people on one side, secularists on the other. The division, however, was not (and even today is not) a simple story of secular, modern, Westernist elites fighting against reactionary, anti-secular, traditional and anti-Western people. Rather, it has been used as a convenient vehicle for reducing many political battles into a single polarity.

Prime Minister Bulent Ecevit, leader of the DSP (Democratic Leftist Party) stood up and went to the podium without the permission of the eighty-six-year-old ceremonial President of the Parliament, Ali Rıza Septioglu. From his pocket he withdrew a prepared speech on what looked like a scrap of paper. He silenced the cacophonous crowd with his loud and stinging remarks:

> This is not a place to challenge the state, no one may interfere with the private life of individuals, but this is not a private space. This is the supreme foundation of the state. Those who work here have to abide with the rules and customs of the state. It is not a place in which to challenge the state. Please put this woman in her place.

It was a defining moment. The state had spoken. Merve Kavakci had always worn her headscarf, including when she applied for an election permit as the Fazilet (Virtue) Party nominee, during the campaign, and when she received official papers indicating her election to Parliament two days earlier. She picked up those papers in front of what seemed like the entire Turkish press corp wearing her headscarf. When asked throughout the campaign, before and after her election, about her intentions, she had always stated clearly that she would continue to wear it as part of her beliefs, that there was no law banning the headscarf in Parliament, and that she would not remove it when taking her oath of office. She was not about to remove it now.

Merve Kavakci was fully focused on trying to remain composed in the face of the riotous atmosphere, although she sat visibly unmoved by the harsh words of the Prime Minister, which were received with applause and support by the members of the DSP, while the majority of the rest of the deputies in Parliament sat in silence. As Stephen Kinzer wrote the next day for the *New York Times*:

> Last week, almost no one in Turkey had heard of Merve Kavakci. Today she stands accused of nothing less than trying to destroy the nation, and Turks are talking of little else. Prime Minister

Bulent Ecevit has begun assembling a new Government, but few seem to care. Even the figure of Abdullah Ocalan, the captured Kurdish revolutionary, who is intensely hated, has suddenly faded from the public consciousness. Front pages of today's newspapers were dominated by photos of Ms Kavacki in Parliament, where her appearance with a headscarf on Sunday sparked pandemonium. Television stations endlessly rebroadcast tape showing legislators shouting insults at her.[2]

The display of rejection in Parliament continued for forty-five minutes until a recess was called. The scene was chaotic and disorganized. At this point, against her better judgement, Merve Kavakci left her seat with the other deputies. Her father was desperately calling to her cell phone to tell her to remain seated, but her phone was turned off. Denied her seat in the Turkish Parliament, harangued by the government, not supported by her party and her citizenship taken away, she would not be allowed to return. A day after the event, Turkey's leading paper asked, 'So who is forcing her to take such an uncompromising stance and thus creating political turmoil?'[3]

The other Turkey: what does Merve Kavakci represent?

The headscarf worn by Merve Kavakci on 2 May 1999 may have ended up being exhibited in the US Capitol as representative of the struggle for democracy and religious freedom, but in Turkey her actions were viewed by the Kemalist bloc as an intolerable threat to Turkey's very existence. Is Merve Kavakci nothing more than a symbol of Islamic fundamentalism and an affront to Ataturk's philosophy of modernism and secularism that is embedded in the Turkish Constitution and the psyche of Turkey's people? The concept of religious freedom may seem to be a simple one for Americans, who approved the first amendment to its Constitution (and the Bill of Rights) in 1791, a logical outgrowth of the many people who settled in America in the seventeenth and eighteenth centuries to avoid religious persecution. But many, if not most, Turks do not see religious freedom from that perspective and have a dramatically different view of democracy based on the particular history and underpinnings of the Turkish Republic. Religion is to be controlled; religion impairs democracy. And thus her short and almost serene walk into the Turkish Parliament met with an explosion of conflict and outrage.

In spite of the fact that most women in Turkey[4] wear a headscarf as part of their religious beliefs, they are subject to life-changing barriers and prohibitions in public, barriers that are not found in other countries in the Middle East or elsewhere, even in France. Headscarved women have been excluded from attending universities and high schools in Turkey for most of the last thirty years, both public and private, denied work in the public sector and consistently discriminated against in white-collar jobs. This is particularly the case since the military coup of 1980, which resulted in the 1982 Constitution created by the coup government and the establishment of Constitutional courts, and since the resurgent crackdown that ensued after the 'post-modern coup' of 28 February 1997.[5] Even the daughter of the President of Turkey, Abdullah Gul, graduated from Bilkent University by attending classes wearing a wig and did not receive her diploma in public so as not to embarrass Bilkent's administration. Neither his wife, nor the wife of Prime Minister Tayyip Erdogan, attended official state functions because of their headscarves. When President Gul broke from that tradition in 2010 on Republic Day the entire general staff of the Turkish Armed Forces boycotted the event.

Turkey's secularism, based on French laicism, which was the foundation of the Turkish Republic, supports the view of the headscarf as a political symbol and specific threat against the Turkish Republic. Laicism, unlike the American view of secularism, subordinates religion to the state and, in Turkey, is controlled by the state. The fear on the part of secularists is that Islamic people want to impose an Islamic state in Turkey similar to nearby Iran. On the other hand, repeated surveys and polls show that devout Turkish people are not interested in establishing an Islamic state and that Turkish women who wear headscarves simply do so mainly for their own personal religious reasons.[6] Put another way, the foundation of the Turkish Republic was based on the repression and control of Islam, along with the suppression of non-Turkish cultures (for example, the Kurds). That repression exists today, even with an Islamic-friendly ruling party, affecting the behaviour of Islamic people who deal with its constrictions in various ways, and continues to result in an incomplete democracy, at least the way the West defines it.

The 'other' Turkey is not just defined as headscarved women. A key example is how vocational school graduates are openly discriminated against. From 1974 to 1997 all students from vocational schools, like other high school students, gained entrance into one of Turkey's universities by taking a national entrance examination. But after the 28 February 1997 military intervention a 'coefficient' system was put into place, administered by the Directorate of Higher Education, YOK, that downgraded the scores of students coming from vocational schools and religious high schools, called Imam Hatip, with a negative multiplier. The rules imposed by the coup leaders were an attempt to lessen the opportunities for 'Islamists' to rise up the career ladder and gain influential positions. In 1997, 49 per cent of students went to vocational and religious schools, but that number has plummeted because of the discriminatory rules in effect since then.[7] Moreover, students of these schools cannot transfer back into regular high schools to remedy their situation. Merve Ozsoy, a twelfth-grader at the Hikmet Nazi Kursunluoglu Vocational High School, in response to a court decision to continue the coefficient system, said she views the situation as a nightmare from which she cannot awake and it 'pushes the limits of disappointed young people'.[8] The coefficient system has been upheld by the Constitutional Court, though the ruling, Islamic-friendly AK Party continues to push reforms to remedy the situation.

Much has been written about the fault lines that beset Turkey. Obviously, there is much to fight over: a modern and developed nation rich in resources, culture and history that sits at the crossroads of Europe and the Middle East with eight countries on its borders. Indeed, its geo-political position has likely contributed to the origin of many conflicts including the modern/secular versus the traditional/ religious. The political and cultural revolution led by Mustafa Kemal beginning in 1923 leaned towards the West, adopting a pro-secular and Western ideology of modernism. This was in response to nineteenth- and twentieth-century Ottoman failures, and after the capitulation to foreign powers that marred its six-hundred-year history of rule over a vast empire that reached to the walls of Vienna.

Turkey's secular establishment or bloc – which includes many Turkish institutions, sectors including the military, civil bureaucracy, higher echelons of the judiciary, business sectors and some educational elite – are protective of the status quo in Turkey and take a pro-West, anti-Islamist position. In particular they cite Turkey's foreign policies under the current AK Party government as examples of a non-Western and Islamic-friendly orientation, which to them explains a similar pro-Islamic domestic policy as a result. However, in reality Turkey's imitation of the West, which started in the formative years of the Turkish Republic, is not rejected by a large part of the population. Nor has Turkey's so-called 'Islamic' government done much Islamizing since it came to power in 2002. The tutelage role of the military and its lack of strong civilian control are legitimized on the grounds of unsecular threats to the secular and modern character of the state. Similarly, Turkey's qualification of individual rights and abrogation of religious freedoms may be admissible in terms of Turkey's own view of democracy, but it is decidedly not democratic in the Western sense. So the paradox is that even the 'West' as a set of values is defined differently in Turkey.

It is a complex conflict, difficult for Westerners to grasp without knowing the context of modern Turkish history. The Kavakci Affair was obviously an internal issue for Turkey, difficult for the West to get involved in. Therefore it is possible to understand why the US ambassador did not voice any opposition against Merve Kavakci being denied her seat, for example, although on other occasions there were statements of concern on other issues and only Islamic countries registered a protest. In the post-Merve Kavakci Affair period, Westerners do not readily understand the deeply embedded fears of Turkey's elite and aggressive form of secularism, but tend to go along with it because it complements fears of Islam after 9/11 and the perception of Islam as supporting terrorism.

Moreover, applying a Western feminist perspective does not help to explain matters more clearly either, in spite of Kemal Ataturk's advances for women's equality. Modern, secular Turkish women have also opposed lifting the headscarf ban and are not sympathetic to the plight of these 'other' women. In fact, many have organized to support women's rights, but specifically not the rights of Islamic women, whom they see as being anti-feminist and a threat to Turkey.[9] They too view Islamic women with disdain, as having a political agenda, as being paid to wear their headscarves or forced to do so by political parties and family members. This disdain can be seen in the stares of modern women at the headscarved girls who shop at Kanyon, the ultra-modern mall on the European side of Istanbul north of the old city, as relayed to me by covered women. And it can be seen in the photographs of women protesting against Merve Kavakci in May 1999. Some of these non-sympathetic women are also academics, even sociologists who research and write about Islamic women for their academic articles. Their feminism and empathy stop with the headscarf.

Secular women have also voiced the fear that they will be pressured by Islamic women to cover their heads if such bans are lifted. There is no evidence to support their fear, which does not discredit their having such feelings, but this fear is often expressed as one of the reasons for perpetuating prohibitions.

One crucial question that occupied Turkey's popular and official agenda was how this woman could possibly be acting on her own? This lack of agency attributed to Islamic women seems to be one endemic barrier placed in front of women who want a voice, or a seat in Parliament, or to teach at a university in Turkey or work for the state. It runs counter not only to Western notions of liberal democracy and human rights, but also to the unique attributes of all humans, of our magnificent individualities. Ms Kavakci, now Merve Kavakci Islam, addressed this issue of a lack of women's agency and Orientalism in *Headscarf Politics in Turkey: A Postcolonial Reading* (Palgrave Macmillan, 2010). She argues in this book that although Turkey is itself in the Middle East, Orientalist assumptions were at the core of the founding of modern Turkey in 1923.

Sympathetic Westerners are often told that applying democratic principles to Turkey does not always make sense because Turkey is different, Turkey is 'unique' and therefore human rights standards do not similarly apply. I have also been told this directly by Islamic men, even by some who are sympathetic to the political struggles of Islamic women and Merve Kavakci specifically: 'Feminism is a Western concept. In Islam it is replaced by the family.' In fact women leaders of the AK Party, including its sole female minister, speak against 'feminism,' which they view as a Western concept, yet advocate the interests of women. And for others, including the military and political parties, the headscarf issue reduces itself to a power struggle against the 'other' Turkey. Turkish nationalism and its definition also make the waters separating the two sides murky, for it is an attribute shared by all sides.

Yet for me clarity comes through living in Turkey and talking with religious people, who seem not unlike religious people elsewhere, anywhere. They want to be part of the middle class, get a good job, raise a family and prosper. Yet they are, also, simply unfortunate. In Turkey they have been politicized as the enemy of the secular state, a by-product of a revolution led by one man with a modernizing vision beginning in 1923, 'modern' for the 1920s, which turned into a forced revolution supported over the years by the Western countries it sought to emulate. Second, religious people are unfairly characterized in a pejorative way as 'fundamentalists' intent on bringing an Islamic state to Turkey, regardless of polls showing that this view is rare among religious Turks. The rise of restrictive laws against minarets and headscarves by European counties and the objection by France and Germany to Turkey entering the European Union come to mind, as well as many instances of Islamophobia in the West, including laws against Shariah in many US states. These views stem from a one-dimensional view of Islam that does not reflect reality, a view amplified by the idea that a 'stable' Turkey with an influential military is better than one that is less-than-stable yet more democratic, led by an Islamic-friendly political party.

As I write these words the midday call to prayer echoes among the apartment complexes where I live, on the Asian side of Istanbul, overlooking the Marmara. It is an almost transparent part of the fabric of this country, like the church bells heard on Sundays in the West, ones I heard every morning where I lived in the USA, calling Catholic parishioners to morning Mass. I am not Catholic, but I got used to it and didn't mind. Practically every neighbourhood in Turkey hears the *ezan* five times a day. The Directorate of Religious Affairs replaced the *ezan* with a Turkish version, which was objected to by religious Turks, but was restored to its original Arabic in 1950 by a new government led by Adnan Menderes. The name *ezan* appears in the Turkish national anthem as well.

Turkey is almost 100 per cent Muslim today; the majority of its citizens are devout and practise its tenets in several variations, including the majority Sunni, as well as Alevis and Sufis. The perception of headscarved women during Ataturk's time has little relevance today. At the time of Turkey's War of Independence they were often rural, impoverished and focused on working in their family's business or in the countryside, raising children and taking care of the home. It was a war that headscarved women also fought. That headscarf, worn loosely around the head and not fastened with a pin, often not tightly covering the hair, was a traditional female custom of the time. But then, 'In the 1990s, a new generation of young women, assertive and liberated but still religiously conservative, began pursuing opportunities that had never been available to their mothers and grandmothers but that, thanks, ironically, to women's liberation provisions of Kemalism, were available to them.'[10] They tied their headscarves differently, competed with secularists in universities and the public and private spheres, and thus infringed upon the secular establishment.

Mustafa Kemal did indeed bring equality to Turkish women (albeit with some qualifiers). He wished to be seen and photographed with them, in their modern Western dress without the *hijab* (headscarf) and *carsaf* (black cloak, like a *chador* in Iran), women who would take part in modern Turkish society alongside men, get educated, drive cars and join the modern world. The fact that they looked modern was important. In the Turkish Republic's view of modernity, appearances mattered. This was certainly for the time a highly modern view of women, not only for the Middle East but elsewhere in the world. This attribute of Ataturk's revolution is often revered today. For example, a large photograph of Ataturk and women in modern dresses is the backdrop at the front desk of the Marmara Hotel in Taksim Square, Istanbul. However, when he died in 1938 he could not have envisioned the 'modern Turkish Islamic woman' who wanted to do almost everything that a secular woman would do except cover her hair, like the headscarved women I saw recently at a Tarkan (a Turkish pop star) concert in Istanbul, singing along with their secular counterparts in the crowd of cheering young people.

There is a class issue here as well in which educated Islamic women do not have an easy time crossing the line to modernity. For some Turks wearing a headscarf is fine for the women who commute to their homes to provide cleaning and cooking services, or who work in offices at night or who clean the streets. But for women doctors, lawyers, computer programmers and professors, wearing a headscarf represents a social and cultural threat. These women are smart, they know what they are doing and thus are perceived as knowingly challenging the secular public sphere. Certainly there are a lot of elements at work in this fear: real insecurities, cultural differences, political power, prejudice and isolation, to name a few. The point is that there is a generation of Turkish Islamic women (as well as men) seeking entry into the middle class whose self-development is stymied by discriminatory laws and practices. Ironically, Merve Kavakci's education level, her elitist family background, income level and her fluency in English did not help her cross the bridge to a new definition of non-secular modernity but rather exacerbated her provocateur label. It is a surprising but key fact to remember.

Today, more than ten years later, the most aggressive secularists in Turkey marginalize Merve by referring to her, as did MHP (Nationalist Movement Party) deputy Osman Durmus in the Turkish Parliament in 2010, as that 'American citizen Merve Kavakci'.[11] But Merve Kavakci is Turkish. She was born in Turkey, as were her parents. Her grandfather fought in the War of Independence, was wounded and served for twenty-seven years. And like thousands of other Turks, as we shall see, she held dual citizenship, which enabled her to obtain a university education and to enjoy religious freedom in America.

There are eighteen million covered women[12] in Turkey today, from a vast socio-economic spectrum, including rural and urban women, illiterate and educated, some of whom stylishly cover their heads with the latest Islamic fashions, drive cars, have profiles on Facebook, and want to become lawyers, doctors, professors and other professions, and join the growing Turkish middle class. Despite some studies that have shown that not all Islamic women embrace a full work-life because of their conservative family values,[13] religious Islamic women have expressed, through their street demonstrations and new human rights organizations, that they want to participate in the modern world alongside their not-so-religious 'sisters'.

While the idea of 'modern Islamic women' may be bothersome or an oxymoron to both secularist women (and men) and some religious Islamic men as well, its increasing presence is a fact. Understanding their struggles and issues of identity is important to bringing the West closer to an understanding of the highly multi-dimensional nature of the Islamic world and Turkey in particular.

Moreover, that understanding is critical for Turkey if it is ever to resolve a chronic and polarizing conflict. The fault lines in Turkey resemble, in some ways, America's up to the early 1960s before the civil rights movement gained cohesiveness and a dynamic leadership. Discrimination in housing was the rule and not unlawful in most states, and if unlawful, those laws were rarely enforced administratively or in the courts. Neighbourhoods were not integrated throughout the USA and there were entrenched, segregated enclaves in the suburbs, north and south, and in the cities were the 'ghettos' that many white Americans managed to avoid. After hundreds of years of separate cultures, there was certainly fear in the air in the suburbs and white neighbourhoods of America, and that fear and friction took decades more to assuage as African Americans progressed slowly into the middle class, discrimination laws were passed, and one by one minorities made inroads in housing, employment and public accommodation. It was a long, arduous, often violent and political struggle. One should not expect Turkey to quickly resolve its similarly deeply entrenched conflicts.

In addition to separate neighbourhoods, gated communities and shopping areas, as well as the sharp difference between major cities and rural areas, consider this: most secular Turks have not attended high schools and universities with headscarved women for much of the last thirty years. Moreover, headscarved women were absent in many professions (lawyers, doctors, engineers) due to educational barriers or discrimination, and the white-collar employment environment was similarly disconnected from the world of covered women, especially in the front offices, managerial positions and jobs that interact with customers (like Turkish Airlines flight attendants). This lack of interaction with an entire group of 'modern' Islamic women who labour at workarounds to advance themselves, whether from lower socio-economic classes or from the up-and-coming middle class, naturally engenders fear and enmity at worst, and lack of empathy at least. This lack of contact in Turkey is enveloped by a level of polemical political discourse that is also severe in the extreme.

A decade after the Merve Kavakci Affair, the explosive issue of the headscarf continues to rage. Merve's name may have left the front pages of the *New York Times*, and her headscarf is long gone from the halls of the US Capitol, but the conflict continues in Turkey unabated. And her name is not only well known and remembered; according to one of Turkey's leading journalists it 'hangs over the heads' of Turkey's ruling AK Party, to this day.[14]

In my first meeting with Merve Kavakci I asked about how she seemed so placid in contrast to the shouting and conflict around her. 'I was determined not to let them see my suffering on the inside and not give them that pleasure,' she said. 'I was elected to represent the people from my district, my constituents, many of whom wore a headscarf. They called me earlier in the day and expected me to represent them and that is what I was intent on doing.' Merve Kavakci became emblematic of this conflict and achieved a dual meaning for Turks. For some she is a provocateur; for others, particularly Islamic women, she is a heroine. Untold numbers of them have named their daughters after her.

The early Republic

Turkey's long and rich history, plus its relatively recent establishment as a republic, provides an overpowering context that hovers just below the surface in the consciousness of its politicians and citizenry. It fuels nationalistic fervour and supports the notion of Turkey's 'uniqueness'. In that sense, Turkey is no different from any other country. Pride in Turkey is fuelled by its history as a great nation.

Merve Kavakci's mother grew up in Istanbul within walking distance of the Haghia Sophia, one of the 'world's greatest architectural achievements',[15] built by Emperor Justinian in 537 and the greatest cathedral of Eastern Christianity. More than a quarter of a millennium before the British established a colony in the Americas, in September 1396, a massive European army of 250,000 men, led by John of Nevers and King Sigismund of Hungary, battled and lost to Bayezid I, the head of the Ottoman Empire, who had a smaller and less equipped army, at Nicopolis in Turkish territory near the Danube. It was the last battle of the Crusades. The Europeans lost more than 150,000 men trying to defeat the Turks, whose empire at that time stretched to the Euphrates.

Then in May 1453, the Ottoman Sultan Mehmet II and his army defeated Constantine after a seven-week siege of Constantinople (today's Istanbul) and after spending a year at the Castle of Rumeli-Hasari that has guarded the Bosphorus since 1452, which can be visited today. After the victory, Mehmet II raced on his white horse through the ruined city to protect the Haghia Sophia from looters and convert it immediately into a mosque[16] (one of Istanbul's major tourist attractions).

A hundred years later, people in Istanbul were observed lowering buckets through their basements to collect water and even fish. It was only then that a massive underground cistern, built by Justinian a thousand years earlier, was discovered. It is still there today, one of the more unusual tourist attractions in this historic city, just a short walk from the Haghia Sophia.

The Ottomans ruled for six centuries, their empire stretching at one time from the gates of Vienna to today's Balkans and Greece, across

Anatolia to Mesopotamia, Syria, Egypt and North Africa. Europeans over the years were terrified of them and their bad reputations live on today in the works of Shakespeare and more contemporary commentators who do not want them in the European Union.[17]

Ataturk established Ankara as its capital in 1923. Situated in a valley on a plateau (2,700 feet) 250 miles east of Istanbul, Ankara had become the headquarters of Kemal's forces during the War of Independence because it was far from the Ottoman, British, Greek and Italian armies that sought to claim their share of Turkey after the Treaty of Sevres in 1920. But its selection also symbolized the changes that were taking place in Turkey after almost five centuries of rule from historic Istanbul[18] and its location as an imperial capital for 1,593 years.[19]

Although Ankara's population was only about 50,000 at the time, the new capital grew to one million by 1968, the year of Merve Kavakci's birth in that city, and is about five million today. It is an overtly modern city, with sleek and immaculate shopping malls, and apartment complexes have seemingly sprung up everywhere, spread out and organized without a centre, as if planning could not keep up with its rapid growth and economic development. It hardly appears historical, compared to the ancient mosques and spires that characterize Istanbul. Yet overlooking the city of Ankara, mostly hidden from public view, is the Citadel, whose walls date from the mid-seventh century. Near those walls is a building that houses an amazing collection of artefacts, the Museum of Old Anatolian Civilizations. It was founded by Ataturk himself as the Hittite Museum while his troops were still fighting the War of Independence. Photographs of the great man visiting the museum in the 1930s adorn the main area on the ground floor.

Ankara's history, and Anatolia, can be traced back 4,000 years to the Hittites, followed 'in the tenth century bc by the Phrygians, and later by the Lydians, Persians, Macedonians, Galatians, Romans, Byzantines, Seljuks and finally the Ottomans'.[20] And just about anyone of significance passed through, from Genghis Khan to Alexander the Great. In summary, Turkey's long-time place in the world is at the centre of civilization – not as a colony but as a colonizer, a major player on the world stage for 1,500 years.

However, by the twentieth century the empire was almost at an end and its grandeur gone. Picking the Germans as allies in 1914 was a disaster, the only bright spot being the Ottoman's victory at the Battle of Gallipoli led by a young colonel named Mustafa Kemal. But by 1918 the country was essentially under the control of foreign powers and the sultan was an 'irrelevant puppet'.[21] In 1920 the Sultan agreed, at Sevres, to allow the allies to cut up Turkey, including the Greek and Italian infiltrations in Anatolia, a section of the country for the French, and independent territories in the east for the Kurds and Armenians.

Three years later, those plans would be all but forgotten. Mustafa Kemal did the impossible, leading an impoverished nation against not only a weak government but also foreign powers, including the invading Greeks, to establish the Turkish Republic. Mustafa Kemal, officially called 'Ataturk' since 1934 ('father of the Turks') was one of the greatest military and political leaders of the twentieth century, in the same category as Mao Tse-tung, who also led his country in a successful war of independence against foreign powers and who had an immeasurable impact on generations of people. It is no wonder that his countenance is everywhere in Turkey today – on all currency, in every business, office and public place, on the side of buildings, on key chains, mugs and blankets, as statues in town squares and in front of important buildings – the list is endless. He was indispensable in making Turkey into a modern state, resembling the West, which was his goal, breaking away from the backwardness and weaknesses of the Ottomans and the religious domination of the Caliphate. When a young Bernard Lewis came to Turkey in 1938 he was mesmerized by how modern Turkey had become, and his landmark book on the history of Turkey that appeared in 1961, *The Emergence of Modern Turkey*, resonates with admiration.

Ataturk's military accomplishments are far outweighed by the one-man Cultural Revolution he led after the Ottoman army and foreign powers were defeated. Seeing a backward country of twelve million mostly illiterate and impoverished people, he set forth on a modernization campaign unlike any other. Early on, he abolished the Ottoman monarchy and shortly thereafter even the Islamic Caliphate, the leader of the Islamic world represented by the monarch, who was put on a train and sent to Switzerland. Although Ataturk appealed to the religious beliefs of the peasants to fight off Turkey's foreign invaders, after the war he took steps to control religion along the lines of the French laicite model. Certainly part of his motivation was that the Caliphate was a great source of political power, not simply head of a religion.

The changes implemented by Ataturk were top-down and had no basis in democratic principles. On the other hand, they were not expansionist, totalitarian; nor were they based on a powerful leader. A semblance of democracy – a Parliament and elections – was left in place. But from the founding of the Republic in 1923 until 1945 the Republican People's Party was the only party, and Turkey was an authoritarian state, directed by Kemal Ataturk until his death in 1938, and then by his successor, Ismet Pasha Inonu. Opposition parties were allowed to form on two occasions, but when they began to criticize the government they were shut down.

Ataturk focused his years as leader of Turkey in establishing a secular and national state[22] in three areas.

- Secularization of the state, education and the law: this was a continuation of a process started by Sultan Mahmut. The Swiss civil code was adopted to replace the institutionalized Islamic law of the *ulema*, the religious schools were abolished, and a Directorate of Religious Affairs was created in 1924 to impose control by the state over religion. (This is far different from separation of Church and state, as found in US law.)

- Cultural change: the religious fez was replaced by the hat in 1925, religious attire was limited to mosques, and Sunday was made the official day of rest instead of Friday. The Western clock and calendar were also adopted. Women were not only given the right to vote, but also encouraged to take part in Western-type occupations, from professional jobs, to pilots, opera singers and beauty queens – a liberation that had obvious non-religious connotations. More importantly, in one decree in 1928, Ataturk replaced Ottoman Turkish script, a version of the Arabic/Persian alphabet, with Latin letters, and went around the country instructing adults and children in the new form of writing. These ideas were not new, and were first proposed as early as 1862, but the recommendations never stuck. Ataturk squashed opposition and gave the entire country just two months to learn the new way of writing. Illiteracy was, in a sense, eliminated as a problem: now everyone was illiterate, including university professors and lawyers, and all would start from the same place. The use of family names was introduced in 1934, at which time Mustafa Kemal Pasha became Ataturk, exclusive to him and his descendants (he had none). During this time Ataturk also took steps to 'construct a new national identity and strong national cohesion'.[23] These steps included altering history to indicate that Anatolia had been a Turkish country for thousands of years; that Turks had helped to create major civilizations in China, Europe and the Middle East; and the adoption of a uniquely Turkish identity separate from the Middle East, without recognition of Turkey's minorities, such as the Kurds.

- Secularization of social life: the most important act here was the elimination of religious schools and courts, and suppression of the orders (*tarikats*) in 1925 along with their related mystical brotherhoods, which touched upon many areas of popular religion, including 'dress, amulets, soothsayers, holy sheikhs, saints' shrines, pilgrimages and festivals'.[24] Resentment by these and other religious movements caused them to go underground. With the increasingly unpopular regime in the 1940s 'the Kemalists politicized Islam and turned it into a vehicle for opposition. One could say that, in turning against popular religion, they cut the ties which bound them to the mass of population.'[25]

Ataturk's reforms were aggressively implemented from the top down without debate in a relatively short period of time, compared to the previous six hundred years of Ottoman-Islamic culture. With fascism and Nazism already rising in nearby Europe, and often-viewed as contemporary models, democracy was not in the equation, and if it were those reforms would likely have not taken place and Turkey might very well be a different place than it is today. On the other hand, as the coming years would illustrate, the old culture would not be easily repressed. Turkey was and still is a Muslim country. The politicization of Islam would take other forms, as would the rise of modernism among Turkey's religious Muslim population, hardly the perception of rural ignorant religious people so abhorrent to Kemalists.

A tenuous democracy emerges
The Kemalist regime was built on and supported by officers, bureaucrats and local Muslim notables and traders, yet the vast majority of the population, peasants and workers, were not happy by 1945 and, in

fact, lacked basic standards of living. Only one-quarter of 1 per cent of Turkey's 40,000 villages had electricity [26] at the time, for example.

Although President Inonu is often given credit for supporting Turkey's first modern, free, two-party elections in May 1950, several factors in the previous five years gave rise to that effort. Turkey was a founding member of the United Nations in 1945, which was committed to democratic ideals. The USA gained preeminent influence at the end of the Second World War, which was a victory for Western democracies. In a speech in 1945 Inonu promised to make the regime more democratic and criticism of the government began openly in Parliament for the first time. Later that year he allowed for a choice among candidates within the Republican Peoples' Party (CHP). New political parties were then created in this relaxed atmosphere, notably the Democratic Party (DP) in January 1946. As the DP gained in popularity, elections were quickly called and the CHP won overwhelmingly, gaining all but 62 of 465 seats in the assembly. But massive vote-rigging and lack of secrecy in the voting led to more complaints by the DP. The DP pressed for democratic reforms after its first convention in 1947 and by 1950 an election law was passed that required the judiciary, not the administration, to monitor elections.

During the time following the Second World War, tension with the Soviet Union emerged. The Truman Doctrine in 1947 brought military and financial aid to Turkey (and Greece) as part of the USA's defence of anti-communist regimes and the start of the Cold War. These factors also supported the move towards democratic reforms, the relaxation of the political climate, and the start of independent newspapers. Both the CHP and DP wanted the religious vote; the CHP even moved to allow religious education in schools.

Inonu, to his credit, allowed for the formation of other political parties and, despite ideas to the contrary by the Turkish military, supported Turkey's first free election on 14 May 1950. To everyone's shock, the Republican People's Party garnered only 39.8 per cent of the vote; the winner was the Democratic Party. Celal Bayar became President and Adnan Menderes became Prime Minister. A fragile democracy had begun. The military volunteered to take control but Inonu, again to his credit, called them off. It was an important first step towards democracy.

Not accustomed to being an opposition party, the CHP fought back but the DP, thanks to American aid and a booming economy, maintained and even increased its lead in the 1954 elections. However, the DP was insecure – it felt that the bureaucracy and military still supported Inonu – and an economic downturn and increase in inflation in the later part of the decade eroded its support, particularly on the part of salaried employees, such as the bureaucracy and military. Menderes' unfortunate response was to become more authoritarian towards the bureaucracy, trade unions and the press, resulting in a split within his party. Menderes was a secularist but used religion to extend his support, reintroducing the call to prayer in Arabic, building thousands of mosques (mosques are built and controlled by the government) and allowing religious broadcasts on radio.[27] The CHP had begun the process of authorizing Qur'an courses and opening up religious schools, including a theology college at Ankara University, and Menderes continued that trend, not fearing religious practice as the Kemalists had, opening religious schools in many cities,[28] and relaxing restrictions on expressions of religious feelings.[29]

However, by 1957 the issue of secularism had intensified. Although the Democrats did not undermine the secular character of the Republic, they accepted the autonomy of religious organizations. 'To the majority of the educated elite (including civil servants, teachers and academics and officers) who had internalized the Kemalist dogmas and who themselves owed their position in the ruling elite to the fact that they represented the "positivist, Western-oriented outlook"; the Democrats were threatening their political power and control of the state.'[30] And 'within the army, which regarded itself as the keeper of Ataturk's heritage, the feeling that the DP was betraying the Kemalists traditions was especially strong'.[31] In addition, Turkish intellectuals saw the relaxation of secularists' politics as a resurgence of Islam, although it was really the masses expressing themselves. Nevertheless, as the CHP continued to attack the DP, Menderes fought back with even more repressive actions. His government banned newspapers from reporting on assembly debates, launched an investigation of the opposition, used troops to stop Inonu from holding a meeting, and carried out disciplinary actions against professors for criticizing the government, all of which resulted in student riots and demonstrations.[32]

The result was that on 27 May 1960 the military implemented its first coup, which had, it was discovered, been in the making for several years. The country was now in the hands of a 'National Unity

Committee' (NUC) headed by General Cemal Gursel, who became head of state, Prime Minister and Minister of Defence with Colonel Alparslan Turkes as Deputy Premier and a key advisor. Although initially greeted with outbursts of joy by students and the intelligentsia, the mood quickly changed. First more than two hundred generals were purged, then almost as many professors were fired. The DP was dissolved, a new Constitution was written to balance political parties that got out of hand, and civil liberties were spelled out. The new Constitution was approved by referendum, 61.7 per cent to 38.3 per cent, a disappointing margin for the NUC however. To the surprise of many, there was 'no return to the strict secularist, or even anti-Islamic, policies of the years before 1945'[33] on the part of the NUC. However, the political use of religion was prohibited in the new Constitution.

The coup government also convened a tribunal, without any legal basis, to try the former regime, which took place on an island near Istanbul in the Sea of Marmara. Hundreds of people were imprisoned, and former Prime Minister Menderes and Foreign Minister Zorlu, despite the pleas of foreign governments, were hanged on 17 September 1961.

By 1965 a new party, the Justice Party (Adalet Partisi) had gained the support of the NUC and, led by Suleyman Demirel, won enough votes to gain control of the government. Demirel managed to hold the JP's party together while emphasizing its Islamic character and maintaining pressure against leftist and communist movements, which included the purging of teachers and arresting of those who published communist propaganda. However, the new Constitutional Court protected civil liberties to some extent and universities, which felt empowered by toppling Menderes, got more actively involved in politics, particularly the 'new left'. Suleyman Demirel would play an active role thirty-five years later in the Kavakci Affair.

In 1968 Abdullah Gul – later to be President of Turkey and another key actor regarding the incident in Parliament – entered Istanbul University. He was a leader of the Turkish National Union of Students (Milli Turk Talebe Birligi), which had a conservative identity at the time. This was the beginning of a chaotic period that saw universities ceasing to function, left-wing students robbing banks, neo-fascist militants bombing homes, paralysing strikes and Islamic political groups openly rejecting Ataturk's aggressive secularism[34] – a situation that ultimately led to yet another military coup three years later.

In March 1968, in Ankara, one of the first headscarf incidents to receive media attention occurred when a woman named Hatice Babacan[35] was expelled from the Ankara University Faculty of Divinity. 'The dean of the faculty's decision to expel Babacan set an important precedent for universities' policies in dealing with veiled students. Presumably, Babacan's style of veiling, with the scarf snuggly framing her face, made her stand out among her classmates.'[36] Upon her arriving dressed that way, her professor told her to uncover or leave; she refused to uncover, citing her faith, and left.

Hatice Babacan lost her arbitration. The expulsion resulted in a boycott by fifty students and hunger strikes outside the faculty building, which ignited a two-month battle in the media with the mainstream press supporting the school.[37] In addition to Hatice Babacan, one of the leaders of that boycott was Saim Altunbas, a man who would later meet the Kavakci family in Erzurum and become a good friend. Ten headscarved students from the school and dozens of male students joined the boycott.[38] The school even shut down during the controversy as the administration planned its next move. The university claimed that the students were being manipulated and controlled by others, including the 'Muslim Brotherhoods', although there is no evidence of this.

The marginalization by the Kemalist press in 1968 of the religious beliefs of Hatice Babacan, a headscarved woman, and their claiming that she was controlled and pressured by others, would be repeated for the next forty years as other cases and incidents involving headscarves played out in the press and society as a whole. From the beginning, as noted earlier, the secularists and Turkish courts viewed such incidents as infringing on the rights of women *without* headscarves, a view that is echoed even today by US educated Kemalists teaching in America. As noted by the *Turkish Daily News* regarding Hatice Babacan: 'In March 1968, President Cevdet Sunay was discussing "inappropriate attempts in some places to make our girls and women cover their heads". In other words, according to this viewpoint, defenders of the Shariah attacked people's freedom of thought and the basic concept of human rights, exerting pressure on women to wear the veil.'

Shariah refers to the 'way' Muslims should live or the 'path' that they should follow.[39] But the secularists in Turkey and elsewhere characterize it as the Islamic law that Muslims want to impose on others or on Turkey generally as their ultimate goal. Secular women and political leaders take the position that for *their* freedom headscarves should be disallowed in universities. Surveys of the Turkish population by TESEV and Gallup have shown over the years that only a very small minority of Islamic people in Turkey wishes to impose Shariah on its population. Moreover, the fears that secular women would be pressured to cover in Turkey have not materialized whatsoever during ten years of rule by the Islamic-friendly AK Party.

Nevertheless, almost fifty years later that same argument of pressure on uncovered women remains. In 2005 the Grand Chamber of the European Court of Human Rights ruled against Leyla Sahin in her case against Turkey for its headscarf restrictions using the same reasoning relating to the fears of secular women. Secular proponents, including judges, often cite this case to prove that Turkey is democratic and that headscarf prohibitions do not violate human rights laws.

Early on, the 'Kemalist state justified its coercive secularism by presenting Islam as the main reason for economic underdevelopment and social malaise that confronted Turkish society in the 1920s and 1930s'.[40] As noted earlier, this inadvertently helped to politicize Islam groups who clearly began to see the state's hostility towards religion, and 'the secular elite considered any attempt by marginalized societal groups to seek representation within the state centre as an example of an "Islamic revival"'.[41]

Hatice Babacan maintained her religious beliefs in spite of her expulsion and would soon cross paths with the Kavakci family. Her nephew, Ali Babacan, is a well-known member of the current Erdogan government in Turkey. Merve Kavakci, born in the same city (Ankara) about the same time, would be the centre of her own media storm thirty years later.

The Kavakci family

Merve Safa Kavacki was born on 19 August 1968 at Mevkii Military Hospital, a nondescript two-storey building at a small military base in the Diskapi section of Ankara. She was the first child of Yusuf Ziya Kavacki and Gulhan Gungen.

Both parents had impressive academic accomplishments by the time Merve was born and both were observant Muslims. Gulhan, her mother, was one of the first university-educated women to wear the headscarf in Istanbul. She graduated from the historic Istanbul Saint George Avusturya Lisesi (Austrian High School) in 1960, a Catholic school whose teachers were nuns. 'My religion was put in the corner those days and repressed,' she told me. 'But I looked at the Austrian nuns and what they were wearing and wondered why could I not wear my religious dress?'

In 1962 she entered Istanbul University, Faculty of Letters, majoring in German Philology. 'In those days it was unthinkable that women who wore headscarves could even dream of going to a university,' she said. There were no specific laws prohibiting headscarves, but given the subjugation of religion in support of Turkish secularism, there was no need. The Turkish military's coup just two years earlier, in May 1960, legitimized itself partly by being a response to increasing religious activities in public spaces, which it saw as threatening its Kemalist programme.[42]

In this repressive atmosphere, Gulhan knew enough not to enter Istanbul University wearing her headscarf. So, during free periods, she would wash her hands (*wudu*), run to the mosque, cover her hair, pray, then return and uncover as she re-entered the university. But by the third year she made up her mind to cover whenever she wanted. She awoke one day, covered her hair and entered the doors of Istanbul University. Somehow the brazen tactic worked and she managed to complete her education, the first headscarved woman to graduate from Istanbul University.

Yusuf met Gulhan when she was an undergraduate student at Istanbul University, where he was working on his PhD. They got engaged in 1966, married in 1967, and then moved to Ankara for Yusuf's compulsory year of military service, where he was a member of the military police – which is why Merve was born in a military hospital.

Two years earlier Yusuf had received his BA in Islamic Studies from the Institute of Higher Islamic Studies (Ministry of Education) in Istanbul and LLB from the Faculty of Law, Istanbul University. He was a Hafiz al-Qur'an, having memorized the Holy Qur'an at the age of ten. He received his PhD from the Faculty of Letters, Istanbul University, Institute of Islamic Research, just before starting his compulsory military service.

Yusuf Kavakci and his new family moved back to Istanbul in August 1969, returning to the house where they were married. He took the position of teacher of Islamic Law for the Institute of Higher Islamic Studies of the Ministry of Education.

These were anything but quiet times in Istanbul. Visits by the US Navy's Sixth Fleet sparked anti-American demonstrations in July 1968. On 16 February 1969 (Bloody Sunday) a massive demonstration of 30,000 people in Istanbul's Beyazit Square was broken up by police and troops, but then was attacked by a counter-revolutionary group wielding knives and sticks, resulting in two deaths. The violence included bombings, robberies and kidnappings, started initially by left-wing groups. 'But from the end of 1968 onwards, and increasingly during 1969 and 1970, the violence of the left was met and surpassed by violence from the militant right.'[43] Colonel Alparslan Turkes founded the MHP (Nationalist Movement Party; Milliyetci Hareket Partisi) in 1969, whose youth organization, known as the Grey Wolves, used street violence and trained in military-style camps to intimidate the left, including teachers and students. Turkes was a fascist advocate of secularism and racist nationalism but started to appeal to Islamic sectors at this time to attract votes. The MHP is still around today, one of three main opposition parties in Turkey.

At around the same time, Professor Necmettin Erbakan became general secretary of a business organization, then became a Member of Parliament as an independent, and finally formed his own party, the National Order Party (Milli Nizam Partisi) in 1970. Gulhan's brother, Orhan (Merve's uncle), graduated from the same high school as Necmettin Erbakan and in 1952 they entered Istanbul Technical University together. They met in the prayer room and became friends. Erbakan would end up playing a major role in Turkish politics and Merve's political life.

Gulhan was planning to stay at home and take care of Merve but Yusuf did not agree and felt that she should pay back society and work. This was hardly indicative of the prevalent patriarchal attitude of conservative religious men, then or now. At the same time, a friend of Yusuf's told him that the German teacher at the Imam Hatip School in Istanbul was retiring. It seemed a perfect opportunity for Gulhan.

But a headscarved woman teaching at Imam Hatip? Once again, Gulhan thought it seemed impossible. One day at Imam Hatip, the principal alerted Gulhan to the impending visit of an inspector from the Ministry of Education. She would have to stay hidden while he was there. Then a knock came on her classroom door and in came the inspector. He was one of Turkey's most famous poets, Cahit Kulebi. At the time he was chief superintendent at the Ministry of Education.

He walked over to Gulhan and said, 'What is the matter? You look frightened. Don't worry, I am a Turk and I am a Muslim too.' Thus Gulhan was able to keep her job.

Gulhan's father, Merve's grandfather, was Ethem Gungen. He was also religious and was close friends with Mehmet Zahid Kotku, a well-known leader of the Naqshbandi order who preached in Bursa and who, like Ethem, spent years in the military during and after the First World War. Gulhan's mother, Merve's grandmother, was Kadriye Gungen. She was born in 1907, and wore a headscarf before she was married, which was at the beginning of the Turkish Republic in 1923 when the new secularism repressed religious practices of all kinds, putting pressure on her and her new husband. She had also memorized parts of the Qur'an and her parents too were very religious, more than all their other siblings. Her father emphasized the need for constant education, not necessarily to progress to a better job, but as an important Islamic value.

Gulhan developed a bond with her new school, its teachers (who knew her husband), the principal and the students, who had great potential but were often from rural areas, awkward and in need of social skills. She had some memories of one particular student, a very talkative fellow with curly hair, who was nominated for president of the school student association. His name was Tayyip Erdogan. Later, he would brag about his Imam Hatip education for the very reason that secularists looked down on it. The schools were viewed as second class whose students could not take exams to apply to the universities, and were for religious people, the 'other'. In actuality, the Imam Hatip schools 'raised many of the future leaders of Turkey, like Erdogan, the majority of the members of his party, and the majority of the mayors across the country'.[44]

It would be thirty years before Tayyip Erdogan would emerge as Turkey's Prime Minister. Meanwhile, on 12 March 1971, Prime Minister Demirel received a memorandum from the Chief of the General Staff that amounted to another military intervention in politics. The government had not been able to stem the rising tide of violence on college campuses. Martial law was eventually imposed, five thousand people were arrested and there were many reports of torture.

In 1975 the Kavakci family moved to Erzurum, where Yusuf joined the faculty of Islamic Studies, then Theology of Erzurum Ataturk University. Gulhan took a position teaching German in the same university. She was accepted wearing a headscarf. Yusuf became Dean of the Faculty (School) of Theology.

Merve attended Ataturk Elementary School in Erzurum, an ancient and cold area in the north-east of Turkey. After her expulsion from the Ankara Faculty of Theology, Hatice Babacan had also migrated to Erzurum, a more welcoming environment than Ankara. Ironically, while not in school, Hatice Babacan taught Merve Kavakci how to read the Qur'an (which is in Arabic). Merve was an exceptional student in both venues. Hatice thought she was the best student she ever had. She even named her new-born daughter after her, an ironic precursor of the many girls later named after her.

The family viewed itself as liberal thinking. The rule was that you could do what you wanted, as long as it was something you could share with the family. And family decisions were subject to a vote, which included children. But even in that environment the young Merve was sometimes a challenge. Outside of school, which prohibited the wearing of headscarves, Merve started covering herself and praying with boys. Then she asked her religion teacher to help her find a place to pray, because the second prayer of the day occurred when school was in session. He replied that he would look for a place for her, but of course he did not because headscarves were not allowed in school. Merve kept asking him if he had found a place, until finally one day the teacher told Merve, 'Let's make believe that you never asked me this, that this never happened, okay?' Merve replied, 'Okay, if this is your answer you will be questioned about it in the hereafter.' She came home upset that day and told her parents what had happened. Her mother replied that in Islam you have to at least try to pray, even though you may not have the opportunity.

Meanwhile, political violence in the late 1970s once again escalated, this time out of control. Some student groups even robbed banks to raise funds. The Grey Wolves and fundamentalist groups on the right fought with leftists. Eighty per cent of high school students could not attend universities because of the scarcity of available places, adding to their stress. Gunmen opened up on 1 May demonstrators in Taksim Square in Istanbul in 1977; by 1979 approximately 1,500 deaths were attributed to political violence,[45] more than 5,000 in total by the end of the 1970s. The result was another coup and this time the Kavakci family would be detrimentally affected.

On 12 September 1980, under the command of General Evren, the military took power for the third time. The Evren government formed YOK, the Higher Education Council, with a strong grip to take control of all universities and their curricula, and to remove left-leaning professors. In 1981 Evren banned headscarves worn by students by means of a National Security Council decree. He personally stated, 'We will not let *basortusu* [headscarves] into the university. We are adamant about that. No one should insist on it. There is no such thing in the religion anyway.' The decree stated, 'Staff and students at the higher educational institutions must be in plain attire that is compatible with Ataturk's reforms and principles' and the 'head will be uncovered and it will not be covered inside the institution'.[46] The actual implementation of the ban was left to the discretion of the universities themselves, resulting in various ways to get around it, including transferring to different universities, wearing wigs on top of headscarves, or hats, and taking examinations without coming to school.[47]

The coup eventually resulted in a new dress code at Erzurum Ataturk University, which included the requirement that hair would be uncovered. Gulhan knew the then Vice-President of YOK, Vecdi Gonul, who was once Turkey's Minister of Defence, so she visited him in Ankara to tell him about her situation, but to no avail. She returned to Erzurum and met with her dean of the faculty, Ahmet Cakir, who asked her to please remove her headscarf because 'we don't want to lose you'. Gulhan replied that she had made the decision to cover many years previously and was not going to change.

Because she was violating the dress code regarding headscarves and not an official law, the university could not officially investigate her; instead they began a campaign to get her to quit. First they reassigned her from teaching philology to teaching at the foreign language school during evening classes. She did not complain and told the administration that it 'would be nice to meet new people'. Then they required her to sit in a classroom and not teach anything, to do nothing. This did upset her but she endured it for two months. The final step was when they cut her salary.

Gulhan told her family that she wanted to resign, that there was no other option. The family took a vote as to what Gulhan should do and they agreed that she should resign rather than be mistreated.

Thus Gulhan left Erzurum for Ankara, to be with her parents. Two days later her brother hired her to work for his international construction company, although she had been an academic and teacher all her life. She had a job, which she eventually learned, but the vocation she loved, her life as a teacher, was taken away from her.

Yusuf was soon to follow. He was told to prevent covered women from entering his classroom, a classroom where they learned about Islam. Notes Merve, 'My father was in his youthful and most productive years teaching and thought it was out of the question for him to even suggest that the covering female students should uncover, so he submitted his resignation as dean of the school.' He left Erzurum on 24 December 1982 while Merve stayed behind with her grandmother, transferring to Erzurum Anadolu Lisesi (an elite school where classes were held in English) for two years to complete her junior high years. She then went to Ankara to join her parents, who missed her.

In Ankara Merve Kavakci attended Ankara Koleji, a private, elite high school founded in 1928 and one of the best schools in Turkey for teaching English well and preparing students for college. She excelled in this environment, as she had at Erzurum Anadolu Lisesi, achieving superior grades. It was around this time that Merve started to wear a headscarf, though not in school, and started praying five times a day.

Merve graduated in 1986 and scored the necessary high grades in university entrance exams to be admitted to Ankara University Medical School.

After her high school graduation, she decided to visit an English teacher who had been a role model for her, and from whom she had learned so much. She bought the teacher a gift to show her appreciation, a standard sign of respect in Turkey, and wanted to tell her about her acceptance to medical school and thank her for all she had done. But this time she wore her headscarf. There was no longer a need to comply with the school's requirements. The headscarf was part of who she was, and school was over. She entered Ankara Koleji and asked to see the vice-principal and her English teacher. As soon as she entered the room, the assistant principal looked at her and said, 'What is this?' Instead of coming to her defence, the English teacher joined in: 'What do you expect, her mother wears one.' Merve was only seventeen and was taken aback and devastated by this insult; she didn't know how to respond. She had known of the red lines that could not be easily crossed in Turkey, and had seen how aggressive secularism had cut short the careers of her mother and father, but this was a surprise attack on her own self-worth simply because of the one square metre of silk that covered her head and neck. The perfect record, the excellent grades, the hard work amounted to nothing if you crossed this imaginary line. Stabbed in the heart, she turned and walked out of the school, never to return again. More than fifteen years later, telling me this story, Merve Kavakci was still visibly shaken.

As the headscarf ban of 1982 started to be implemented at various schools and universities, it soon became a political issue that drove a wedge between secularists and religious people and generated protests across the country, especially in Ankara, the capital city. Then, in the post-coup elections of 1983, Turgut Ozal came to power as Prime Minister, via the Motherland Party (ANAP, Anavatan Partisi), with centre, right and Islamic support, and advocating religious freedom. With Ozal's influence, YOK lifted the headscarf ban if women wore a *turban* in a modern way, but the definition of '*turban*' was vague at best. This vagueness prevented its adoption, plus it did not meet the criteria for covering as religious people interpreted the Qur'an. Moreover, some institutions, including Ankara University Medical School, refused to admit students no matter how they wore their headscarf.[48] The state bureaucracy and judiciary promoted the perception that headscarved women had their own political agenda and that they were being exploited by extremists. Many pointed to neighbouring Iran and its new Islamist Republic that came to power in 1979 as evidence of the threat they represented to Turkey.

In 1984 the *Danistay* (Council of State) ruled against one Hatice Akbulut, declaring that if educated female students chose to cover their heads it was 'espousing a state system that is predicated on religion' and 'antithetical to women's liberation'.[49] Her appeal for being denied entrance to her university because of her headscarf was thus rejected. The argument would be the recurring one: covered women are being manipulated by others to act in a provocative manner. In December 1986, the Higher Education Council tried to stem the protests, stating, this time, that it was 'mandatory for students to wear modern clothing at all times', but left the interpretation up to university administrators.[50] The protests and conflicts continued. Then the Parliament passed legislation letting students wear any attire they wanted. This was met with a veto by President Kenan Evren (yes, the general who led the coup in 1980). In response to that veto, Parliament passed another bill in 1988 allowing headscarves for religious beliefs. The President had run out of vetoes and appealed to the Constitutional Court, which threw the law out. The rejection was met with yet another law lifting the ban. This time the Constitutional Court, although seemingly lacking jurisdiction to interpret the substance of laws, interpreted the law granting freedom to wear what you want as not allowing headscarves.[51]

In summary, regardless of what the liberal-conservative Ozal government tried to do, the Kemalist state (courts, bureaucracy, state institutions), which in Turkey is separate from the ruling government, was not about to lift the ban. Moreover, when allowed, universities tended to go their own way, and that was generally to support the state (which funded them) and the military (whose past infringements on academic institutions were well known).

In her first year, Merve managed to complete her studies because the ban had not yet been put officially into effect at Ankara Medical School but the environment was increasingly hostile. As Merve says:

> One day I was in an exam during freshman year. The professor was walking around and we were all busy with writing. She came and stopped by me and I realized she was standing next to me. And this was a few days before the ban was reactivated so I was wearing my headscarf. She quietly asked me why I was wearing it. I had to stop answering exam questions and in a low voice responded, 'Because Allah, the Creator commends me to do so.' She did not seem satisfied with what she heard. She reacted: 'Come on! Somebody must be paying you to do so. Is it Iran or Saudi Arabia who are paying you?'

To avoid the ban that was imposed in her second year, Merve would wear a wig over her headscarf and drive to school using the unguarded faculty entrance in a car provided by her uncle for that very purpose. The wig looked 'horrible and absurd,' she told me, 'and I hated it.' Then, at one point, the ban was totally imposed. She pulled up to the gate with classmates in her car and the guard stopped her. 'You can't come in,' he shouted. Merve looked at him, seething with anger. Everything she had worked for all her life – her studies, the endless hours of reading and working at home, the envying of her cousins as they each went off to college, the entrance exams, the other graduations, triumphs and awards – they were all gone now, all wasted, stopped by a person with little education at the gate of a university, because of her headscarf.

Because of their faith, Merve and her parents had reached roadblocks in Turkey that had become insurmountable. Protest demonstrations were held all over the country by religious students, women and men, who objected to having their careers cut short by Turkey's aggressive secularism, but to no avail. First her parents and then Merve would visit the United States, and eventually settle in Richardson, Texas, near Dallas. It was Yusuf's idea. He was invited to be an Imam, a religious leader, at a Muslim community centre there. They left everything behind – their friends and possessions, their culture and all they had worked for – to find some religious freedom in the state of Texas.

Merve Kavakci married in 1988, after which she attended Richland College and then the University of Texas in Dallas earning a BS degree in computer science in 1993. She marvelled at her freedom. One day she came home after visiting a local mall and told her mother with amazement how she walked past a woman who simply said 'hello' to her without so much as a double-take, just walking on by without a second look.

Indeed, religious freedom in America was something Merve would get used to, making the lack of it that much more intolerable on her return to Turkey.

In 1994 Merve Kavakci, after completing her BS degree in Computer Science, did want to return to her native country. She and her husband had divorced and she was now a single parent. She left her parents and sisters and moved back to Ankara with her daughters, Fatima and Mariam. They lived in the family flat in the Mebusevleri area of Ankara. Merve says:

> I returned to my home country so that my daughters would speak Turkish, learn our customs and spend their elementary school years in Turkey because it is during this period that children develop their personalities. Now with my grandmother and uncle taking care of me, Ankara was home again. My aged grandmother, who had also raised me when my mother had been a teacher in Istanbul, now was taking care of my children. I would hug her often and joked that there was no running away from us.

It was Merve's maternal uncle, Orhan Gungen, who gained her a high-level, though non-paying, position working for the Welfare Party that facilitated her return to Turkey.

The Welfare Party was founded in 1983 by Necmettin Erbakan as the third party of the Islamist National Outlook Movement, which he originated and which had represented Islamism in politics since 1970.[52] Merve wanted a position in which she could freely wear her headscarf and the Welfare Party presented the perfect atmosphere. As a US-educated bilingual Islamic woman, Merve would find it difficult, if not impossible, to secure a white-collar position in companies and organizations that were not part of the Islamic community – a level of discrimination that persists today in Turkey. In addition, the party could use her obvious intellectual abilities and language skills.

Turan Gungen and Necmettin Erbakan graduated from the same high school in Istanbul and in 1952 Turan's brother, Orhan, and Erbakan entered Istanbul Technical University together, studying structural engineering. Orhan went on to launch a highly successful construction company, one of the first Turkish companies to do business in other countries. Erbakan completed his PhD in mechanical engineering and soon began a long political career.

It could be said that Merve Kavakci had a 'pedigree' background for politics, even though women, and in particular the ones who covered themselves, had never risen to decision-making positions in the party nor run for office. Her uncle, Turan Gungen, was active politically all his life. Orhan was also close friends with Temel Karamollaoglu, then Vice-President of the Welfare Party, who described Orhan as one of its founders.[53] Over the years, Orhan received several proposals to run for office – including, at one point, from Suleyman Demirel – but turned them all down to focus on his family business. Merve's mother and father were also well known in Islamic political circles.

It was an opportune time for her to start working for the party, a time when Islamic political organizations and activism on the part of Islamic women were on the rise. In the Welfare Party organization men and women worked separately, with women playing a key role interacting with other women in neighbourhood meetings to support Welfare Party candidates, an approach that fitted with Turkey's conservative culture regarding interaction among men and women. It was a perfect fit for Merve, who excelled in this environment and who needed also to raise her young daughters, Mariam and Fatima. on her own. She was head of Foreign Affairs in the Women's Commission of the Welfare Party starting in 1994 and then for the Virtue Party when Welfare was shut down in 1998 by the Constitutional Court. She accepted, on the condition that she would be allowed to bring her four- and five-year-old daughters with her to work. It was the best option for her. A headscarved computer engineer would be unlikely to find work, and she was happy to be accepted and valued in a welcoming environment. Orhan was confident that Merve could handle the job, which included travelling overseas and giving presentations. 'She was so talented,' he told me at his home in Ankara. 'As a child her ability to learn was amazing. She was determined to work and study from an early age and was an excellent student, plus her English was perfect.'[54]

Notes

1 Pronounced *Kavahkcha*. Ms Kavakci recently married and is now known as Merve Kavakci Islam.
2 'Islamic Woman in a Headscarf Suddenly Galvanizes Turkey', 4 May 1999, *NY Times.*
3 *Turkish Daily News*, 4 May 1999.
4 TESEV (Turkish Economic and Social Studies Foundation) and other surveys, including a research report by *Milliyet*, put the figure at over 60 per cent. The Organization for Women's Rights against Discrimination (AKDER www.ak.der.org) can provide a comprehensive statistical study of the impact of the headscarf ban in Turkey for those interested.
5 On this date, the National Security Council issued an ultimatum to the ruling government to clamp down on 'Islamic activities' in public, which it attributed to the leading party of the coalition government, the pro-Islamic Welfare Party (Refah Partisi).
6 See, for example, 'No Real Threat to Secularism, Says TESEV', *Journal of the Turkish Weekly*, 24 November 2006, and surveys by Gallup, including 'Headscarves and Secularism: Voices from Turkish Women', *Journal of the Turkish Weekly*, 2 August 2008, among others. The political meaning of the headscarf is derived from the early Turkish Republic and Ataturk's cultural reforms, not from the motivations of covered women.
7 *University World News*, 3 March 2010.
8 *Today's Zaman*, 3 March 2010.
9 Women's Participation Issue and Analysis of Woman Organization Structure in Turkey: A Comparison of KADER (Association for Supporting and Training Women Candidates) and Türk Kadınlar Birliği (Turkish Women Union).

10 Stephen Kinzer, *Crescent & Star*, Farrar, Straus and Giroux, 2001.
11 http://www.yurthaber.com/haber/mhp-kirikkale-milletvekili-osman-durmus-kendisini-savundu-262007.htm
12 This figure is based on percentage surveys conducted by TESEV; see www.tesev.org.tr.
13 Dilek Cindolu and Gizem Zencirci, 'The Headscarf in Turkey in Public and State Spheres', *Middle Eastern Studies*, December 2008.
14 Interview with Dilipak, 21 January 2010.
15 *DK Eyewitness Travel Guide: Istanbul*, Dorling Kindersley, 2007, p. 72.
16 'Mehmet's own army was far from mono-ethnic. Turks were in the clear majority, but there were Kurds, Arabs, Persians and plenty of Christian European irregulars: Hungarians and Italians, Greeks and Germans', Chris Morris, *The New Turkey*, Granta Books, 2005, p. 13.
17 'Their defeat of the Serbs on the Blackbird Field in Kosovo in 1389 was a battle which still inspired thoughts of revenge in Slobodan Milosovic six hundred years later', Morris, p. 13.
18 Bernard Lewis, *The Emergence of Modern Turkey*, Oxford University Press, 1968, p. 261.
19 Philip Mansel, *Constantinople*, Penguin Books, 1997, p. 412.
20 Wikipedia.org/wiki/History_of_Ankara.
21 Morris, p. 28.
22 The basis of this material can be found in Erik Zurcher's *Turkey: A Modern History*, IB Tauris, London, 1997.
23 Zurcher, p. 199.
24 Zurcher, p. 200.
25 Zurcher, p. 201.
26 Zurcher, p. 215.
27 Morris, p. 67.
28 Kinzer, p. 62.
29 Zurcher, p. 244.
30 Zurcher, p. 245.
31 Zurcher, p. 245.
32 Zurcher, p. 245.
33 Zurcher, p. 245.
34 Feroz Ahmad, *Turkey: The Quest for Identity*, Oneworld Publications, 2003, p. 134.
35 Hatice Babacan is the aunt of Ali Babacan, Turkey's Minister Responsible for the Economy (at the time of writing).
36 Dayla Rogers, 'A House of Mirrors: Representations of Veiling in Modern Turkey', senior thesis, University of Michigan, 2006.
37 Ibid. Dayla Rogers also cites Cihan Aktas, Tanziment'tanat Gunumuze Kilik Kryafet ve Iktidar I and II, Istanbul, Nehir, 1889 and 1990.
38 Interview with Saim Altunbas, Ankara, 21 April 2010.
39 Karen Armstrong, *Islam, A Short History*, Phoenix Press, 2000, p. 50.
40 M. Hakan Yavuz, *Islamic Political Identity in Turkey*, Oxford University Press, 2003, p. 55.
41 *Ibid.*
42 Yavuz, p. 63.
43 Zurcher, p. 70.
44 Merve Kavakci, *Headscarf Politics in Turkey*, Palgrave Macmillan, New York, 2010, p. 135.

45 Zurcher, p. 263.
46 Kavakci, p. 51.
47 *Ibid.*
48 Kavakci, p. 53.
49 Kavakci, p. 56.
50 Gul Ceylan Tok, 'The Securitization of the Headscarf Issue in Turkey', International Studies Association of Ritsumeikan University, *Annual Review of International Studies*, 2009, p. 123.
51 Tok, p. 124.
52 Umit Cizre and Menderes Cinar, 'Turkey 2002: Kemalism, Islamism, and Politics in Light of the February 28 Process', *The South Atlantic Quarterly* 102:2/3, Spring/Summer 2003. Copyright 2003 by Duke University Press.
53 Interview with Temel Karamollaoglu at Saadet Party Headquarters, 19 April 2010.
54 Interview with Orhan Gungen, 23 April 2010.

2

Islamic Mobilization
and Its Response

In 1993, a year before Merve's return, President Turgut Ozal, leader of the ANAP party, died suddenly of a heart attack, allowing his rival, Suleyman Demirel, to become President a month later. Tansu Ciller, who became Turkey's first woman Prime Minister, replaced Demirel as the leader of the centre-right True Path Party (Dogru Yol Partisi). Ozal's death likely helped the Welfare Party fill the void left by a weakened ANAP, which had received wide support, including from Islamic communities.

Nonetheless, the rise of Islamic-friendly parties in the 1990s, the Welfare Party (WP) and its successor the Virtue Party (VP), was a sign of significant economic and social change in Turkey, which culminated in the current ruling AK Party's ascent to power in 2002. In spite of cultural and religious control by the state, religious Muslim communities survived and prospered through their own networks. One big example is the Fethullah Gulen movement, which claims to be a non-political example, and has set up its own schools, companies and business networks in Turkey and dozens of other countries, and whose holdings today are valued at US$20 billion. The formation of the MUSIAD organization (Independent Industrialists and Businessmen's Association), similar to a Muslim Chamber of Commerce, is another, in response to its secular counterpart, the Turkish Industrialists and Businessmen's Association (TUSIAD). The first ever meeting of the heads of these two business organizations did not occur until 13 May 2010, another clear example of the polarization that exists in Turkey.

Wendy Kristianasen, the veteran writer on politics in the Middle East for *Le Monde*, wrote the following regarding a new generation of people in Turkey and their views:

> If the ideology of this generation is a touch simplistic (Islamic communities taking over from the nation-state), they are

nonetheless informed by an impressive knowledge of Western as well as Islamic thought. Pluralism, human rights, freedom and social justice are their slogans. Islamist intellectuals, feminists, high-flying professionals, Anatolian entrepreneurs, all the elements of Turkish Islam are harnessing the unstoppable vigour of modern Turkey to bridge the gap separating the 'newcomers' from Asia Minor from the Istanbul elites.[1]

Erbakan's WP gained 19.1 per cent of the vote in municipal elections in March 1994, doubling its previous support, thanks to its 'excellent grassroots organization' and strength in metropolitan areas; more importantly, 'six of the fifteen largest Turkish cities, including Istanbul and Ankara, were taken over by the WP'.[2] These cities represent huge resources and political power. Tayyip Erdogan, running for the Welfare Party, was elected Mayor of Istanbul in 1994. Seventeen of the thirty-three local municipalities in Istanbul were also controlled by the Welfare Party, plus two hundred municipalities across Turkey.

The Welfare Party's success in the municipal elections of 1994, and particularly the legislative elections of 1995, 'shocked the political establishment'.[3] But it is important to note that the party set itself apart from all other Turkish political parties in the organized ways it garnered support and developed relationships with its constituents. This characteristic is important:

> Unlike mainstream Turkish parties, which are notably elite in their orientation and lack substantive organic ties with their voting base, Welfare was able to develop substantial support at the grassroots level through an extensive organizational structure. For example, provincial organizational committees were further divided into district committees, which reviewed neighborhood organization through periodic inspections. Neighborhood organizers appointed street representatives that served as Welfare's presence at ground level even in the poorest neighborhoods. Party representatives were also careful to attend communal events, often distributing municipal welfare services in visible but very local forums.[4]

This was not a top-down imposition of party rule but a micro-managed, bottom-up campaign that touched one voter at a time – the essence of representative democracy. The Welfare Party's success in the 1994 elections was a 'game-changing' event that would have lasting effects not only on Turkish politics, but also on the nature of Islamic support for political parties. As Head of Foreign Affairs for the Women's Commission, Merve Kavakci gave speeches in Europe and the Middle East supporting the mission of the Welfare Party and its successor, Virtue. She usually gave similar speeches, espousing unity among the Muslim *ummah* (Muslims around the world), explaining the need to live in peace with non-Muslims, describing for the audience the struggle of the Islamic parties and people in Turkey, and promoting the role and importance of women to the Welfare Party's success in the 1990s. She used verses from the Qur'an in all her speeches and translated them afterwards. She also spoke of the need to stand up against Zionism.

A few years hence, these speeches would be turned into a major controversy. The Turkish government and mainstream media, anti-Islamic sectors in Washington, DC think tanks and intelligence agencies tried to pull out segments of Merve's speeches to create fabrications or discredit her, by trying to link her to the groups supported by the organizations she gave speeches to, and to the people in attendance. These speeches would become the centre of media smear campaigns, distracting voters from the fact of her election and assassinating her character.

Islamic women in the party

An indispensable part of the WP's success was due to the hard work of women in the party. In Istanbul alone they comprised 52 per cent of party members: 1,265,000 women.

The struggle of Merve Kavakci is the struggle of Islamic women in Turkey and cannot be understood without realizing the plight of these women, their political activism and the fact that they were fighting battles on two fronts: a rigid understanding of secularism from the Kemalist elite (which included the state, military and bureaucracy); and patriarchal attitudes on the part of Islamic men generally and in the Welfare Party specifically, but also quite palpable and visible among secular men. She became symbolic for these women, and for this significant movement, which can be termed as the cause of religious freedom and women's rights. This may be why Merve would sometimes also gain the support of non-Islamic women, many of whom had their own concerns at the time (and now), who had begun organizing in the mid-1980s, particularly against repression at home.

One of the most valuable works on this subject is by a social anthropologist, Jenny White, who spent years in Turkey interviewing men and women involved in the Islamist movement.[5] Her on-the-ground research clarifies the motivations and involvement of women in the Welfare Party and the nature of this support. Getting hit from both sides with discrimination and subjugation, Islamic women felt empowered by political work and were 'very much interested in using party activism to advance the position of women, particularly through work outside the home'.[6] They were motivated to play active roles even though they were paradoxically subject to discrimination within their own party:

> Activists in the Women's Branch did not have the power to affect the party's practices by voting on party policies or even by setting up job training courses for women. Yet they believed that the party would give women the opportunities they sought. After all, as the head of the Women's Branch had pointed out, women themselves, through their party activities, had become independent and competent, left their houses, 'found' themselves. At one level, this is an elevation of women and an expression of the party's avowed principle of not making distinctions (between men and women, veiled and unveiled women, social classes, ethnicities, and so on). On another level, while women were given status in the party, they were not given access to administrative or financial decision-making, except within their own tightly organized but autonomous hierarchies. The party projected an ambivalent message. For instance, while Mayor Erdogan supported women working, women were only loosely incorporated into the party structure and there were no women in the highest positions.[7]

In America, where both discrimination and civil rights laws are well established, this type of practice is called a 'double standard'. The men in the party were simply reflecting their own values, as Professor White's interviews confirmed. Nevertheless, 'despite their isolation from the centre of power and policy-making, female Welfare Party supporters were extraordinarily successful in popular mobilization'.[8]

One of the foremost activist Islamic women in Turkey today is Sibel Eraslan, a lawyer and columnist. In the 1990s she was the head of the WP's Women's Commission in Istanbul and later she would help manage Merve's campaign. She was a key person in mobilizing the women's vote for the 1994 elections, gaining the powerful municipalities of Istanbul and Ankara. She led a force of 18,000 women workers who interacted with 200,000 potential women voters. Yet after the victories in March 1994, Sibel Eraslan was not given any position within the newly elected WP administration and was expected to go back home to look after the kids. She told Tayyip Erdogan, the newly elected mayor of Istanbul, her feelings about the 'dismissal of women after the election'.[9] This was the plight of Islamic women workers during this time, critical to the party's success yet treated in a patriarchal and unequal way compared to men.

Prime Minister Erbakan

In elections on 24 December 1995 the WP received 21.4 per cent of the vote, ahead of all other parties – 'a true watershed in modern Turkish history'.[10] Not surprisingly, although the WP was in the driver seat to lead a coalition, the other political parties refused to form a government with the Islamists. Plus the military, press and major business organizations, including TUSIAD, all came out staunchly against any government with the WP.

Yet contrary to uniformist views of the Islamic supporters of the Welfare Party, a survey during this time found that 41 per cent of those who voted for the WP viewed themselves as secular, and 'regarded Ataturk as the first among the great men of all time, even before the Prophet'.[11] Certainly the WP was mainly Islamic-friendly, as was most of its leadership. The state's harsh measures against Islamic people, their symbols and activities, including the headscarf ban in universities and state employment, which had a detrimental effect on the career aspirations of Islamic women, formed the core of their constituency. Nevertheless, their approach to garnering local support by working with non-party organizations, as well as their middle-of-the-road-looking advertisement campaigns designed by a professional marketing company, helped them to gain the support of non-Islamic people as well. In spite of this, they were summarily mistrusted by all the other political parties.

President Demirel asked Erbakan, as was tradition, to attempt to form a coalition. But this partnership, between ANAP and WP, failed due to pressure from the military. This was followed by a brief coalition between ANAP and Tansu Ciller's True Path Party (TPP), which had gained just less than 20 per cent of the vote. Yet this coalition also fell apart after four months when the ANAP started to investigate Ciller for alleged corruption. Finally, Erbakan made a nefarious deal with Ciller that was shady from anyone's viewpoint: he agreed to stop Parliament's investigations into her alleged unlawful dealings if she entered a coalition with the Welfare Party. She had 'campaigned on the platform that she was the salvation for a secular Turkey threatened by the rising tide of "fundamentalism" and that she would never form an alliance with the Islamists'.[12] However, this was a deal she could not refuse.

As a result, on 28 June 1996 Necmettin Erbakan became Turkey's first Islamic Prime Minister; Ciller was to take over two years later.

Things seemed peaceful at first, but the nation was watching and waiting, as were Western countries, to see how the Erbakan government would act. The army was not pleased and, in anticipation of problems, fired officers with Islamic leanings. The new coalition seemed to go out of its way to avoid confrontation in political appointments, and Erbakan's previous anti-Israeli and anti-EU rhetoric stopped.[13] 'Tansu Ciller could not afford to break it up with the accusations of corruption hanging over her head like a sword of Damocles and Erbakan could afford to wait, while his support in the country continued to increase. In fact, mid-term elections in 1996 consistently gave him over 30 per cent of the vote.'[14]

Merve Kavakci's work for the party continued domestically. When she was working during the summer of 1996 for the upcoming elections in Istanbul – to garner more support for Tayyip Erdogan from non-WP districts – she was dismayed at the prejudices of and misconceptions she heard from secular people. She attended rallies during the mornings, then met with small groups in the afternoons and evenings in people's homes, accompanied by Erbakan's wife and daughter, and Erdogan's wife, Emine. Some of the questions appalled her. Are religious people against democracy? Do they have normal lives at home like other women? Many of these women had for the first time the opportunity to talk to conservative women in a frank environment and were surprised to see what they were really like, as opposed to their preconceived notions. Merve saw this as making progress and thought these women were happy to have met them.

Meanwhile, the print and television media, dominated by the Dogan and Bilgin conglomerates, constantly attacked the new government. Erbakan was criticized for visits to Iran and other Muslim nations, although previous Prime Ministers had done the same. But he then made a big miscalculation by embracing Muammar el-Qaddafi in a visit to Libya, who blasted Turkish foreign policy in front of him as he sat quietly and listened without response in a tent on the outskirts of Tripoli. The press had a field day:

> Mass-circulation newspapers carried banner headlines like CATASTROPHE IN LIBYA, NIGHT OF SHAME and QADDAFI'S RAVINGS. A report in the secularist paper *Sabah* began, 'A barefoot Bedouin stood in front of Erbakan and the Turkish delegation last night and hurled insults at Turkey.' Even the Islamic-oriented *Zaman* was scandalized, with its correspondent writing: 'Qaddafi's bitter words had the effect of a machine gun being fired at Erbakan. It was as if an atom bomb had fallen on the tent.'[15]

After almost thirty years involved in politics in Turkey, which is a young democracy, Necmettin Erbakan's actions during his short-lived term are difficult to understand. The striking fact is that he came to power with just 21 per cent of the vote yet acted as if the whole country was behind a change in foreign policy from the West to the Middle East. Perhaps we can attribute this to the political immaturity of Turkey, and its short history of democratic institutions and practices. In America when a new president is elected with a narrow majority it is said that he has a slim 'mandate' and must therefore work hard with the opposition party to effect change. Erbakan had no mandate whatsoever, had barely one-fifth of the votes, yet he attacked the other political parties as 'hostile to religion for [the last] thirty years'.[16] He replaced Kemalists regularly with his own party loyalists, encouraged those with radical Islamist views in the Anatolian countryside, espoused worldwide Muslim solidarity, and disavowed any human rights abuses in Turkey.[17] Instead of balancing Kemalism with democratic initiatives that could benefit those with deep attachments to religion as well as those with few religious inclinations, he managed to alienate all sides, exacerbating fears that existed for decades, which were fuelled and intensified daily by newspapers and television programmes.

Erbakan's opposition took the change in power as all-out war. On the one hand, 'The Kemalists did not utilize this historic moment [Erbakan's election] as an opportunity to form a new social contract based on tolerant secularism, democracy, and the rule of law.'[18] On the other hand, the government seemed to upset the traditional balance between the government, the military and the business cartels. This was borne out by the sale of state assets per International Monetary Fund pressure to privatize Turkey's institutions to the Dogan Cartel after the coup, assets that were sold for much less than they were worth. Erbakan cut off access to state resources, engendering ideological attacks that were more likely a front for the loss of these cosy relationships. In Turkey, as in other countries, power politics and economic self-interest are often embedded in ideological conflicts.

Turkish and Western writers list the many missteps of the Erbakan government leading to the post-modern coup process that began on 28 February 1997. They include: attempts to lift the headscarf ban that prevented covered women from entering universities and working for the civil service; inviting the leaders of traditional Sufi orders in their religious attire to a fast-breaking dinner held at the Prime Minister's residence; and the change in foreign policy, and local support for the Iranian ambassador, who gave a fiery pro-Islamic speech in the town of Sincan where flags of Hamas and Hizbullah (Islamic radical groups) were displayed and which resulted in tanks rumbling through the centre of town (the military insisted that they had got 'lost'). In hindsight, even though the commentary from academics makes sense, it would be unacceptable to suggest that such actions justified a military coup, actions that would not be viewed as justifiable in any modern democratic country in the West. It is a major flaw in Turkey's democratic state that the Turkish military views itself as the entity to solve supposedly unsolvable conflicts, conflicts whose resolution could not be left to 'irresponsible' politicians, in their view. One wonders even today if it is not this 'tutelage' by the military that has given rise to much of the incompetence and immaturity in Turkish politics. Certainly Erbakan made political mistakes, but so did George Bush and Tony Blair. We don't hear commentators explaining away military coups in their countries on the basis of leaders' mistakes.

The '28 February Process'

Can democracy thrive in a country where the military plays an active role in politics? Every fifteen years or so, since the beginning of multi-party politics in Turkey, the military has interfered in the political process and taken over for a couple of years, eradicating parties it did not like and arresting thousands (in 1980 more than 650,000 were swept up). In Turkey, military coups have been supported by secular Turks, to varying degrees, and that was certainly the case with the one in 1997.[19] When I bring up this subject in my own conversations with Turks they often seem to shrug their shoulders and state that occasionally the military has to act, particularly to stifle the 'Islamist threat'. It is relatively easy for academics and commentators to intellectualize in a detached way the coups that have occurred in Turkey, seen as a natural outgrowth of its military beginning, adoption of an aggressive form of secularism, unstable politics and rise of Islamist political movements in the Middle East. We cannot expect Turks to have the same sensibilities as Americans, whose closest bout with a military takeover came with vague threats during the Kennedy Administration in 1963 and the imagined 'Seven Days in May' in 1964. America has a long history of putting the military in its place, from General MacArthur during the Korean War to General McChrystal for comments reported recently in Rolling Stone magazine. Clear civilian control of the military, starting with General George Washington checking with the Continental Congress before he embarked for Boston to New York City during the War of Independence, has been axiomatic from before America was a country.

Things are not just different in Turkey, they *feel* different. The military's presence is never far away. Their offices and barracks line the main highways in Ankara with soldiers in military fatigues and weapons at the ready guarding entrances. Often their facilities are in beautiful locations, such as the military social club and installation on the Marmara Sea in Fenerbahce on the Asian side of Istanbul, or in Harbiye and Tarabya on the European side. Other military facilities are located in prime coastal areas where one would expect to find a luxury hotel not military base. Signs in Turkish and English around such installations indicate that taking photographs of their facilities is unlawful, which sometimes an unfortunate tourist neglects to take seriously. And statements, comments, warnings and threats from generals are also voiced in the media against various groups, including the press. The current state of the military's influence in politics will be discussed in the Afterword.

Just two years before Merve Kavakci's nomination for Parliament, the Turkish high command of the armed forces issued demands by means of the National Security Council during one of their monthly meetings directly to Prime Minister Erbakan on 28 February 1997, to block Islamic activities in public in almost every sphere. In a country where the military undertakes to defend against internal as well as external threats and has massive presence in the institutions that define these threats, it is expected that they become engaged with political issues that, after all, make up 'internal' or 'external' threats. Likewise, in Turkey the military has been involved in making or breaking governments, as well as public campaigns against political Islam and writing its own bills, especially beginning with the 1995 elections.[20]

The coup on 28 February is called a 'process' in Turkey because the military's direct role, as well as long-term effects, have continued over time, attested to by the lengthy debates every 28 February on the topic of democratic reforms. It is also called the 'post-modern' coup, one that lasted until 2002 when the AK Party came to power. Regardless, the military is often viewed as possibly coming out of their barracks and meddling in the affairs of state directly. Its presence also creates an atmosphere of self-censorship in Turkey, along with laws that limit free speech.

The coup process reversed the post-1980 atmosphere in which Islam was incorporated into public discussions with open negotiation between the secularists and Islamists, and instead 'revived the myth of a homogenous nation and society'.[21]

This was not a coup of guns and bullets, but rather threats by the military, briefings of the mass media, academics and judges, and public pronouncements and conferences on the threat of Islam and Kurdish nationalism to the state. It was a cultural and political war against Muslim sectors of society, the mayors they elected and the budgets they controlled.

The relentless attacks and distortions by the media during Merve's campaign two years later can be traced in part to the nature of the '28 February Process' that was engineered by the Turkish Armed Forces (TAF). Before the intervention, the TAF invited journalists, academics and judges to conferences to let them know about the threats to Turkey they saw coming from Islamists and Kurds. Once the coup occurred they took steps to silence the opposition. The military continued to 'work very closely' with major media cartels such as the Dogan group, which publishes the dailies *Hurriyet* and *Milliyet*, and leading business and university administrators in justifying the need for military intervention and civilian purges because of alleged 'national security threats'. 'Without the need for even cursory evidence, the army declared 19 newspapers, 20 national television stations, 51 radio stations, 110 magazines, and 1,200 student hostels as constituting the "reactionary sector".'[22]

A summary of the 28 February actions is as follows.

> All primary and secondary school curricula were altered so as to emphasize both the secularist history and character of the Republic and the new security threats posed by political Islam and separatists movements. Teaching on Ataturkism was expanded to cover all courses taught at all levels and types of schools. The secondary school system for prayer-leaders and preachers (*imam hatip*) was scrapped and an eight-year mandatory schooling system was introduced. Appointments of university chancellors since 1997 were pointedly made from among staunch Kemalists. Teaching programmes on Kemalist principles, the struggle against reactionism, and national security issues were also extended to top bureaucrats and prayer leaders. Finally, military institutions and personnel were actively involved in administering the programs.[23]

Moreover, laws were changed so that national security concerns dominated the areas of anti-terrorism, media, political parties, education, civil rights and liberties.[24] Teaching the Qur'an to those under twelve years of age was also banned. A few months' later 300,000 demonstrators gathered in Istanbul to protest against the closing of Imam Hatip Schools, and massive demonstrations occurred elsewhere protesting against the headscarf ban and other promulgations by the military. The response to these demonstrations was further threats by the military to use force against Islamist groups, which led Erbakan to finally resign as Prime Minister on 17 June 1997.

Closing of the Welfare Party

On 16 January 1998 the Constitutional Court shut down the WP and banned Erbakan from political activity for five years. It became the fourteenth political party to be banned in Turkey by the Court since 1983. The Court cited statements from the WP about the right to wear headscarves in the universities as evidence of its violation of secularism and its non-acceptance of Kemalist doctrine, which, it proclaimed, is 'the way of life' in Turkey. This use of the 'independent' courts, which favour Kemalism and espouse secularism to alter laws and counter liberal policies, is a continuing practice and one that the AK Party is today trying to reverse with constitutional reforms. The Turkish Constitution refers to the 'principles of secularism' and loyalty to 'the nationalism of Ataturk' throughout, allowing court members to freely interpret those clauses as they wish.

Tayyip Erdogan

Tayyip Erdogan became the Prime Minister of Turkey in 2003. He attended the first and most important Imam Hatip School in Istanbul – religious, vocational schools that are administered by the state – where, as noted earlier, Merve's mother taught him. Growing up in tough neighbourhoods in Istanbul he once sold *simits* (Turkish bagels) on the street. He was an excellent soccer player but did not join a professional team because he refused to shave his Islamic beard.[25] He joined Erbakan's Welfare Party and was one of the younger generations of intellectuals in the party 'who did not seek to subordinate democracy to a particular interpretation of Islam' and who 'conceded that, in a democratic political system, Islam in various forms will be one voice among a number of competing visions'.[26] He won the mayoralty election of Istanbul in 1994 and is today the charismatic Prime Minister of Turkey, its best known and sometimes highly controversial leader, and head of the moderate and Islamic-friendly AK Party.

But in the wake of the 1997 coup Erdogan was vulnerable because he 'was one of the most popular politicians in the country' who ran Istanbul honestly and efficiently.[27] And so the State Security Court brought about his arrest for reciting a poem by Ziya Gokalp, 'a nationalist icon for early Kemalist leaders'. One of the verses he recited was:

> Turkey's mosques will be our barracks, the minarets our bayonets, the domes our helmets, and the faithful our soldiers.[28]

Merve Kavakci met Erdogan shortly before he was due to serve his sentence. He appeared with her in Istanbul and supported her campaign, and his wife campaigned with her when calling on women. Merve often sought his advice, even twice visiting him in prison and cited her admiration for him when interviewed, as we shall see. 'He is part of the family,' she told me, and they remain in touch to this day.

Unfortunately, many Western writers have not bothered to explain Erdogan's jailing and viewed it, by default, as legitimate. However, his arrest was not about a traditional poem – references to Islam and calls to prayer can also be found in nationalist songs and even the Turkish National Anthem (the eighth stanza) – but had everything to do with political power struggle and removing potential opposition.

The Virtue Party

It was in this environment that the Virtue (Fazilet) Party (VP) was formed as the WP's successor, under the leadership of Recai Kutan. Needless to say, it was fearful from the beginning of being shut down by the secular establishment. The VP tried to redefine itself in terms of human rights and democracy, and as an advocate for admission into the European Union, which would more likely protect it from closure based on anti-secular grounds. Many of the young reformers in the VP were averse to saying or doing anything that would bring about closure, but also were sincere about a more moderate, less Islamic-oriented platform which would yield a greater chance for success from a broader constituency.

Not surprisingly, Erbakan and Kutan's tone became conciliatory[29] shortly after the 28 February intervention. The VP also employed a consensus-seeking strategy, expressing no discontent over the undemocratic nature of the crackdown on Islamic identity. Kutan went as far as declaring that 'they will not be a party to any conflict' and that 'they will not bring up the issue of the headscarf even though it is the right thing to do so'. He even lent some legitimacy to the '28 February Process' by indicating that they understand the TAF's sensitivity on secularism. It must be pointed out that this obedient stance was motivated by the VP's massive sense of insecurity – so much so that on that particular point, the party even asked the opinion of the chief of staff about its political programme.[30]

Certainly these views can be attributed to military pressure. As Kutan lamented to me during an interview, 'We give them guns and then they use them against us.' Although the VP tempered its Islamic message, very little seemed to change with the closing of the WP and its replacement by the VP. Its supporters and participants across Turkey were the same. However, there was divisiveness in the party leadership from the beginning. Erbakan was viewed by younger constituents as a 'dinosaur' and a 'creature of the state'.[31] The rising star of the VP was the new Mayor of Istanbul, Recep Tayyip Erdogan, whose populist style contrasted sharply with Erbakan's old-school elitism and, for that matter, Kutan's. He also embraced what Jenny White called 'vernacular politics', the mobilization of horizontal networks in Islamic communities. He walked the streets and was seen in the neighbourhoods, at local barber shops and restaurants – a highly charismatic man of the people who lives today, as Prime Minister, in a nondescript neighbourhood in Ankara.

Erdogan's political views – until his conviction in January 1998 by the State Security Court for 'promoting religious hatred' – were less ideological and more pragmatic in a bottom-up sense. Even his political opponents admired the honesty and efficiency with which he ran Turkey's largest city. But the military saw him as an obvious threat. He was sentenced to ten months in jail and banned from politics for life, although both sentences would later be reduced. In the meantime, Abdullah Gul, Erbakan's Minister of State and government spokesman, who played a big role in formally restructuring Virtue from Welfare, became the new representative of the young constituents who favoured Erdogan. Gul obtained his doctorate from Istanbul University in 1980, then taught at Sakarya University for three years before working as an economist for the Islamic Development Bank. He entered Parliament in 1991 running at the invitation of the WP. Jenny White described Gul's moderate views:

> Insisting that the party had changed even from the days of Erdogan's tenure, Gul supported tolerance of different lifestyles, arguing (in response to an interviewer's question) that such issues as whether or not a woman wore a bathing suit in public were personal decisions and of no interest to the party. He supported gender equality and expressed an interest in attracting the support of what he called 'contemporary modern women who accept a lifestyle like that found in developed countries'.[32]

After Erbakan's resignation, Mesut Yilmaz became the Prime Minister as head of the Motherland Party (ANAP). He resisted with a good deal of courage the TAF's prerogative to define internal 'Islamic' threats, to the consternation of the military, and implemented hardly any of the military's directives. But by November 1998, he lost a vote of confidence because of alleged underworld ties in the bidding of state contracts. Suleyman Demirel, the President, nominated Bulent Ecevit of the centre-left Democratic Left Party (DSP) to become Prime Minister. The military supported Ecevit and the new government prepared for elections to be held in April 1999.

Notes

1 Wendy Kristianasen, 'New Faces of Islam', *Le Monde diplomatique*, July 1997.
2 Zurcher, p. 311.
3 R. Quinn Mecham, 'From the Ashes of Virtue, a Promise of Light: The Transformation of Political Islam in Turkey', *Third World Quarterly*, Vol. 25, No. 2 (2004), p. 342.
4 Mecham, p. 343.
5 Jenny B. White, *Islamic Mobilization in Turkey: A Study in Vernacular Politics*, University of Washington Press, 2002.
6 White, p. 234.
7 White, pp. 239–240.
8 *Ibid.*
9 *Ibid.*
10 Erik Zurcher, *Turkey: A Modern History*, IB Tauris, London, 1997, p. 313.
11 Sami Zubaida, 'Turkish Islam and National Identity', *Middle East Report*, No. 199, June 1996, p. 10.
12 Feroz Ahmad, *Turkey: The Quest for Identity*, Oxford University Press, 2003, p. 169.
13 Zurcher, p. 315.
14 *Ibid.*
15 Stephen Kinzer, *Crescent & Star*, Farrar, Straus and Giroux, 2001, p. 71.
16 Kinzer, p. 70.
17 Kinzer, p. 70.
18 M. Hakan Yavuz, *Islamic Political Identity in Turkey*, Oxford University Press, 2003, p. 42.
19 Zurcher, p. 300.
20 Umit Cizre and Menderes Cinar, 'Turkey 2002: Kemalism, Islamism, and Politics in Light of the February 28 Process', *The South Atlantic Quarterly*, 102:2/3, Spring/Summer 2003.
21 Cizre and Cinar, p. 312.
22 Yavuz, p. 246.
23 Cizre and Cinar, p. 312.
24 *Ibid.*

25 Rogers, p. 38.
26 Yavuz, p. 226.
27 *Ibid.*
28 *Ibid.*
29 Yavuz, p. 248.
30 Cizre and Cinar, p. 323.
31 White, p. 145.
32 White, p. 147.

3

A Covered Candidate
Runs For Parliament

———

Prior to the elections in April 1999 President Demirel stated that if the Virtue Party and True Path Party won the election 'the state would act'.[1] He stated, 'The military belongs to the people. If the state fails to defend its military against criticism there will come a point when the army will take matters into its own hands and defend itself.'[2] The 'state' in Turkey is not the government, but the governing institutions, the military, the bureaucracy and the courts. Just two years after the coup, the tutelage role of the military was obviously intact.

Shortly before the nominations, more than two months before the elections, an article appeared in the newspaper *Milliyet* by journalist Hasan Cemal that supposedly conveyed the mood at Virtue Party (VP) headquarters, in view of the President's threats:

> The anti-VP circles' propaganda line, which boils down to, 'The VP would not be allowed to come to power even if it won the election; do not vote for the VP because your ballots would be going down the drain', is upsetting VP officials ... What will the VP's election campaign be like? There are those who want to take a radical line during the election campaign. But Necmettin Erbakan, the former leader of the now-defunct Welfare Party, his close associates, VP Chairman Recai Kutan and the 'pro-change' wing of the VP all favour a moderate stance. They do not want to clash with the February 28 process. They do not want a confrontation with the military. They want the election campaign to be conducted on the basis of specific, substantial issues and projects rather than with religious slogans. *They do not intend to nominate any headscarf-wearing candidates for Parliament.*[3]

Milliyet was supportive of the coup process, yet it is logical that it was presenting what the VP leaders were saying at this time, objectively, though not perhaps what some of them were thinking. There was no sense clashing with the military before the nominations. Just one day earlier Demirel had stated: 'Do not turn the election campaign into a reckoning with the "28 February Process"' – a warning issued to the VP. He added: 'It is very difficult to make an assessment of the VP in the Western sense. The VP has a visible part and an invisible part. If the two had been the same, there would have been no problem.'[4] This was once again a reference to the so-called 'hidden agenda' of Islamic-friendly parties. Meanwhile, Prime Minister Ecevit distributed a circular urging governors and prosecutors to prevent any attempt to 'politicize religion' including regarding the 'dress code'. Kutan fought back against these comments, arguing publicly that the VP is a party for both religious and non-religious citizens of Turkey.[5]

This was the repressive environment in which Merve Kavakci would be nominated to run for the Parliament in the first election since the 1997 coup.

The Kavakci time bomb

Stephen Kinzer has written that Merve's nomination was a tactic by Erbakan to create havoc in Turkey, 'a clever bit of revenge after he was thrown out of politics',[6] that 'Kavakci was his time bomb ...'[7] Another standard assumption is that Merve was nominated at the 'last minute' by Erbakan – a notion that has been picked up and disseminated as truth by journalists and academics alike, and of course secularists. Jenny White has written: 'Although Erbakan found himself more and more isolated within the Virtue Party, he continued to try to manoeuvre party activities and policy from behind the scenes, including orchestrating Merve Kavakci's ill-fated confrontation with Parliament.'[8] This view of her candidacy has held to this day because it also fits well with the Kemalist view of Merve Kavakci as an 'agent provocateur' and perhaps because it seems reasonable.

But these views do not reflect what really happened. Historical mistruths have a way of becoming 'fact' and impairing our full understanding of historical events by their repetition, but sometimes they do not hold up with more analysis over time. In the case of Merve Kavakci, the notion that her nomination was a plant from Erbakan, a vicious vengeful tactic to raise hell, simply supports the view that Islamic politics are disingenuous, and that the Islamic politicians' stated objectives are never what they really are. On the contrary, they are viewed as a subterfuge to take power and impose an Islamic state or cause a provocation. The simple 'blame-it-on-Erbakan' view unfairly deligitimizes a grassroots political movement and de-emphasizes its support for a legitimate candidate. As we shall see, Erbakan was indeed directly involved in running the VP, contrary to legal prohibitions from doing so, and he did support Merve's nomination, as Dr White has stated. However, there is no evidence whatsoever to characterize and explain the nomination of a covered woman as a provocation on the part of Erbakan or the Virtue Party, despite its objection by a military-dominated government and, for that matter, society. And Stephen Kinzer is hardly alone. I have heard this view of Merve Kavakci's nomination from Turkish political scientists as well as American scholars, from some Islamic intellectuals and even from some students at well-known universities in Turkey who were ten years old when the event occurred. In books and even academic articles this depiction often lacks a footnote. I politely challenged one such comment by an American academic in one of her articles, who then told me she couldn't remember the source and wasn't sure about it. I have never seen any such source. The damage this speculation has done over time to Merve Kavakci's persona is real and has brought about her unwarranted bad reputation.

Regarding the so-called 'last minute' nomination of Merve before the 1999 elections, most of the parties waited until the deadline to make their decisions, 24 February at 5 p.m. Literally thousands of candidates had to be selected by the parties, ranked onto lists, and submitted, also for all-important local elections, including Istanbul and its districts. Bulent Ecevit, leader of the DSP, stated that whichever party wins the Greater Istanbul Municipality will either come to power or be the major partner of a coalition.[9] Virtue Party leaders took their time in devising their list of candidates, based mostly on a multi-level array of feedback from grassroots representatives and local supporters. The Virtue Party and the True Path Party waited until the last day to announce candidates for Istanbul mayoralty districts as well, wanting to be sure their candidates were the ones most likely to get elected, based on local surveys and feedback.

Yes, Erbakan was directly involved despite the prohibitions against him. Recai Kutan confirmed in my discussions with him that Erbakan was actively involved in the party regardless of his ban. His directing the party behind the scenes was not a trivial matter, for in Turkey political parties are not democratic entities. Erbakan's agents in the VP were Kutan and Oguzhan Asilturk, as well as, unofficially, his wife and daughter. This angered the younger members of the party, including Abdullah Gul and Tayyip Erdogan and fostered much dissension, as we shall see later. (The reformist wing of the VP displayed its growing power at the first VP convention on 14 May 2000. Even though its leader, Abdullah Gul, lost the party leadership to Kutan, the narrow margin of the conservative victory demonstrated that a pro-reform movement within the VP was fermenting.[10])

Tayyip Erdogan was also a part of the reform movement, although he was in jail at the time of the election on 18 April 1999. The goal of the reformers was to lead the party with a new, modern perspective, and one that would not be abrogated by the military and closed down by the Constitutional Court. In fact, both Erdogan and Gul resigned at the next party congress[11] and eventually went on to form the ruling AK Party.

Within the Virtue Party by this time there was also a rising tide of feminist aspirations of women who were facing barriers from the patriarchal attitudes of men in party management. That is why the Virtue Party nominated seventeen women for Parliament in 1999, several of whom wore headscarves from different cities, and one of whom was Merve Kavakci representing Istanbul's Anatolian (Asian side) district.

According to Merve, 'the Virtue Party, unlike its predecessor, the Welfare Party, was supposed to be the transitional party of democratization of the political Islamist movement, but it was so short lived, so ephemeral that it did not establish itself as a transitional party'. And it was very much a male-dominated party up until this point – like all other parties in Turkey – whose double standards and patriarchal attitudes towards women did not spare the women with headscarves within the party. These women were tired of working in the background and wanted to be represented in executive committees and in particular as candidates for office, something that is missing from commentaries from this time period. As Merve Kavakci explains:

> One of the reasons the party was nominating women this time
> around was to transform the political agenda into a more democratic

image, and to claim a new identity. We were going into the elections quickly, and there were thousands of women who were part of the women's commission, thousands who were starting to push from the bottom up. These women did not get paid and were poor – I have seen them with holes in their shoes – and they were not as fortunate as me to have a car and a grandmother to take care of children at home. They travelled from city to city, buying their own bus ticket, sometimes travelling for eighteen hours, to come to the headquarters, where they were criticized for not working hard enough, then went back and started knocking on doors to support the party.

To become a modern, democratic organization, the party opened itself up to prominent women who did not cover, people like Nazli Ilicak and Oya Akgonenc. However, there was no doubt in anybody's mind that the headscarved women who brought the party to power in 1997 would certainly be asking, 'What about us?' There was a tremendous pressure to finally nominate headscarved women for office, so much so that the leadership thought it wise – if not warmed up to the idea absolutely – to go ahead and do so. I was one of the more fortunate ones to enjoy some of the benefits of the party, travelling around the world, meeting world leaders, which helped me to grow on my own. And so within this context my name and some of the other names were coming up. Women within the party were finally being considered as nominees.

Merve's viewpoint is borne out by on-the-ground surveys and investigations by social scientists at the time, and increased activism and frustrations on the part of Islamic women. The most prominent is Jenny White's classic and invaluable study covering the period between 1994 and 2002, focusing on Islamist activists in Umraniye, a working-class and traditional neighbourhood of Istanbul which was typical of Merve's constituency:

Female Welfare Party supporters were extraordinarily successful in popular mobilization and it is widely acknowledged that they were in large part responsible for the Welfare Party's success in working-class neighborhoods like Umraniye in the 1994 and 1995 elections. In the month before the 1995 elections, in Istanbul alone, the Welfare Party's women's commission worked with 18,000 women and met face to face with 200,000 women. They worked person-to-person, building cells of local women attached to the Women's

Branch that, in turn, was guided by the party and took its direction (and much of its financial support) from there. By 1997, women made up a third of party membership in Istanbul.

However, at the time almost no women were represented in the party administration and the women's branches and commissions had no formal status within the party. This latter fact clearly irked some of the women activists, but they assured me that this would change in the near future ... Male party activists generally deflected questions about the lack of women in the party's formal administration by retraining the question on the issue of banning headscarves in university. This disguised internal divisiveness with the artful unity of political symbolism. When pressed about the importance of education for women, these same male activists stated simply that women's main role was to be mothers and homemakers and that women should be educated because it would make them better mothers. Many local male activists categorically resisted the idea that women could or should work outside the home after marriage.[12]

It was a 'time bomb' in the way that Rosa Parks refusing to give up her seat to a white person on a bus in Alabama, or James Meredith trying to get into the University of Mississippi, was a 'time bomb'. The nomination was reflective of a rising tide of Islamic women, particularly in Istanbul, who were responsible for the Welfare Party's initial success, and later the Virtue Party. And although the Virtue Party eventually responded to the need for representation on the part of women, its male leadership was conflicted and their patriarchal views of women obvious. This was yet another barrier that Merve Kavakci had to deal with within her own party and tried to overcome. In this respect the party was a miniature of the larger Turkish society: conservative, male-dominated, and patriarchal. The men in the party were uncomfortable with women as co-workers, although women were required to recruit the participation and votes of other women. The men were used to seeing covered women as their wives, children, daughters, and revered mothers, not colleagues. Transitioning from those views to treating professional covered women was, as Merve described, 'a work in progress'. Party leaders were also unsure of exactly how to treat these young women in a professional context, as an equal who thinks and criticizes as they do. This is still the case in Turkey today, a male-dominated society with the lowest female employment rate in Europe, and a host of inequality issues relating to women, including honour killings and discriminatory employment practices.

As noted by Jenny White:

> While many activist women I interviewed in Umraniye were engaged in the Islamist project in order to carve out new areas of autonomy within the traditional expectations of their community, male activists in the next office were motivated in part by a desire to reinforce traditional female roles and to enhance their own autonomy vis-à-vis women, for instance by supporting polygamy, which is illegal in secular Turkey. Party leaders deflected public statements on divisive issues, allowing differences in the lower ranks between men and women activists to be attributed to personal points of view.[13]

Although the Welfare and Virtue Parties were outwardly different in their orientation and in some of their leadership, their participants and certainly constituencies were virtually identical based on the same community and cultural underpinnings, and the same people in Islamic communities across Turkey. Merve's father was highly respected and her uncles were active and influential in supporting both parties. Family and personal ties were everything in this version of politics and Merve's language abilities and representation of the Welfare Party overseas at international conferences added to her reputation.

One such close friend of the family was Temel Karamollaoglu,[14] a high-placed official in both parties, and who at the time of this writing was Vice-President of the Saadet (Felicity) Party. Merve refers to him as her *amca* (uncle). I interviewed him in his office at Saadet Party headquarters, a small, square four-storey building on a back street in Ankara, where he readily answered my questions in perfect English. The Saadet Party can be viewed as the conservative wing of the Virtue Party after it was closed down, and stands in contrast to the towering AK Party building that originated from the reformers of the Virtue Party who are now in power in Turkey.

Mr Karamollaoglu also did not agree to the claim by many that the selection of Merve was made by Erbakan to cause problems. 'I think it is just supposition; there was no intention of that kind,' he said, noting that other covered women were also candidates. 'And we never thought that the problem that we faced could arise when she was elected, because there is no clause either in the procedures of the Parliament or the election law or any other law that ladies need to wear a certain type of clothes.' He added: 'We never thought it would cause a problem because when she submitted her photograph she was covered, and the court that runs the elections accepted it, so there was nothing wrong and as I said, in the internal procedures of the Parliament there was nothing. It would have been a step in the right direction for the normalization of Turkey.' He viewed that matter as the other side making it into a big political issue to harm her and through her harm the Virtue Party, adding that the acting head of the Parliament, Septioglu, 'was determined to let her swear in as a Member of Parliament but unfortunately it did not come to that point'.

Regarding how the nomination was made, its timing and the involvement of Erbakan, Mr Karamollaoglu gave the following responses:

> No, it wasn't last minute – for one thing they forget perhaps that Merve's uncle was in the past one of the founders of the party, so she was not alien to the party at all and her father was a very close friend of mine as well and we knew her mother earlier, and so it was not just a last-minute selection. Plus Merve had the potential of really serving the core of the party, not just for her but for the party it was a gain. Her uncle has always supported our policies, he accepted and he worked for us – he was involved in the earlier parties because we had the problem of a few parties banned by the constitutional court. So no, it was not a last-minute selection and decision.
>
> I was involved in the decision as well. We have a very wide systematic process. It starts in the constitution provinces – there are eighty-one in Turkey – first they make an assessment, a few hundred in Istanbul at first, then they reduce it to a certain number and then it comes to the executive committee. We establish ten or fifteen committees and we interview every one of the candidates. The committee has three members, and then points are assigned and then there is a short list. We generally have in all the provinces surveys to see which candidates they prefer, and then the area committee decides who will be considered.
>
> Of course Professor Erbakan, being the leader of the party, has a big influence and his decisions are generally accepted, but there is discussion and very rarely does he make a decision contrary to the executive committee. So she was selected let us say. It was not just a decision of Professor Erbakan, because it was not just

Merve Hanim, there was the head of the women's committee in our party, she was one of the candidates as well, in Ankara. Our women worked harder than men; it is necessary, especially in Anatolia. You can of course relay your message to the masses, men and women, but women do not mix with men in most of the villages so you have to work harder door to door and the ladies they really worked hard.

Of course the covered women wanted to be represented. We wanted some of them to be elected to be candidates to work harder, but when there is some kind of position taken especially by the courts, it causes a big problem unfortunately.

Mr Karamollaoglu suggested that I speak to Recai Kutan, who (at that time) worked for Esam, the research arm of Saadet. Through a translator Mr Kutan said, 'Someone had to take the risk to nominate her and we have no regrets about that. There were female candidates in the time of Ataturk in 1937 [though not headscarved]. Our position has always been very risky, ethical, with spiritual values.'[15]

Kutan's job at the time was almost impossible: Erbakan was trying to impose his views on the party, while reformers, such as Erdogan and Gul, were objecting to his directions. In addition, the military's presence hovered over everyone, a fact of political life in Turkey. A year before Merve's nomination, which was just a year after the 1997 coup process started, when Recai Kutan was speaking to a Parliamentary group meeting of the Virtue Party, students with headscarves and beards in the audience carried banners that protested against their inability to enter universities. One by one he read their banners out loud, interrupted after each one by applause. 'He spoke against the claim that women who wear headscarves do so for a certain ideology and not because of their beliefs, that "reactionary" claims were artificial and that the same game has been played since the 1950s. Kutan said that in real terms, they wanted to have democracy, nor only for themselves but for everybody.'[16]

In summary, the nomination of Merve Kavakci to run for Parliament should not be characterized as a last-minute ploy by Erbakan to cause havoc or to be provocative. As noted above, it was not last minute. More importantly, after speaking with many people within the party, who had direct contact with Mr Erbakan, including those who were present when the decision to have headscarved candidates was made, there is nothing to indicate that the decision was anything less than genuine, to 'do the right thing' for covered women. For this, Mr Erbakan deserves credit and admiration. Being provocative was not Erbakan's style, despite some missteps in politics, and not a wise motivation when building and starting a new party. But it was, most definitely, Mr Erbakan who originated the idea to have covered candidates and made the selection of them when preparing the lists for the election. Kutan, Gul, Erdogan, Sener and others, regardless of the obvious importance of covered women in the party, did not push for headscarved candidates. These 'reformers' had been burned before when Welfare was shut down and they did not want to cause problems. To the best of my knowledge there was only one known advocate in the party's leadership who supported covered women as candidates other than Erbakan and that person was, in fact, a secular woman named Nazli Ilicak.

Yet, although banned from politics, Erbakan was, nevertheless, directly involved in the Virtue Party's decision-making process. His daughter and wife took part directly in Virtue Party affairs by making calls and holding meetings, by constant communication with Recai Kutan, its nominal leader, and making all key decisions, including the final list of Parliamentary candidates and the all-important order of the list.

The specific nomination of Merve Kavakci should be attributed to her previous work in the Welfare and Virtue parties, as well as her qualifications and family connections, the increasing influence of and pressure by Islamic women in the parties to be represented. Plus Merve was one of the best known active participants in the party. Given that Islamic women brought success to both parties during elections in the 1990s, and the fact that the Virtue Party nominated non-covering secular women in 1999, there was an obvious need to respond to the Islamic women's desires to be nominated and treated by the party on a par with secular women. Because of the critical aspect of covered women's support, it would be difficult to solely nominate secular women, such as Nazli Ilicak, as will be seen below, while ignoring the headscarved women of the party. That was also the view of Abdurraman Dilipak, one of the most important contemporary Islamic writers in Turkey, who told me that the Virtue Party had to nominate a headscarved candidate because it had included secular women in the party's administration, such as Nazli Ilicak.

And yet, only one person in power considered these factors to the point of favouring, recommending and pushing for headscarved candidates, and that person was Necmettin Erbakan.

The youngest candidate

She was thirty years old, a single mother with two small children, yet idealistic, hard-working and on all accounts incredibly energetic.

On that Saturday morning in which her nomination was announced, Merve awoke with the normal commotion at home, telling her kids to get ready and not be late. After morning prayers she told her grandmother not to worry because there was a meeting in the morning at party headquarters that might continue into the afternoon and that she would call her as soon as she had a chance.

Merve's young daughters, Fatima and Mariam, and her grandmother, were living together in the house in the Mebusevleri district of the Ankara, where Merve grew up and spent her high school years. Her grandmother was a very spry ninety-two at the time – holding the family together, taking care of her granddaughters while Merve worked for the party.

The meeting was held quarterly with representatives from around the country crowded into the party headquarters. Around noon, with a break for lunch, Necmettin Erbakan's daughter, Elif, approached Merve to talk. Elif was on the Women's Committee of the party responsible from Istanbul. They went outside looking for a quiet place. As they approached the elevators, Elif said that the head of the committee wanted to talk to her but she preferred Elif to do it instead. She continued by saying that the party's General Administration Committee had discussed the possible women candidates for Parliament, and it was decided to include covering women – women who wear headscarves – as well. They recognized that the party had received much criticism in the previous election due to their lack of women candidates. She added that Merve's name was mentioned in this meeting, and she wanted to know her thoughts about running for Parliament.

Elif's comments made Merve's heart pound. She had long thought that the women who helped to bring the Welfare Party to power should be represented and knew the Virtue Party was drawing the same criticism, especially since it was clear that uncovered women were going to be nominated. Merve thanked Elif for the party's consideration, told her she was honoured and wanted time to think this over. Elif replied, 'Okay, but you are to be formally nominated by the Head of Women's Committee and I hope you accept this offer because you would be a good representative for women.'

The Kavakci family traditionally discussed and voted on major decisions among family members – including children – and friends. It was not yet morning in the USA, so instead of phoning her parents in Richardson, Texas, Merve called her cousin Ethem and asked him to relay this news to her uncle, Orhan Gungen, for serious thought.

She returned to her meeting too excited to focus or take part in any discussions, except for an update on the party's foreign relations activities. She called her children on her way home, telling them that she had something important to talk about with them. She told her grandmother at the dinner table, and then asked her children what they would think of their mother becoming a Parliamentarian and whether they would like it. She added that this would be a very time-consuming job and might lessen her time with them, but that the party had never had a female Parliamentarian before. In response, her daughter, Fatima, slowly looked away from her plate and towards her mother, thought for a few moments, then said, 'I hope you're not thrown in jail' – and then continued eating. Merve froze and stared at her eight-year-old daughter.

She called her parents later that night and asked them to think over the idea. They were happy but surprised by the news. That weekend passed with heavy phone traffic between Ankara, Istanbul and Dallas. In the meantime, the Head of the Women's Committee, Leman Aksay (who was also nominated), called Merve. She told Merve of her reluctance to take part in the elections because she was a young mother and wanted to spend time with her two babies. Merve could not convince her otherwise.

That weekend Merve discussed with friends of hers who were knowledgeable in the law about legal barriers to headscarved officials. She was encouraged by what she heard: that there were no laws against her attire in the Supreme Law or Parliament's internal regulations. The fifty-sixth item in the Parliament Internal Regulations stated that all Parliament members and staff needed to wear jackets and ties and women were to wear a two-piece suit. She then discussed the nomination with her family, who all agreed with one exception – her middle cousin, Kerim. Everyone else wanted her to accept the position

On Monday Merve called Elif Erbakan with her acceptance. She then met with Elif and her mother, Mrs Nermin Erbakan, for tea, told them that her decision was made after a family discussion, and expressed her hope that this next step would bring nothing but goodness and that she needed their prayers. To this Nermin Erbakan placed her teacup on the table and, with a smile, told Merve that she had earlier expressed her sadness to Elif because of the great responsibility that being the 'first' would bring. She told Merve that she was worried about the role the media would play in her life, how biased the media could be and how public her personal life would become. Merve knew that Erbakan's wife had seen the ruthless face of politics and had experienced prejudiced people and difficult, sudden, unexpected political changes for many long years. She listened and nodded her agreement. Mrs Erbakan added that 'it was time to show our people that a pious person could also be modern, highly educated and knowledgeable of foreign languages and dress in a modern way' and that Merve would successfully fulfil this position.

Merve Kavakci idealistically believed that she could play a role in bringing together the two conflicting groups in Turkey as a covered Parliamentarian, although she was initially reluctant to take on that responsibility. She came to believe that her support for these 'other' women at the centre of legitimate power in the country would set an important example for Turkish society. She knew full well how modernity, culture and education had been monopolized in Turkey by a select few. Merve:

> Kemalist and 'secularists' reduced being Western or contemporary to merely being in Western clothing, a group with no tolerance for their fellow humans who happen to look or think differently, and who sometimes cannot even bear their existence. For years they put down fellow Turkish people who were intimately tied to their religion. They called headscarved women 'spider-heads' (orumcek-kafali). They saw the Turkish women who covered due to the commandment of their Creator as only worthy of working in the fields, as janitors in schools or cleaning ladies in their houses. They criticized covering women at every chance because of the way they dressed, and even violated their basic human rights by preventing their education.

As Merve listened to Nermin Erbakan, she became more enthusiastic and decisive. She started thinking about the days in which her mother was forced to give up her faculty position because of her headscarf and saw her campaigning and election to Parliament as a worthy task. She asked Nermin Erbakan what would happen if the secular bloc did not accept her. After gently placing her teacup on the saucer on the table and turning towards her, Mrs Erbakan said that if such a thing happened then they would show the whole world how two-faced they are and how they respect human rights only when it suits them. Merve thought about what she said as she left the Erbakans' house.

The next day Merve called a close family friend, a person whose views she respected, Professor Besir Atalay, who is now Turkey's Minister of the Interior, and asked to meet him. He urged her to come right away. Their family friendship went back to their many years together with his family at Erzurum Ataturk University and continued when the family moved to Ankara. Atalay had been forced to resign from his position of university president. She visited him on a warm February day, joined by two of his journalist friends who were familiar with Turkey's media cartels. They warned her to be ready for accusations and slander, and that her life was about to change dramatically. So Merve's initial excitement about her nomination was gradually replaced with apprehension about what lay ahead for her.

She later found out from Elif, who had spoken to her father, Erbakan, that she would be representing Istanbul's first district. Why was this information continuing to come from Erbakan's daughter and not party officials? As we shall see, the men of the party were not inclined to meet with her directly; women were used to communicate to other women, a practice embedded in Turkey's male-dominated, conservative society. It also shows Erbakan's direct involvement in the day-to-day running of the Virtue Party, contrary to his being banned from political activity.

Her election would depend on how many votes her party received and her position on the list of VP candidates. Because Merve was the fourth candidate on the VP's list for her district, a relatively high-ranking position, it was likely that she would be elected with decent showing by the party. The number of deputies elected to Parliament depends on what percentage of votes the party receives for each district, not each candidate. Parties that do not account for at least 10 per cent of the total votes from the entire country, however, lose their seats, which are then proportionally given to the parties that did gain 10 per cent of the vote.

Nermin Erbakan called and gave her instructions on how to proceed, to go to the district record-keeper and then to the district court office to receive her residency and 'good-standing' papers. Merve did so then brought her applications to a very crowded Virtue Party office in Ankara.

On the final day of nominations, as Merve was about to leave for home, she heard her name in the list of nominees of Istanbul being read by an officer at party headquarters. As Merve explains it, she sneaked out – so the media did not get a chance to see just who she was and that she was a covered woman. She took a taxi and called her parents in the USA, but they were not at home, so she left the following excited message: 'Your daughter is becoming a Member of Parliament, and you are not even home.' The taxi driver had a puzzled look as he asked her if she really was going to be a Member of Parliament and how old she was. Merve was just thirty, but she smiled and told him, 'old enough'.

The next morning the Turkish newspapers wondered about this unknown Virtue Party candidate. The other high-ranking women on the list – Nazli Ilicak and Oya Akgonenc – were well known and not covered. Meanwhile, Merve enjoyed her freedom during this brief period of anonymity.

***

It was a rainy, September Saturday in Washington, DC and we were in Merve's modest office at George Washington University where she is a lecturer in Political Science. Merve's sister, Ravza, and her daughter, Fatima, had joined us because the Kavakci family is inseparable from Kavakci the individual. I placed my recorder in front of Merve and we began by travelling back eleven years to the start of her Parliamentary campaign. She gazed into the distance, as if looking into the past, and calmly, slowly and articulately recalled that time.

> I remember there was a feminist organization, KADER, that supports women in politics and as a member of the Virtue Party we were always part of that group attending their meetings. My name was not out yet but I knew that I was going to be a candidate,

so I attended that meeting and I remember all the women who wanted to become mayors, *muhtars* (local administrators), and members of Parliament – very ambitious, Kemalists – and I was sitting next to one of them, a very stylish woman, and we were on swivel chairs and she just turned her back towards me when I sat next to her; she just turned her back and it was so natural. It was so natural.

This is what every woman who wishes to wear a headscarf because of her religious beliefs deals with in Turkey: being shunned, objectified and mistreated without regard to her true character, her qualities, abilities and worth as a person. It is something that Merve wears along with her headscarf, a square metre of silk that weighs more than it seems, and in spite of the years of discrimination, the infinite number of moments of daily suffering, there is never a sign of acceptance of this treatment by her words and tone of voice. Because it is so clearly unfair, there seems to be perpetual amazement in her voice recalling one incident after another. To accept it at any moment is to give in to its permanence. So, instead, it is worn, every day, with a quiet determination, a look into the distance, and a peacefulness that comes with following your feelings and beliefs regardless of the obstacles presented in everyday life.

***

With elections due to be held on 18 April 1999, in just six weeks, Merve prepared to leave for Istanbul, her election district. But before she left Ankara, she had some questions for Abdullah Gul, whom she knew from their working together on the Foreign Relations Committee. Her worries were increasing. They met one afternoon in his office and he congratulated her and said he thought she was the right choice when he had heard of Merve's nomination. She thanked him, and then asked him, since he had just attended the high-level administration meeting of the Virtue Party on that day, if there were any discussions at this meeting about the strategies to be implemented in case she was elected and started facing problems. He replied with a half-helpless, half-gloomy smile that there was really no strategy in this party, and that everything was a last-minute effort, adding that he was telling her this because she was now one of them. She was astonished by his response. Then, as she was about to leave, she told him about an upcoming interview she was to have with the *Washington Post* in the next hour and National Public Radio (in the US). As Head of Foreign Affairs for the Women's Commission she had many dealings with the foreign press. At that moment, Gul suggested that she cover her hair in a different way during the interview, gesturing with his hands to indicate the way grandmothers traditionally tied their headscarves under their chin. Merve told him she didn't think that style would suit her, and wondered why on earth it would even matter to change her style of headscarf when she talked to the international media. Actually, she did the interviews and they went well. The US press asked substantive and meaningful questions and she provided her answers, which were reported without distortion, unlike what was to come in Turkey.

Merve Kavakci in public

With the announcement of the names of the nominees, questions began pouring in from the media about the identity of this new candidate. Because Merve already had several media contacts, they had her mobile number and were calling day and night trying to get as much information as possible. However, Merve often declined to speak with them, knowing what an unfriendly media could do. This cautious approach was probably the best course for her to take given her inexperience and the lack of direction coming from her party, which was underfunded, indecisive and split at the management level.

The party chose 8 March at the World Women's Day Programme organized by its Istanbul branch for her first day of public appearances and in front of the media. The anticipation was such that one of the newspapers had printed a picture of a fully covered woman, in a *chador*, with Merve's name in the caption.

Merve picked up Elif Erbakan at the airport, who was also Istanbul's inspector for the party and was handling a breakfast event at the Florya Social Complex where the nominees would be officially introduced to the press. She thought to herself, 'This is it; they are going to know who I am.' Numan Kurtulmus, the head of the Virtue Party for Istanbul, was to announce the Istanbul candidates. He gave the opening speech and then invited the Parliamentary nominees from the Istanbul region one by one to the stage. Group pictures were taken. After Merve left the stage to return to her table, several media members stuck their cameras in her face until her diminutive yet forceful and protective sister, Ravza, raced in between and pushed the cameramen back. It was just the start of a media onslaught.

After the completion of this introduction, Merve went to the Cemal Resit Rey Convention Hall together with the other women in the party. An army of media people, writers, photographers and videographers awaited them, haranguing her even as she sat in the first row trying to listen to the speakers. Ravza shooed them away. Merve delivered a speech on the vast difference between women's education in Turkey's developed regions versus the countryside, but was dismayed that the next morning *Hurriyet* newspaper placed a large picture of her on its front page, introducing her not as a computer engineer but as a technician, and totally ignored the speech she delivered.

Lost in the coverage of the 'Merve Kavakci' affair was Merve's campaign for her office; the content of that campaign; her interaction with potential voters; and her search to represent her constituents' interests in Parliament. When I first asked Merve about the nature of her campaign, she said that 'Americans will get this, they will understand immediately.'

Istanbul is an enormous city of 2,000 square miles, more than six times larger than New York City and, today, with almost twice as many people. It straddles two continents, divided by the Bosphorus Straits, which becomes a river of activity, commuter ferries crisscrossing all day long and commercial ships moving their cargo between the Black Sea and Marmara day and night. The Bosphorus Bridge connects the European side on the West to the Asian side in the East, also known as the Anatolian side – Anatolia being the central part of Turkey formerly called Asia Minor. The first district of Istanbul is on the Anatolian side, and Merve travelled across the Bosphorus Bridge in heavy Istanbul traffic at least twice a day, often having to go back to the second and third districts on the European side as well, whose Islamic VP constituents wanted to see for themselves their headscarved candidate.

Given the events of the previous two years, following the post-modern military coup, the presence of a headscarved candidate became big news on a daily basis. Because of the intense press coverage Merve was soon instantly recognizable and there were thus increasing demands for her to appear at party events. She was constantly on the move, giving speeches in mass gatherings, then meeting with groups of twenty to thirty women at tightly packed tea parties hosted by a member of the party, where she was mostly accompanied by Tayyip Erdogan's wife and Erbakan's daughter; once again women being designated to interact with other women. Merve also attended numerous openings, ground-breaking ceremonies and ribbon-cutting events with the Mayor of Istanbul and other people from the party.

The young candidate was plunged into a political maelstrom, yet held herself with grace and dignity and continuously tried not to be ruffled by all the attention. For this she may have seemed to some as too focused and non-human, but in reality and in person Merve Kavakci is as kind-hearted and human a person as anyone. Yet the press, reflecting the standard outlook of the establishment, de-humanized her, typecast her as an Islamic woman with an 'agenda', and increased tensions steadily during the campaign, after the election and after the incident in Parliament.

Though young and inexperienced, Merve knew what was happening, knew that the Kemalist-military establishment threats were real, yet sought to convey a series of messages that espoused democracy and women's rights, and specifically countered the stereotypes of backward Islamic women in Turkey. The content of her campaign, however, seems to have been completely lost in the record of what happened.

Although in her campaign she attacked the opposition, she realized that after the 1997 military intervention, Islamism (meaning the politicization of Islam) was viewed by the military as a security threat; thus she addressed issues of liberties, but not in the openly religious context to avoid their wrath. She believed in what she was saying and the need for democratization in Turkey, but she could not and did not specifically mention the issue of religious freedom. However, she talked about the need to establish the rule of law, civil liberties, transparency and accountability in Turkey's political system, and how Turkey's human rights record needed to be corrected. She saved the topic she was most passionate about, women's rights. Merve:

> I wanted to be recognized as a young woman who the Turkish Republic brought up and produced. It was my way of resisting the opposition as defining me as a backward woman, the 'other' woman. I am not a backward woman; I was produced by this Republic. And it was a way to deal with the patriarchal aspect of

Turkish society for the regime went hand in hand with a patriarchal system in keeping women where they were. The progress it brought was minimal, and only confined to particular groups of women, not the whole female society, which can claim equality but only to a certain point.

Merve would join the last thirty minutes of five-hour-long campaign events to give her speech, then run to the next event or tea party. The tea parties would sometimes be in very up-market houses and at other times in run-down apartments of the economically disadvantaged. Depending on the neighbourhood and districts, issues dealing with city concerns, such as clean running water, infrastructure and roads, were usually responded to by the imprisoned Mayor's wife, Mrs Erdogan. But others wanted to meet Merve and find out who she was. Some secular women liked her and were impressed with her having studied in the USA yet decided to return to Turkey, and indicated they would vote for 'someone like her' for the first time. Others simply stared, as if an alien had crossed their path, as she gave out roses to shop-keepers, went to barber shops where men were getting haircuts (an activity unheard of for a covered woman), and even handed out roses and pamphlets to the men. In the beginning of her campaign she brazenly entered a McDonald's and spoke to patrons who were eating; when they told her 'We support you, we love you', she was flushed with happiness – especially in the districts where the Virtue Party was strong.

Headscarved women complained to her about their bad treatment and the problems they were having at universities. They pressured her about the headscarf ban and whether the Virtue Party would lift it. With non-stop coverage in the press, as the election approached this issue was amplified, many asking her, 'Of course, you are going to lift the ban, right? There is this provision that prevents women from wearing the headscarf, so you will work on that, right?' Merve hoped that if she could enter Parliament, the party might become powerful enough to facilitate that. She answered, 'We will do our best,' but thought to herself that it might take some time. Yet once she made such a promise, she felt complete commitment to it.

Early on in the campaign Merve met Ali Mufit Gurtuna, soon to be the next Mayor of Istanbul, and Reyhan Gurtuna, his wife and political leader in her own right. The three of them began campaigning together in Umraniye, a large working-class district near Uskudar on the Anatolian side of Istanbul that regularly provided Islamic-leaning parties with support. The enthusiastic crowds numbered in the thousands and energized Merve. At one political rally she first supplicated in prayer – 'In the name of God, the Most Gracious, the Most Merciful' – then walked out onto the platform to a chorus of applause, a sea of headscarved women in front of her, and was almost overcome with joy. Years later she could hardly describe the euphoria she felt, her connection to the crowds of people and campaign workers, most of whom were unpaid, and the love they expressed for her. They would give speeches at one programme after another, at ground-breaking events for a park or civic centre, meeting after meeting in a whirlwind that included the three of them crossing back and forth to the European side, whose populace complained about not having a covered woman candidate of their own. They had to replace their old slow car for a faster one, racing over the Bosphorus Bridge several times a day. They would start around 9.30 every morning, attending large open-air public meetings arranged by women, joining house discussions or visiting businessmen and then barely making it back to their homes very late at night.

Wherever Merve went she was accompanied by her sister, partner and protector, Ravza; her press assistant Muzeyyen Tasci; and her driver, bodyguard and all-round problem-solver, Osman Ulusoy.

Osman Ulusoy was assigned to provide professional, armed protection as soon as Merve was nominated – especially because she was a headscarved candidate.[17] He was a strong, silent type, with a sharp jaw right out of central casting, trusted today by high-ranking elected officials and VIPs. He said that Merve got special protective treatment because of the tension that the coup process had created two years earlier and that, because of Merve's popularity, some of the crowds were enormous. At Caglayan Square, for example – a huge open area on the European side of the city – a massive gathering of a quarter of a million people met for a Virtue Party rally, wildly applauding Merve when she spoke, showing their love.

When the campaign started Merve wanted the party to provide an assistant who could help her with programmes during the day, answer one of her three cell phones, and attend meetings with her. Ravza, who worked in the Istanbul Women's Commission, ended up taking the job because no one suitable could be found. At the time, Ravza's daughter Erva, whom she left with their grandmother while out all day, was just three years old. Merve's own daughters were with their other grandmother in Ankara, along with Merve's mother who had arrived immediately from Dallas to support her campaign. Merve called her daughters at every chance she had between meetings. She missed her children but enjoyed the campaign and the adrenalin it created.

***

As noted earlier, a key organizer of Merve's campaign was Sibel Eraslan, lawyer, writer, intellectual and activist, who played a major role in the Welfare Party's growth as head of the Welfare Party's newly formed Women's Commission in 1989 until Erdogan's election as Mayor of Istanbul in 1994.

Sibel Eraslan's life changed the day she started to cover in her last year at Istanbul University, which caused trauma in her very secular Kemalist household, headed of course by her father, then a colonel in the army. Not every Turkish family fits into the stereotype of one camp or the other.

I met with Sibel Eraslan and Yildiz Ramazanoglu, one of Turkey's best-known Islamic activists and journalists, in May 2010. We sat in a café overlooking the Bosphorus from the Anatolian side of Istanbul, near Uskudar on a beautiful Sunday morning. While ferries rumbled past and well-to-do patrons drank tea and feasted on a traditional Turkish breakfast of olives, tomatoes, cucumbers, cheese and *simits*, I was struck by the serious focus and presence of these two women, who spoke of the events of the 1990s as if they had just happened.

Sibel described how Merve's unique candidacy as a woman with a headscarf resonated with both men and women at her rallies, how thousands of women would chant 'we are women, we are strong and we exist' during her speeches, and how she was the strongest candidate in terms of her educational and family background and experience in America:

> Her nomination was accepted by the authorities and there were no problems in the beginning. She was very important in the Turkish

psyche and difficult to repress. Of course there was some tension during the campaign but it was hibernating, the tension that arises from the fight over women's bodies as symbols, the fight between the Westerners and the Muslim politicians.

Her candidacy was very important for the first district constituency and they were euphoric about her because they identified themselves with Merve and that was a dream for them, a dream that would come true. In fact there was an explosion of new-born babies named Merve, and it became a name for some shops, even for a coal store and a grocery. Tradesmen were also using the name of Merve for their businesses. It shows the excitement, the societal acceptance, that men also took part. But women were unstoppable and the places where she gave speeches were packed with spectators wanting to hear her.

Although she had all these elitist background characteristics, she had this ability to reach out to the poor and aggrieved part of the population. We would enter the homes of some very poor families, real poverty, and she did it with ease, she didn't mind. Some of these places in the first district were PKKs [Kurdistan Workers' Party, a terrorist group] and were not very secure areas; men would not enter, but women wearing a headscarf could go. But we could not take Nazli Ilicak there because she didn't wear a headscarf and she was different.

Sibel Eraslan told me that one million people voted for Merve, but that they were considered 'non-existent', and her eyes then welled up with tears.

***

Nazli Ilicak is one of the most prolific and courageous independent journalists in Turkey today, a secular, non-headscarved woman with a lifelong commitment to democracy. She was also a Virtue Party candidate representing Istanbul's third district, which includes the European district of Bakirkoy. She was part of the party's large advisory committee of fifty people, not the small executive committee, but her inclusion in the committee at all could still be viewed as a slight to covered women – who dominated the female workers in the party and yet were not represented in the committee – and as another indication that Islamic men had a hard time dealing with covered women in a management capacity. Nazli was well known then, a columnist for an Islamic paper,

Yeni Safak, and the host of a political programme on Channel 7, an Istanbul television station friendly to Islamic sensibilities. She was listed third as a candidate, making it likely that she would be elected. Targeted by today's Turkish military in coup plans, sentenced to prison for a mild criticism of a judge, and a continual proponent of democracy and non-discrimination in Turkish society, she can often be seen today on news talk shows, when she is not writing her column for *Sabah*.

She regularly campaigned with Merve (even though they were representing different districts of Istanbul) and they developed an enduring friendship. Early on in the campaign Merve met Nazli at a party meeting and she soon became her unofficial 'big sister'. Unlike other secular women in Turkey at the time, even in the party, Nazli Ilicak was an unwavering proponent for the human rights of covering women everywhere. The first day they met, Nazli invited Merve to her home that evening, along with Emine Erdogan. Nazli Ilicak, as we will soon see, would play an instrumental role in the story of Merve Kavakci's run for Parliament.

The young campaigner, Merve, was deeply moved by new and life-changing experiences as she interacted with the people of Istanbul during March and April 1999: she met with many different types of people from the Istanbul neighbourhoods of Umraniye, Sultanbeyli and Samandira, heavy supporters of the Fazilet Party, as well as people from the districts of Moda, Kadikoy and Adalar, whose views were generally opposite and in the Kemalist camp. The warm bond she felt with those who were already pro-Virtue Party was immediate and familial, from young and old, men and women. Their acceptance of her was total, as they had never doubted she would represent their interests. The elite, secular people of Istanbul who had never given the Virtue Party a chance approached her with curiosity at first, questioning who she was and where she came from. She met them personally at tea parties. She felt that as they saw her close up and listened to what she had to say, they began to understand her better. Merve: 'I remember a middle-aged, sweet lady told me in a house meeting that there wouldn't be any problem if every covered woman were like me. I told her that all those covered women were like me and most were even better, but there are few chances to meet and be around them. She agreed and added that Turkey needed young, dynamic, educated, well-mannered women politicians like me.' Perhaps not all secular people were so open-minded, but Merve Kavakci remembered those who were with fondness. At the very least this belies the notion that the Virtue Party was monolithic in its support and that its voters were only Islamic.

Besides the election campaign work, foreign press members took most of her remaining time with their interviews. The world's attention turned to Turkey. Merve was meeting with the foreign press either after a public meeting or by special appointments in the party building or in house meetings. Naturally, the main subject was the headscarf. Those interviews gave her the chance to discuss the issue in its entirety.

The Turkish media

The nature of the media in Turkey at the time of Merve's candidacy may be difficult for Americans to grasp. Imagine, if you will, politicized, unethical tabloids run by cartels that support the military-led coup process and the secular bloc that they cultivated prior to 28 February 1997 and continuing thereafter. The mainstream media moulded events to fit its political views, emphasizing what it wanted to support those views, using headlines to editorialize, leaving out important information. Opposed to the mainstream media was a much smaller group of Islamic-friendly media, subject at this time to threats and intimidation from the military.

Throughout the campaign the press coverage, particularly from the mainstream secular media, was unrelenting in its questioning Merve about whether or not, if elected, she would wear her headscarf in Parliament. After the election, and after the incident in Parliament, the torrent included almost daily instances of fabricated news, using bogus statements and facts in both the printed media and television, and non-stop biased reporting. As noted earlier, the coup of 28 February 1997 was a 'process'. The military 'briefed the press' before the coup, shut down publications after the coup, and even paid and directed press coverage, often based on their own intelligence gatherings, including wire-taped conversations from Merve's phone. A conversation Merve had one afternoon would show up in a front-page article the next day. (Even now in Turkey journalists claim that 72,000 people are having their phone conversations monitored.)

Years later, Ergun Babahan, *Sabah*'s manager before the coup, and Dinc Bilgin, ex-owner of *Sabah*, admitted that they wrote the news according to the wishes of the military, and as a result of the paper's other business interests which may or may not have coincided with corruption in the military.[18] A few months later, a well-known journalist, Mehmet Ali Birand, also confessed to blatant bias: 'For us [for a majority of members of the secular central media] the priority did not belong to democracy or Parliament. The General Staff was more important than both. And this was quite normal. This was the way we were raised. Pro-coup thought penetrated our genes without our even knowing it. We would unquestionably acknowledge the superiority of our commanders.'[19]

The media had also played a key role in running stories of the dangers of 'Islamic fundamentalism' with encouragement from the military prior to the staging of the 28 February intervention. Their cultivation of the media cartels, along with state offices, the courts and prosecutors, had helped them to pull off the fall of the Erbakan government. Now they took aim at 'agent provocateur' Merve Kavakci with as much enthusiasm. One of the reasons the cartels had actively supported the 1997 coup process was that they hoped to benefit from IMF requirements to privatize state-owned businesses. For example the Dogan Media Group, which owned *Milliyet, Radikal* and *Hurriyet*, bought the state-owned energy company, POAS, for only US$1.26 billion, even though it was worth US$4.3 billion. Erbakan's Welfare Party was the only voice to object and stand in the way – and thus became a target. To promote their nationalist and secular qualifications, and facilitate the corruption of their owners and their cosy relationship with the military-influenced government,[20] journalists attacked Kurdish and Islamic movements and in particular the Welfare Party and its successor, Virtue.

The cartels were accustomed to supporting the military and attacking what they labelled as anti-secular forces in Turkey, which were for all practical purposes made into 'internal' enemies of Turkey after 28 February 1997. One of the very few independent papers was the English-language *Turkish Daily News*, which I have cited often in this book, though it changed ownership soon afterwards.

Another important factor, noted by Professor Kim Shively (who studied this time period) is related to news about Kurdish separatism at the time. The secularist politicians and the press labelled Merve Kavakci as having ties with radical fundamentalist groups and claimed that she was being manipulated from forces outside of Turkish society. President Suleyman Demirel's subsequent charging of Merve with separatism (*boluculuk*) was 'a particularly strong one in the Turkish context'.[21] And the rest of the country followed suit after the incident. By linking Kavakci to the Kurdish conflict, Demirel was certainly drawing on the deep-seated attitudes of Kemalists, who see both Islamists and Kurds as threats to Turkey's national identity and integrity. More explicitly, he was 'capitalizing on a particularly strong wave of nationalism that pervaded Turkish public rhetoric in response to a series of galvanizing events occurring just prior to the 18 April 1999 elections – the pursuit and capture of Kurdish separatist leader Abdullah Ocalan, which united much of the country in a great show of nationalist fervor'.[22]

Ocalan was captured in February 1999 in a daring raid with the help of the US Central Intelligence Agency, causing a surge of nationalistic pride in the press and population as a whole, just when election campaigning started. According to Shively, putting Merve in the category of outsider and agitator helped attribute to a 'lack of agency' in characterizing her actions. In other words, it was assumed that she was manipulated by others. There was no need to understand her views or give them credibility. This viewpoint was so entrenched that it was universally adopted by the Turkish secularist press; her statements were discounted or ignored by the courts, and there was no effort to present, uncover or understand her views.

Shively notes that one politician argued that Kavakci was a mere 'toy' of Erbakan's and that Kavakci attempted to counter the accusations made against her of being an agent of outside forces, in one instance claiming, 'This quality does not apply to me but is more appropriate for those who did not allow me to take the oath.' Yet the media – most prominently the mainstream newspaper *Hurriyet* – claimed that Kavakci had not written this statement but that it had been formulated by someone else from the Virtue Party. Even Kavakci's words were taken not as her own but used to demonstrate that she was exploited by others. Again, Kavakci was reduced to 'an object of manipulation with no will or agency of her own'.[23] Unfortunately, not only was this perspective adopted by large sectors of the population in Turkey towards headscarved women, but also it was sometimes picked up by Western journalists and reported without an opposing view.

Notwithstanding the fact that this period was at the height of the post-28 February intervention, the lack of objectivity on the part of the Turkish press deserves further illumination, particularly because of the damage it has done not only to Merve Kavakci and the Islamic movement generally, but to their perception outside of Turkey by Western media. Of course there are other factors in play influencing public opinion and politics, but the Turkish media's lack of objectivity and professionalism – still an issue today (though there have been some improvements) – was a determining political factor in its own right detrimental to the democratic process. During this time it was its own major political actor.

Many media studies have been undertaken analysing bias in different countries, relating to various issues, such as gender, ethnicity and war. One such scholar, Dr Esra Arsan of the Communications Faculty of Istanbul Bilgi University, notes the sources of news manipulation during the Merve Kavakci incident by tracing Turkey's early modernization project, built 'on the ruins of a Muslim, religious empire' that helped to create a 'fear of collapse of the nation state by the Islamist fundamentalist' in Turkey's public sphere, resulting in 'racialized and stereotyped discourse woven into the everyday practices of journalists and editors in Turkish news media'.[24] She cites the works of Michel Foucault (the French twentieth-century scholar and philosopher) and the Dutch academic Teun A. Van Dijk, who viewed the representation of knowledge ('discourse') as power, creating meaning through language. Social power is rewarded to those who control meaning and public discourse. In Turkey in the 1990s the mainstream media exercised overwhelming power in how they represented 'knowledge' relating to Merve Kavakci. It is a vivid example of the importance of a free press in democratizing movements.

A reflective Merve Kavakci, now academically trained and with the benefit of time, from her office at George Washington University, articulated and analysed her experience. She wondered if she herself contributed to how she was portrayed in the media:

> That depersonalization, part of how generally the orientalist depersonalizes Muslim women, and Muslims in general, traps them into certain typologies. In this case, the Kemalists have depersonalized me very very much and actually maybe to an extent I also contributed to it. The fact that I appeared to be resilient,

as if I were not affected by their attacks; my friends brought this criticism to me: 'Merve you appear invincible and the human side of you does not show, your head is up and you are not crying.' I remember that I had very fashionable sunglasses and I was at an opening of a park with the Mayor of Istanbul; the next day I saw myself in the newspaper with this austere look on my face, and I looked like this person with a hidden agenda or something. I was amazed at how they, the media, manipulated the images to portray me in a different light, rather than appearing like a fashionable, nice-looking woman [they saw me as] a scary, indignant one probably with an agenda in the background. I remember Nazli Ilicak twice commenting. 'Merve, you don't cry, you appear like you are invincible; that is why they attack you more.'

That human part of me was not able to come out, I suppose. I did not want to show them my vulnerability to start with and I am a person with a certain dignity and honour. I hate to show others if I fail at anything; I want to have my own internal process of dealing with it particularly regarding the Kemalists who are trying to bring me down. I would not give them the pleasure of seeing me collapse before their eyes.

And yet, Osman Ulusoy, her driver and bodyguard, told me that on several occasions Merve would break down and cry in the back seat of her car, something the public only saw once when she was questioned about her children and shed a single tear for all to see, wearing a yellow headscarf.

Yeni Safak interview

In addition to the foreign press, Islamic-friendly newspapers gave Merve a forum to convey her views and supported her right to run and be elected. Adem Figan of *Aksiyon* 'argued that Parliament's rules of conduct do not explicitly bar the presence of the headscarf in Parliament'.[25] And in a lengthy interview of 14 March in *Yeni Safak*,[26] a well-established daily from Istanbul, Merve answered at length several questions on her views. The headline of the full-page interview was 'I Will Enter the Parliament As Lady Virtue' (*Meclis'e 'Fazilet Hanim' olarak girecegim*). The translated interview provides a detailed record of Merve Kavakci's views during the campaign, even though most of the Turkish public was probably not exposed to them, nor would have taken them seriously.

Q: *As a headscarved deputy will you be able to represent everybody including those without a headscarf?*

A: Yes, of course, *inshallah*. First of all I am foremost a deputy of the Fazilet (Virtue) Party. Since this party is open to everyone, Alevi and Sunni, I will have to be a deputy for everyone.

Q: *Is this your view as an individual or as a member of the VP?*

A: I do not discriminate among people. I accept and love people as people first and will be a representative of both women and men, and I will be a representative of all women without any discrimination. There are important problems for women in Turkey and I will carry them with me to the Parliament in a very serious way. In the meantime I will try to be a representative of the young people as well ... If elected I will be the youngest person in Parliament.

Q: *How did you think of entering politics?*

A: I have always been interested in politics because it affects your environment and everything around you.

Q: *How did you decide to be a deputy?*

A: They were discussing if we should have a woman candidate, headscarved or not, and my name was mentioned. It has something to do with the maturation of the party. Then I thought whether or not I could do it, then I said with happiness 'yes'. It's a job that requires a lot of work and sacrifice for working women.

Q: *On whose behalf are you going to engage in politics? Does it include uncovered women? Who has priority?*

A: Of course it includes uncovered women because the Virtue Party is on the side of democracy, human rights and full freedoms and rule of law; therefore it has uncovered candidates; they work just like me. Covered women are not given priority. If I enter the Parliament as a woman I will represent both, the whole female population. Their political views and appearance do not interest me. I think it's senseless to waste time by having a hang-up on these questions. The appearance of people does not interest me I cannot expect everybody to look like me and I have no right to expect that and people who think like us are in no position to take an interest in people's dresses, opinions and views. We already live this problem and we are suffering from this problem. We need to broaden the horizons of Turkey's future, we have to reduce the tension in Turkey on this issue and open the way to the future and this can only be possible by the instituting of human rights, freedom and justice. I don't find it useful or productive for Turkey to be obsessed with who is covered and who is not.

Q: *What did America contribute to your outlook regarding politics, human rights and freedom?*

A: I learned quite a bit. First of all America opened my horizons. You find out that different people with different colours and different ideas live in this world. You see this richness. After having seen this richness you realize how unthinkable and crazy it is to try to shape people into one single mould. Of course, in America democracy is well understood. People respect each other's freedoms. There is something called freedom of religion. People respect your beliefs and thoughts. This is very beautiful. It broadened my horizon. *Inshallah*, human rights, freedom of conscience and thought in Turkey will come to resemble America's. In addition, America first of all gave me a university education that I could not have in Turkey. The fact that I was able to get my education there shows the difference between the two countries.

Q: *What is your response to people who say that the 'headscarf should be kept out of the Parliament'? People want the headscarf to be in social and political life, but some others are trying to exclude headscarved women from social life by not allowing them into schools and the public sphere. Everybody knows these are not legal practices but they still exist.*

A: Yes you are correct. We are almost unable to go out in the streets. You cannot get a driver's licence or a passport wearing a headscarf. It's as if people are saying, 'Go stay in your house, go work on a farm and become invisible to us.' They have no tolerance for us. Whereas tolerance means maturity. They may think like this about us, but this is very wrong. We need to show them that they should respect the outfit, views and beliefs of those who do not think like them in a democratic way. It is not possible to please everyone but I think the time has come for us to demonstrate another view. Let's see if our nation will send people who dress and think like us to Parliament. They may not want to; they may say 'we don't want you' and they have a right to think that way. We would respect this. Whether or not the will of the nation will be realized, we will see on the morning of 19 April.

Q: *There are those who do not pay much attention to the national will in this country. What if they do the same and close the doors of Parliament to you?*

A: Then we will go as far as we can within the law in a manner that is becoming for us, in the best, balanced way. *Inshallah*, I expect that they are a small group; that the majority will act with common sense and say, 'this is shameful'. We are talking not about civil servants, but deputies. If they prevent it, a great scandal would result. The 18 April elections will be a test of whether or not we have been democratized.

Q: *You have said you are the kind of person who would embrace the uncovered women as well. As you know, it is very important in politics to be convincing. Will you be able to convince the non-headscarved women and those who do not share your thoughts?*

A: It is not 'whether I can'. I am convincing them. It is a personal thing. People I talk to and meet are supporting me. They like me being a woman and young. This is happening for the first time in Turkish history. In 1935, there were eighteen women deputies. On the seventy-fifth anniversary of the Republic, the number has declined to thirteen. The lack of women in politics is working to my advantage. I am receiving support. I treat people equally. I do not distinguish between headscarved and non-headscarved. I act sincerely.

Q: *The political sphere is new for the headscarf. If you enter the Parliament you will be the 'first' and will go into history. What do you feel?*

A: I am worried, to put it bluntly.

Q: *What are these anxieties?*

A: I have personal anxieties about passing into this kind of lifestyle. My anxieties have to do with my understanding of responsibility. One has to be productive. I have to represent all the people living everywhere in Turkey, all women urban or rural. My anxieties are in this sense. I must confess it is not as if I am not proud of being the first.

Q: *I saw a picture of you in a paper wearing make-up. Your dressing style is also very casual and sporty. Is it correct to say that you are a headscarved woman who feels modern?*

A: First, let's get back to the paper. They have worked on that photo.

Q: *You mean it's been photoshopped?*

A: Yes, they have thickened the eyebrows, coloured it, added some make-up. Only my smile was real. As for my using eyeliner, I do and I will continue using it. But, that has been made thick too. As for how I dress, I like dressing casual. You could see me in a skirt and jacket as well as in pants and a trench coat. I have a yellow as well as black coat. Besides, the concept of modern is too nebulous. Let's not think of this as being modern or not modern. I am extremely respectful of people's dressing, beliefs and thoughts. For me Islam means modernity. Islam means technology and science. If Islam only meant staying at home, doing housework and not going out, it would be too easy. Islam is also difficult too. The Muslim religion compels us to be the best and reach the best in this world. For this reason, Islam means contemporariness and modernity. It means not interfering in whichever way people dress and express themselves. It means carrying on your lifestyle and the way you believe is right.

Q: *Let's say you entered Parliament and took the oath. What will be the first thing you would do?*

A: I would pray for this to serve the goodness and welfare of people. I don't know much about the ways in which Parliament operates; I guess I would be doing commission work and have various other duties suitable for my skills. I am very interested in international relations, for example, and in helping women, all women, and young people. I would work in the direction of the mission of Virtue (Fazilet) and of what it believes.

Q: *So, you will enter Parliament as 'Lady Virtue'?*

A: Yes, yes, I will enter as Lady Virtue.

Q: *Is there a politician you take as your model?*

A: There is Tayyip Erdogan. I take him as a model. The services he delivers and the fact that he does not discriminate between people are very admirable.

Q: *Once headscarved women enter Parliament, what would change in Turkey's political life?*

A: Pluralism, polyphony and colourfulness would come. Horizons would widen, because every headscarved woman would bring the voice of the people. This means carrying the pluralism, colourfulness and richness of Turkey into Parliament. It would mean more democratization.

Q: *Some will perceive this as shattering secularism to pieces?*

A: They shouldn't. Those who perceive it like this can only be 'laicists' [a French term used in Turkish to indicate the dogmatic, almost unsecular and partisan way some secular people defend secularism – *laikciler*]. It seems to me we need to define secularism (*laiklik*) in correct ways now. This has nothing against secularism (*laiklik*). In reality, I should be looked at not as a headscarved woman but for what I can contribute to the country and Parliament as a headscarved person.

Q: *When you enter Parliament, if you meet an unbearable pressure to take your headscarf off, what would you do?*

A: This will not happen. I cannot compromise on my headscarf. Moreover, this would be a great shame (*ayip*) for Turkey. If people elect me there, they will want to see me there. In this situation, those who pressure me will have to answer to the people. I would do everything in my power to enter, but I would never remove my headscarf.

It is unfortunate that Merve's interview occurred the day after a terrorist bombing in Istanbul at the Blue Shopping Mall in which thirteen people were killed. It was given no discernible attention in the mainstream press. Other bombings occurred across the country. The PKK (the Kurdistan Workers' Party) was blamed for the attacks and threatened to bomb tourist sites too, declaring the entire country a war zone. This brought about heightened security measures across Turkey and travel warnings from Western countries. More important, it impacted the election as well, supporting the military's fixation with internal and external security and taking votes away from the Virtue Party because of its tension with the military and MHP's constant campaigning that the military would not let the party come to power anyway.[27]

The other woman with a headscarf

Once the identities of the candidates were announced to the public, the ones wearing headscarves who, in particular, had a good chance of being elected because of their position on the ballot list,[28] were asked the inevitable question: 'Will you remove your headscarf when entering the Turkish National Assembly?' One of these women was Nesrin Unal of the jingoist Nationalist Action Party, also known as MHP. Party sympathizers were almost united in support of lifting the headscarf ban in universities and ran in 1999 on the slogan: 'The head-covering issue will be resolved not by cowards but by real men.'[29] However, beginning in 1997, leader Devlet Bahceli sought to bring the party to a more centrist position, though many in his party disagreed. Regardless, he asked Nesrin Unal to take off her headscarf when in Parliament and she agreed, stating from the outset when asked if she would uncover her head that although she did not want to, she would uncover because she felt that the needs of the nation were more important than her religious feelings.[30]

On the other hand, Merve Kavakci, from the outset, was unequivocal, as the interview on previous pages shows, as do statements quoted later in this book

Could there be any other answer from Merve Kavakci? After briefly wearing a wig, she did not take off her headscarf for medical school, nor did her mother as a teacher, nor would her father tell his students to remove their headscarves. Her grandparents were similarly devout Muslims. The family had already paid a dear price by leaving Turkey and going to America for religious freedom. Regardless of the political inferences a headscarf in Turkey implied, the Kavakci family's religious beliefs had nothing to do with politics and were consistent and central for their entire lives, as they still are today.

Yet, while Merve may not have visibly shown to the public and the press her feelings about the tidal wave of enmity against her coming from the press, she definitely felt it – but she persevered. With the elections fast approaching, the media cartel was trying to increase the tension by putting out false news, and by a consistent campaign of slander that shook her on a daily basis. Then, digitally falsified demeaning photographs of her were being replaced with questions of whether she would uncover or not, together with false news of statements she supposedly had made. On the last day for candidates to announce whether to withdraw from the elections, as she stepped into Tayyip Erdogan's office to pay him a visit, a reporter from the newspaper *Radikal* called asking her for a response to the news they published regarding her 'declining to enter the elections'. Her initial response was outrage and an increasing anger that only fuelled her determination. The fact that she was honest and had participated in the campaign with pride – and had nothing to hide – didn't seem to matter to the press at all. It was a new experience for her to be bombarded every day with accusations and criticism, but over time she embraced it like a badge of honour. As with other leaders who derive strength from her followers, Merve Kavakci grew stronger and stood taller, with the added strength of her faith. She came to realize that the mainstream media in Turkey would never make peace with her regardless of what she said and did, so she developed a strong inner sense of patience and perseverance. She was exhausted by the campaign and by the attacks, but over time she held onto the feeling that she could overcome them.

On the other hand, the Western press, as Merve had anticipated, was fair in its reporting. On 18 April, the day of the election, the *Dallas Morning News* published a half-page article, 'Candidate's Headscarf Highlights Turkey's Church–State division' and quoted Merve, Ali Bayramoglu and Necla Arat in a 'balanced' article. Ali Bayramoglu was then, and is still, a highly respected journalist; Necla Arat was then, and is still, an aggressively Kemalist academic-turned-politician. Regarding Merve: 'Speaking in English honed to fluency by five years in Dallas, her political talk is of the need for more social benefits for the poor, better educational rights for women and the importance of strengthening Turkey's democratic institutions. "I want to be a voice for women in Turkey, for all women – to push for more democratic rights, freedom of speech, freedom of belief," she recently said.'

Then the article quoted Necla Arat: 'She can say openly that she is on the side of secularism, but they have their own kind of secularism, and the reference is Islam and Islamic principles and not democracy … Their dreams are to use democracy to bring an Islamic state.'

The goal of journalists to be 'objective' rather than 'truth seeking' aside, once again, this is the standard Kemalist response used to disenfranchise major blocks of people from the democratic process: their intentions are not what they seem. They aim to take over. Yet, as was also noted by the author of the article, 'Female Parliamentary candidates were barred last week from appearing in televised debates if they keep their headscarves on.' Not letting covered women debate on television was an example of Turkish secularism and its view of democracy during the coup process. Now that practice on state television has changed because there is an Islamic-friendly ruling party in power, although other restrictions, such as prohibiting employment for the state bureaucracy of covered women, have not.

In the Turkish Constitution the state's interests are set above those of individual rights, which is the opposite of the Constitution of Western democracies in which 'the state exists secondarily to the universal principles of human rights of all citizenry'.[31] In 2010 a referendum resulted in 58 per cent of Turks approving several changes to the Turkish Constitution and after Tayyip Erdogan's third victory in 2011 a new Constitution is on the agenda to be written and submitted for approval by Parliament. It remains to be seen if serious changes to civil–military relations, party closures and prohibitions regarding the headscarf will result.

At the time of Merve's election campaign, the two sides could not be more different, as if operating in different worlds. Merve Kavakci is campaigning on a platform of democracy, freedom and women's rights to thousands of people on the Anatolian side of Istanbul, with a sea of covered women chanting, 'We are women, we are strong and we exist.' On the other side, the military is regularly issuing warnings about the 'dangers of Islam-based politics and cautioning the public not to vote for the Virtue Party'.[32]

I asked Recai Kutan if he ever had any direct contact from the military during the campaign and up until the incident in Parliament. His response was a definitive 'no'. But an informed source, a Member of Parliament who witnessed directly what was happening at this time, told me that Kutan was repeatedly receiving threats on the phone directly from General Cevik Bir, who led the 1997 coup. After the election military people were openly making comments, publicly and in private, about the need to preserve the secular state.

Discussions of democracy abound from within the USA, Turkish and global contexts, and Merve has written extensively and given presentations in many forums on the subject, including women and Islam, and secularism as a requirement for democracy, especially from the perspective of Western democracies. Kemalists are often defensive on the subject of democracy and argue that Turkey is 'unique', located at the edge of the Middle East, and that in the post-9/11 world precautions must be taken against Islam.

Questions about party support

The split in the Virtue Party at this time was practical, ideological and eventually would impact current Turkish politics. On one side was Erbakan. In spite of his having been forced to resign as Prime Minister by the 28 February coup process, banned from politics for five years, and starting his Welfare Party again as the Virtue Party, albeit different in some respects, Erbakan was still a key player in the Virtue Party. Recai Kutan, the Virtue Party leader, and Temel Karamollaoglu, his second in command, told me as much when I interviewed them, as noted above. It is also evident that Erbakan's wife and daughter were actively involved, and he was making recommendations and orchestrating matters by phone.

Erbakan's involvement was a dangerous move, one that continued to burn in the hearts of the secularists and the military. More importantly, for the young reformers in the party – namely Tayyip Erdogan and Abdullah Gul – Erbakan's involvement could bring an end to not only the Virtue Party but also their political careers. The tone and language of the campaign, modified from a direct endorsement of Islamic concerns as the Welfare Party to the Virtue Party's protestations for human rights and democracy, mattered little and convinced no one in the military and the secularist camp. The reformists not only viewed Erbakan's involvement as a threat to the party but also saw his meddling as hindering intra-party democracy, although their motives were likely self-serving given that Turkish political parties are not generally perceived as being run democratically, either then or now.

The party was also divided on another issue: delaying the elections. Erbakan persuaded Kutan to allow Virtue deputies, aligned with other members of Parliament, to favour postponing the elections, based on polls that showed Virtue's support lacking. Erbakan was also hoping that a delay would buy time to remove his political ban and perhaps have him lead the party into the next elections.[33] On the ideological question, there were those – notably the reformists – who felt that the headscarf issue would also raise the ire of the military and further endanger the party's status.

Tayyip Erdogan met with Merve and her cousins in his office shortly before his imprisonment. Merve wanted to get feedback from him on her work. He looked at her and said politely that he did not agree with her nomination – that is, the nomination of a headscarved woman. He pointed out how ruthless the media was, but his main concern, which he told her, was that in the coming days the party might not be behind her. She was floored. He offered to help her as much as he could up until his prison term started on 26 March, and after that he would do what he could. He advised her to start an election office in every district to establish a flow of information to the voters. She listened to this advice but knew it would be too costly and impossible.

Combined with Gul's previous interpretation, Erdogan's evaluation of the party stuck, and her hope for success almost evaporated. Now she had more to worry about, fearing lack of support from her own party. Her mission became more daunting, the objections to her headscarf coming from everywhere, which also made her mission more sacred and important.

On one of her trips to Ankara, Merve wanted to visit the party headquarters and meet with Recai Kutan. She thought how nice and motivating it would be if some high-level party official called and asked her how she was doing, but no one ever called. Despite her numerous attempts to ask for an appointment, the meeting never took place. The young campaigner began to see the party's situation as very critical, and the way the press was handling her situation as threatening. Perhaps Kutan agreed with how Karamollaoglu described the situation to me: that there was merely limited criticism in the press; that she had submitted her application with a photograph and it had been accepted. 'We never thought it would cause a problem,' he said.[34] Others expressed similar views: that since her candidacy had been approved and she was allowed to campaign, why would there be problems later if she were elected?

On the other hand, Merve's driver and armed bodyguard, Osman Ulusoy, painted a different picture. He was hired by the party to provide special protection to Merve because of her headcover and the tension it would create in the post-coup environment. Mr Kutan's comments seemed incredible to him, given that fact of the press coverage and the rumours about alleged calls to him from the military. He was witness to the daily tensions. The Virtue Party campaign was hardly flying 'under the radar' and Merve's increasing worries at the time, regardless of her newness to the political process, also attest to the increased tension. Merve worried that a group in Parliament were extremely opposed to her, regardless of the legality of the elections, but, somewhat naively, thought the matter would be settled 'behind closed doors'.

So what was being addressed behind closed doors? Merve was completely left out of the decision-making process in the party and treated, not surprisingly, in a patriarchal way by its male leadership. During my interview with Kutan I brought up, on Merve's behalf, the issue of his lack of response to her questions and requests to meet. He brushed them aside and said that there were more important things on his mind at the time.

**

Nuh Mete Yuksel is officially known as Ankara State Security Court (DGM) Prosecutor, although his career mission seems to be Chief 'Persecutor' of Islamic people. With just three weeks to go before the elections, on 22 March, he filed a closure case in the Court of Appeals to ban the Virtue Party. In Turkey there is no grand jury system to hand down indictments, which gives prosecutors a lot of power. They file their own indictments, which then have to be approved by the courts. Yuksel embodied the worst of aggressive Turkish secularism. Two years earlier he had asked for the death penalty for Faruk Akcan, who unfurled a banner of the outlawed Kurdistan Workers' Party (PKK), and for Giyasettin Mordeniz, who supposedly told Faruk to cut down the Turkish flag. A year earlier, on 24 February 1998, he had also sought death for former Welfare Party deputy Sevki Yilmaz for his activities against the Constitution and against secular democratic order, and sought thirty-year sentences against twenty-four other people, including mayors and heads of civic organizations.

Yuksel was not seeking anyone's death in this case, just the closure of the party before the elections. In a six-page filing, Yuksel claimed that the Virtue Party was the successor to the Welfare Party, and was thus in violation of the Turkish Constitution. He also alleged that the Virtue Party had tried to persuade the Parliament to abolish Article 312 of the Political Parties Law by having the bans of Erbakan and Erdogan lifted. This move against the party, because it advocated changing a law as grounds for closing a political party, made a mockery of the functions of political parties that are, after all, about making and changing laws!

Nevertheless, two days later Kutan fought back, requesting that Justice Minister Selcuk Oztek dismiss Yuksel for 'misuse of office' by leaking investigations to the press, making hasty arrests and exceeding his responsibilities, since party closure cases can only be filed by chief state prosecutors. Unfortunately, the state prosecutor who helped close down the Welfare Party, Vural Savas, also launched his own investigation against Virtue, asking for the names of all the Welfare Party members who switched to Virtue before Welfare was closed.

The prosecutors had a decent case in this area, regardless of the undemocratic nature of Turkey's party closure law. Erbakan *was* involved, by even meeting with VP deputy Yasin Hatipoglu, a deputy speaker of Parliament, at his home on 27 March, and by helping to resolve the deadlock in Parliament by trying to extend the election date, contrary to the direction of VP leaders. Ironically, the party did make a concerted effort to tone down its religious appeal, but everyone knew that the substance of the membership and followers of both parties were the same. If anything, the VP's new moderate stance tended to turn off former Welfare supporters, yet did little to assuage the state from going after it.

The move to shut down the party was just one pressure facing the VP leadership at this time, putting them in a real bind. Another big problem was that they could not control thirty-four pro-Erbakan deputies who wanted to delay the elections, nor Erbakan's phone calls and meetings, nor involvement by his wife and daughter, which threatened the party's very existence.

This also truly angered the military. The move by VP members was aimed not only at postponing the elections but also at removing Article 312 of the Turkish Penal Code, which bans 'inciting hatred among people based on race, ethnicity and religion'. Virtue Party deputies wanted to remove the article to stop the prosecution of Erbakan, who they thought might end up facing the death penalty[35] because of it. Vural Savas, the person who shut down the Welfare Party, received a 'courtesy' visit from Deputy Chief of General Staff Hilmi Ozkok and four generals at this time. The Chief of General Staff, Huseyin Kivrikoglu, declared, after a meeting with President Demirel, that the elections should proceed and Article 312 should not be amended. 'Turkey cannot tolerate this. We believe that prudence and serenity will be the winner sooner or later.'[36]

Eventually, the misbehaving VP deputies relented. They were not able to garner enough votes in Parliament to amend any laws, and the elections remained on schedule.

On 6 April 1999, a reporter for the *Turkish Daily News*, Zeynep Erdim, interviewed Merve and Temel Karamollaoglu at a lunch arranged by Nazli Ilicak at her villa in Beylerbeyi, an exclusive neighbourhood in Uskudar bordering the Bosphorus on the Asian side of Istanbul. There were two lunches actually. At this one, no alcohol was served out of respect for the Islamic people present; another was held for non-covered candidates, with alcohol. This English-language paper was independent at the time and not yet part of the Dogan group. Here are some excerpts from the article:

> 'I believe Turkey's going to take a real test on democracy on April 18,' Kavakci said in fluent English, adding that it is unfair that while 70 per cent of women in Turkey wear headscarves, someone who wears the same attire is unable to have the right to represent people in Parliament …
>
> 'In the [Parliamentary] bylaws it doesn't say that you can't wear a headscarf,' said Kavakci, explaining that the only requirement is to wear a two-piece suit, a requirement that they have no problem adhering to.
>
> Kavakci and Tekdal base their argument for being allowed to serve in Parliament while wearing their headscarves on both Parliamentary bylaws and on Mustafa Kemal's famous statement, 'Sovereignty belongs unconditionally to the people.'
>
> However, when asked if they are prepared for the probable reactions against their attire, their answers are unsure and hesitant. Kavakci said she believes that other parties will support her.
>
> Whenever the two women candidates seem at a loss for words, Temel Karamollaoglu, a member of the VP General Administration Council (GIK) and a long time politician, took over the job of answering. 'I hope no one will be able to interfere. I hope that there will only be criticism, but I don't think that anything will happen in Parliament. There might be a crisis, but I hope not.'
>
> With all of these hopes, the VP's position on the forthcoming post-election crisis seems to be vague and limited to 'wishful thinking'.[37]

The 'wishful thinking' article of 6 April 1999 mentioned another headscarved VP candidate, representing Ankara's first district, Aysenur Tekdal, who was also expected to win a seat in Parliament but did not.

Campaigning with Nazli Ilicak

With the election drawing closer the tempo of the campaign accelerated. The pace of the campaign was making it difficult for Merve to keep up in her memorization work – she was a *hafiz*, a Muslim who had completely memorized the Qur'an. Demands were increasing for reprints of Merve's posters and she was being asked to speak at more rallies.

Meanwhile, in the Sultanbeyli district the people were showing their conservativeness by not publicly displaying women's pictures and thus had not hung any posters of Merve Kavakci. The term 'conservative' is used in Turkey to mean religiously conservative. Islamic-oriented and Islamic-friendly parties are all, to a varying degree, 'conservative', focusing on religious, community and family values. Sultanbeyli is one of Istanbul's most conservative districts, and thus gave extensive support not only to the Virtue Party, but also to municipal and civil organizations that provided food and services for the poor and needy. The VP rally in the Abdi Ipekci Sports Centre in the Sultanbeyli district was one of the largest of the campaign. After the singing of the Turkish National Anthem, Nazli Ilicak took the stage and invited all the women candidates to join her, along with Recai Kutan. She then spoke to the crowd and said, 'We are entrusting ourselves to you [looking at Kutan] while Merve is entrusted to me, all right?' The crowd cheered wildly and shouted 'YES, YES!' Nazli was a tireless, fearless supporter – both with her voice and with her pen – not only of Merve Kavakci but also of all covered women, whom she viewed as unjustly treated. It's not possible to overemphasize just how unique Nazli Ilicak was in Turkey at the time, and she remains now a secular advocate for the rights of headscarved women. Nazli and Merve stayed at the front of the stage and threw carnations to the crowd. Returning to their seats, the public pushed towards them in waves trying to get their signatures on party flags. Then a young man had them pose for a photograph and said, smiling and happy, that he wished that they would always stay together. The implication was that while the unity of secular and non-secular people was wonderful in his eyes, for many others it was unacceptable. Merve was taken aback by this wish, and thought: wasn't this what the Turkish public wanted in the first place? More than a decade later, while living in Istanbul, I have many times seen young headscarved and uncovered women walking arm in arm, or hanging out together at Starbucks. Perhaps things are slowing changing in Turkey.

At a big open-air rally in Caglayan Square, tens of thousands of enthusiastic supporters greeted the VP candidates, including Merve Kavakci. It also was full of enthusiasm. After the speeches by the Head of the Istanbul District, Mayor of Istanbul and Head of the VP, she distributed carnations and embraced the public. There too the public was happy to see Nazli and Merve together. A man who was carrying his wife on his shoulder was shouting, 'We love you like this!' while young women with headscarves were trying to catch the carnations they threw. Merve viewed the crowd's response as the enthusiasm of brotherhood and togetherness, a firm belief in the struggle for human rights, and a desire to carry Turkey towards togetherness and goodness by the covered and uncovered, young and old, women and men.

On 17 April, after a busy day, the campaigning stopped at Sultanbeyli, in the middle of a programme at 5 p.m. in compliance with the election regulations.

It had been an intense six weeks, a whirlwind. For Merve Kavakci it was the unforgettable experience of a lifetime, running around Istanbul, interacting with thousands of people. It galvanized and transformed her. She remembered the people from Sultanbeyli and many other places, people who showed their love for her. She knew well that for the past eighty or so years they had been ostracized and marginalized as the people of a particular religious culture and background, looked down upon and subject to restrictions, particularly since the 1980s. Their wives, children and grandchildren had to deal with the headscarf issue in the streets and the universities, and Merve began to feel she was everyone's daughter.

But at the same time, Merve had to deal with the double standard that conservative men from within her party seemed to have in their treatment of her, and even the coldness of non-headscarved candidates. The only bright spot in that category had been Nazli Ilicak, a single, fearless example of someone who fought for the rights of others. In addition, Merve continued to be worried about the media attention she was receiving as the prominent headscarved candidate, which was turning increasingly nasty, and for which the party did not seem to have any strategy or plans.

As Merve and Ravza were driven home that day to their apartment on the Asian side of Istanbul, little did they know how much worse things would become for them in the party, in the press and in the Republic of Turkey.

Notes

1   Erik Zurcher, *Turkey: A Modern History*, IB Tauris, London, 1997, p. 302.
2   *Turkish Daily News*, 11 February 1999.
3   Cited in *Turkish Daily News*, 6 February 1999, italic emphasis added.
4   Quoted in *Milliyet*, Derya Sazak, 5 February 1999.
5   *Turkish Daily News*, 10 February 1999.
6   Stephen Kinzer, *Crescent & Star*, Farrar, Straus and Giroux, 2001, p. 77.
7   Kinzer, p. 78.
8   Jenny B. White, *Islamic Mobilization in Turkey: A Study in Vernacular Politics*, University of Washington Press, 2002, p. 145.
9   'The Race for Istanbul', *Turkish Daily News*, 25 February 1999.
10 M. Hakan Yavuz, *Islamic Political Identity in Turkey*, Oxford University Press, 2003, p. 249.
11 Marvine Howe, *Turkey Today: A Nation Divided Over Islam's Revival*, Westview Press, 2000, p. 217.
12 This information is based on chapter 7 of J. B. White, *Islamic Mobilization in Turkey: A Study in Vernacular Politics*, University of Washington Press, 2002.
13 *Ibid.*
14 Temel Karamollaoglu was Mayor of Sivas during the Madimak Hotel Massacre on 2 July 1993; he is a former Welfare Party Member of Parliament and Deputy Chairman of its Parliamentary group. Interview occured on 19 April 2010.
15 Interview, 21 April 2010.
16 *Turkish Daily News*, 18 March 1998.
17 Interview with Osman Ulusoy, 9 May 2010.
18 http://www.taraf.com.tr/nese-duzel/makale-bu-ulkede-basin-hukumet-de-kurdu.htm; http://www.taraf.com.tr/nese-duzel/makale-basindaki-ajanlari-bilirdik.htm; http://www.taraf.com.tr/nese-duzel/makale-gazetecilerin-parali-ajanlik-kavgasi.htm; http://www.solforum.net/content/ergun-babahan-%E2%80%98and%C4%B1%C3%A7-iftiras%C4%B1-bilerek-at%C4%B1ld%C4%B1%E2%80%99-nese-d%C3%BCzel-taraf.
19 Betul Akkaya Demirbas, 'Media's Role in Coups under Spotlight as Veteran Journalist makes Confessions', *Today's Zaman*, 20 May 2011, p. 1.
20 M. Hakan Yavuz, 'Cleansing Islam from the Public Sphere', *Journal of International Affairs*, 1 October 2000.
21 Kim Shively, 'Religious Bodies and the Secular State: the Merve Kavakci Affair', *Journal of Middle Eastern Women's Studies*, Vol. 1, No. 3 (Fall 2005), p. 53.
22 *Ibid.*
23 *Ibid.*
24 Esra Dogru Arsan, 'Representation of the "Other" in Turkish News Media: Islamists and Kurds', Green College, Oxford, Reuters Foundation Paper No. 193, Michaelmas/Hilary 2001–2002.

25 Shively, p. 55.
26 Yeni Safak, translated by Umit Cizre, 14 March 1999.
27 M. Hakan Yavuz, *Islamic Political Identity in Turkey*, Oxford University Press, 2003, p. 253.
28 In the Turkish Parliamentary system votes are cast in districts for the party, not individuals, and the number of representatives relates directly to the number of votes cast. Kavakci's election was expected because the Virtue Party did well in Istanbul.
29 Metin Heper and Barry Rubin (eds), *Political Parties in Turkey*, Frank Cass, London, 2002, p. 35.
30 Shively, p. 50.
31 Shively, p. 61. See also Mustafa Erdogan, 'Religious Freedom in the Turkish Constitution', *Muslim World*, 89: 377–388, 1999.
32 R. Quinn Mecham, 'From the Ashes of Virtue, a Promise of Light: The Transformation of Political Islam in Turkey', *Third World Quarterly*, Vol. 25, No. 2 (2004) p. 347.
33 *Ibid.*
34 Interview with the author, 19 April 2010, Ankara.
35 *Turkish Daily News*, 19 March 1999.
36 *Ibid.*
37 *Turkish Daily News*, 6 April 1999.

4

The Election

On 18 April 1999, Merve Kavakci voted in an elementary school in the Icerenkoy district of Istanbul. The media had obtained the news beforehand, went to this school before her arrival and escorted her while she was voting. She then travelled from one voting station to the next. In the evening, she and other candidates met in the party's Istanbul headquarters building. As midnight approached the results started to come in. Although enough votes were cast for the Virtue Party to elect Merve, overall the party did not meet its expectations to perform at least as well as its predecessor, the Welfare Party, had in 1996, which had been enough to lead a new government as part of a coalition.

The results were as follows:

- Prime Minister Bulent Ecevit's Democratic Left Party (DSP), 22 per cent, 136 seats
- Nationalist Movement Party (MHP), 18 per cent, 129 seats
- Virtue Party (VP), 15.4 per cent, 111 seats
- Republican People's Party (CHP), 8.72 per cent, no seats because the party did not achieve the 10 per cent minimum required to enter Parliament.

A little more than 87 per cent of eligible voters took part in the 18 April elections in Turkey, with more than thirty-one million votes cast.

The disagreements within the party had certainly had a negative effect on how people voted. The notion that the Virtue Party would not be allowed to run a government if elected because the military would intervene, as MHP had argued during the campaign, may have also had a negative impact. This was logical given the fate of its predecessor party. The obvious conflicts between Erbakan and his allies and the reformers over when to hold the elections may have also contributed to fewer votes, although the party was successful in local elections.

Ecevit had been Deputy Prime Minister in the coalition government formed after the resignation of Erbakan in 1997, but that fell apart in 1998 after the former Prime Minister's (Yilmaz) ties to the underworld were exposed. Now President Demirel nominated Ecevit to be Prime Minister, who had the full support of the military and his party had come out ahead.

The outcome led *Sabah's* Gulay Gokturk to describe the results as follows:

> When I look at the two parties that came out winners, I see that Turkey will face a period in which a totalitarian mentality will carry weight rather than pluralism, anti-democratic views will become more influential than in the past, the tendency to become inward-looking will resist the trend towards globalization and statism will gain strength as opposed to liberalism. Let us hope that this period will pass without damaging the country too much.[1]

In fact, the militant nationalism of the DSP and MHP virtually eliminated the political centre, and this 'had grave implications for efforts to institutionalize Turkey's already weak democratic process'.[2] And grave implications for Merve as well. It was the politics of fear that had won out in the election, reinforced by the Kurdish terror attacks and claims for religious freedoms, seemingly reinforcing each other. 'The results of the 1999 national elections did not remove the shadow of the Turkish military but rather has it looming ever larger over the new coalition governments.'[3]

The 'reality' of Merve Kavakci surfaces

As news of the election results spread across the country, the Merve Kavakci story expanded and grew; picked up by the media before the election, it escalated with the realization that she would refuse to remove her headscarf when entering Parliament to be sworn in, which she was asked about continually. The question about her headscarf was no longer a possibility, a hypothetical, but a reality. Issues to be tackled by the new Parliament – such as unemployment, inflation and embezzlement – vaporized in front of the renewed torrent of campaigns against her on television and in the press. The tension seemed to increase daily. And it became a common story comparing Merve Kavakci and Nesrin Unal. This article in the *Star* newspaper was typical:

She Will Take Off Her Headscarf

The MHP has adopted a clear stance on the headscarf issue. The top MHP officials' position on this issue boils down to, 'Our newly elected deputy, Nesrin Unal, will of course take off her headscarf when in Parliament. Whatever Parliament's rules are, the MHP will comply with them. This is our custom.' MHP Deputy Chairman Sevkat Cetin said, 'We have talked with her and persuaded her to do that.' What will the VP leadership do? The first headscarved VP deputy, Merve Kavakci, has no intention of taking off her headscarf. In fact she is preparing to cause the first crisis for the new Parliament by showing up with a headscarf on the first day of the new Parliamentary session.

Note the biased characterization of Merve Kavakci: 'she is preparing to cause the first crisis for the new Parliament'.

Similarly, *Sabah* reported:

Newly elected MHP Deputy Nesrin Unal says that her aim is to serve the people, and not staying outside Parliament and creating tension, that she is against exploitation of the headscarf. Newly elected VP deputy, Merve Kavakci, on the other hand, says, 'I will neither resign nor take off my headscarf.'[4]

And the *Turkish Daily News*, in an article by Zeynep Erdim on the many female deputies elected to Parliament, related how 'Merve Sefa Kavakci, a young computer engineer educated in the United States, has previously stated that she will not take her headscarf off during Parliamentary sessions' but that Nesrin Unal, elected under the MHP banner from Antalya, 'is reportedly ready to take her headscarf off when she officially becomes a deputy'.[5] The Kavakci–Unal comparisons in the press were common.

The other question on everyone's mind was how the government would react. The press sought out Ali Riza Septioglu who, at eighty-six, was the oldest Member of Parliament and thus would be its ceremonial president for its first session. Septioglu declared unequivocally that 'whatever the law requires, I have to implement. Nobody is above the law.' However, noting that everyone was asking him about the deputies wearing headscarves, Septioglu said that he had no answers: 'I cannot make a comment without looking at the regulation.'[6]

What is that regulation? Septioglu did not seem to know at this time. Given his advanced age, we can excuse him for this. However, others seemed equally confused or wished to convey a distorted answer. Article 56 of the Parliament's dress code seemed clear enough: 'The Parliament speaker has to wear a white bow tie and a black vest under a black frock coat. The deputies, ministers, Parliamentary civil servants and other public personnel in the General Assembly must wear a suit and tie, while women must wear two-piece suits.' But the newspaper that interviewed Septioglu quoted 'Parliamentary officials' as stating that although there is no such regulation about headscarves, deputies should not wear them, noting that 'there are many unwritten rules and everyone should obey them'.[7]

During one interview at Nazli Ilicak's house, a Turkish journalist, Mehmet Ali Birand, mentioned earlier for his confession years later that he succumbed to military influence over journalism, said to Merve: 'I bet the military will never let it happen, they will never let you take office.' Merve was shocked and dismayed. She told the reporter that she believed 'in the way that Ataturk thought about the rights of women' and that 'at the end of the day democracy would prevail and they would have to abide by the rules'. Meanwhile, constituents were continually calling her asking what she would do, even questioning her commitment to being a devout Muslim, which she took as an insult – all of this was due to the constant polemics in the media.

As the intensity of media coverage increased, it seemed to Merve that all of the internal and external problems of Turkey would be resolved if she would only remove her headscarf before entering Parliament, otherwise Turkey would regress a thousand years. Her family – parents, cousins, aunts and uncles – were all upset over what was happening, but eventually it became part of their daily life as well. The Arifan radio station, which had been very supportive, dedicated an entire programme to the subject. In a 10 p.m. interview, Mustafa Basoglu, a well-known trade unionist, was asked by Muhammed Emin Genc whether Kavakci would be uncovering or not. He answered that he did not think so and said, 'Merve, my daughter, don't you uncover!' But Arifan was a tiny,

Islamic-friendly station with little impact compared to the mainstream media.

Meanwhile, Nesrin Unal was appearing frequently in the press, saying just the opposite. Merve called her soon after the election to congratulate her, then a second time, to tell her that she thought her statements to the press were very harmful to the people she represented, and to convey her hope that she would not be uncovering when she entered the Parliament. Merve appealed to her that if they stuck together and did not compromise their principles – especially since the people had voted for them as they were – there was nothing in the law against wearing a headscarf in Parliament, which was clearly evident in Parliament's policies and regulations. Nesrin Unal, according to Merve, 'took our conversation in a different direction and became aggressive with me'. She angrily told Merve that her parents were not highly educated like Merve's, and the conversation became so heated that her husband had to intervene, politely, and then the call ended.

Nesrin Unal had a medical degree from a Turkish university, but seemed jealous of Merve's parents and their educational background. This may relate to the fact that professional women with headscarves had not previously made their presence known in the public realm, yet Merve's mother had, and thus Merve had an advantage. Regardless, Nesrin Unal became the example of the 'good Turk' who loved her country and validated the secularist approach and tradition in Turkey, in contrast to Merve Kavakci, who was perceived as causing a crisis. The two contrasting behaviours were frequently described in the press. Interestingly MHP, Nesrin Unal's party, had campaigned that they would be 'man enough' to 'solve the headscarf problem' in the universities, probably to get votes from this huge voting segment. However, ultimately, they pressured Nesrin Unal to remove her headscarf when she entered Parliament. Eleven years later, when campaigning against a constitutional reform package referendum, CHP also tried to appeal to headscarved women, stating that they would 'seek a compromise' and solve this chronic issue. That promise also turned out to be specious. The 'compromise' was for Muslim women to show some of their hair when they covered to avoid making a political statement, a position that was derided by the Islamic community. Merve may have had significant support among the Turkish population but Nesrin Unal's behaviour reinforced the views of the opposition press and the military and provided a counter-example for the public that was already against her.

***

Merve had about a week to pick up her permit from the state in Istanbul that would officially make her a Member of Parliament, and then go to Parliament to take her oath. So in the meantime she returned home to Ankara to meet with her family and strategize, she hoped, with Recai Kutan and others in the Virtue Party. She was under great strain from all the unwanted press coverage and felt the media was being successful in unbalancing the public, many of whom unquestionably believed whatever they heard or read in the press. Nevertheless, despite all her efforts to get an appointment with Kutan, he could not or would not meet with her for the next three to four days. She postponed her return to Istanbul for one more day and waited by the phone in case he called, but he did not. Perhaps the reason related to what Merve had told me about the party members not knowing how to deal with her, a bright and intelligent headscarved woman, or perhaps this was once again an example of patriarchy or simply a real underestimation by Kutan of what could happen. Regardless of the reasons, Merve would always remember being ignored at this important juncture in her election.

While impatiently waiting, she and her cousin visited Aydin Menderes to seek his advice. He was a VP deputy, the son of the former President, Adnan Menderes, who had been executed by the military in 1960 – someone she respected for his political experience, and a former classmate. Unfortunately, the most advice came mainly from Menderes' wife, who told her to wear something like a wig when she entered Parliament. To that comment Merve just smiled, since she was a guest in her house. Menderes would be another key Virtue Party member who would not support Merve when it mattered – something she was not aware of at this time. So she attempted once again to seek the advice of another member of the Virtue Party, the future President of Turkey. She met with Abdullah Gul at the ANAR Research Centre. She voiced her concern that she would end up alone in the middle of the controversy with no one in the party to support her. In Merve's words: 'With his usual gentleness he told me not to worry in vague sentences, the meanings of which I really didn't understand.' Thus, in the wake of the start of a major political fracture between the secular bloc and the Islamic community, one that would gain the attention of all of Turkey and many other countries, Merve Kavakci could not get the attention or concern of her party. She returned to Istanbul more worried than ever.

The party in disarray

The common view that Merve was being manipulated by the party should be placed alongside what key party leaders were really doing at this time, which appears to be nothing – that is, essentially ignoring her. Although Gul had told her after her nomination that she was 'one of us now,' in fact she was not. She was not in the party's inner circle, nor was she fully aware of the splits that had occurred before the election, and the subsequent pressure on the leadership due to the party's poor election performance. These factors, combined with the pressure by the government and the military, at the very least preoccupied the party leadership, and at worse placed it in disarray. Gul had hinted at this before the election and was hardly providing any help after it.

I asked both Kutan and Karamollaoglu about the party being split before the election and they both denied it. In addition, Kutan did not recall Merve wanting to meet with him and stated that if there had been an issue her uncle Orhan Gungen would have contacted him – yet another example of patriarchy with regards to women, or forgetfulness, or both. Kutan was thrust into a difficult, if not impossible, leadership position. He and Karamollaoglu seemed as honest as politicians could be given that they were still employed by a political party, Saadet, when I interviewed them. But it is clear that splits in the party existed and this resulted in a lack of clear direction and strategy regarding Merve's and the party's complete underestimation of the situation that was about to occur.

At a press conference in Ankara after the results of the general election were announced, this being held with local elections that year, Kutan emphasized how well the party had performed locally – VP candidates in mayor's races had won 23 per cent of all the municipalities in Turkey, including Ankara's new mayor, Melih Gokcek. Kutan defended the party's national results by pointing out that the VP had been founded only a year and a half ago, that it had received less money from the Treasury than it should have, and citing also the 'special circumstances' of Vural Savas' attempt before the Constitutional Court to close the party, all of which affected the results.

Regardless, the press compared the performance of the Virtue Party to that of its predecessor, the WP, and from that perspective Virtue failed, losing 5 per cent of the vote, or one-third of WP's support. It was pointed out that walking a fine line on the headscarf issue during the campaign had caused the loss of it grassroots support, particularly in Konya and Kayseri, where attendance at rallies was low. At some rallies the crowd shouted 'Erdogan, Erdogan' when Kutan was speaking – more evidence that the split in its leadership was hurting the party. On the other hand, it was clear that an overly aggressive VP could bring about its closure and downfall.[8] The party wavered and was stuck in the middle.

Given the bind the Virtue Party was in, it was no surprise that it could provide little guidance for Merve. It had none for itself and was being criticized by its reform-minded leaders. Less than a week after the election, *Sabah* reported:

> Former Istanbul Mayor Tayyip Erdogan, who had been elected on a Virtue Party [VP] ticket and is now serving a sentence in Pinarhisar prison, said, 'The VP deserved this election defeat, because it failed to fulfil its promises and distanced itself from the people. And it has been taught a lesson.'[9]

There is no way of knowing if Erdogan actually made this statement, however. The same day, *Milliyet* wrote: 'Kutan caught in a cross fire – both the Erbakan wing and the Erdogan wing of the VP up in arms against VP leader Recai Kutan.'[10] That type of report was typical and appeared in most of the papers.

The *Turkish Daily News* printed a long article on members of the party who might challenge the leadership of Kutan in its upcoming convention in the autumn, and focused on the need to eliminate the influence of Erbakan and the inefficiency of Kutan. Cited were Bulent Arinc, as well as Cemil Cicek, Abdulkadir Aksu and Ali Coskun, who publicly denounced the interference of Erbakan, and noted that 'political circles within and outside the party see VP Kayseri Deputy Abdullah Gul as a more appropriate candidate for leadership because of his moderate nature'. The article rings true: the four individuals cited all went on to have successful careers as ministers in the AK Party government. Meanwhile, the report found that 'wishing to avoid the same fate as their predecessor, the Welfare Party, many VP deputies are insisting that no chance be given to anyone in the party presenting a strictly Islamist portrait' and that the convention contest 'will come down to the uncompromising, strict Islamist Erbakan or the more moderate Erdogan'. The article noted that the real test would come on 2 May 1999 relating, of course, to Merve Kavakci:

> The first test related to the ongoing internal instability within the VP will be experienced during the swearing-in ceremony for the new Parliament, when the two new female deputies with headscarves may or may not uncover their heads. The VP is not expected to demonstrate a moderate attitude towards this issue, and the tenacious ones within the party will use this as a chance to display their power. If this fight is won by those Islamists who prefer to promote their ideology with harshness, then those who want to avoid closure of the party are expected to resign.[11]

Meanwhile the *Star* also reported the following, under the headline: 'The French Media to Cause the VP's Downfall':

> Renowned news magazine *Le Point* has said, on the basis of documents, that the Virtue Party [VP] had received from Iran a [US]$500,000 contribution to its election campaign. The news has had a bombshell effect in Ankara, stirring State Security Court [DGM] Chief Prosecutor Nuh Mete Yuksel into action immediately. Letters have been written to the French foreign minister and the security director. First a statement will be obtained from the correspondent who wrote the report, then a complaint will be filed with the Constitutional Court, demanding the VP's closure.[12]

It seemed as though everything and everyone was closing in on the Virtue Party just a few days before the swearing-in ceremony.

Merve returned to Istanbul to pick up her election permit in the final week of April. According to Turkish law, deputies start their duties as soon as they receive their permits from the city for which they were elected. After that moment, they are official Parliamentarians with all the corresponding rights. Thus on 27 April 1999 Merve and her contingent rode to the City Election Commission Building in the Sirkeci neighbourhood of Istanbul to pick up her permit. Concerned about being attacked by the press on the way in, she spoke to her father's good friend, Ismail Kahraman, who was also a VP Member of Parliament, and suggested they all go in together. They arrived with Nazli Ilicak and were immediately surrounded by cameras. Merve Kavakci picked up her permit after shaking the officer's hand and signed in. On the one hand she was exhilarated, but she was also worried about leaving the building and being harried by the press, who would, she felt, distort everything she said. Microphones and cameras were thrust into her face as Osman Ulusoy, leading the way, followed by Ravza, Merve and Nazli Ilicak, left together. In the evening she and Ravza watched themselves on television – it seemed that every station in Turkey broadcast Merve Kavakci, a headscarved woman, picking up her election permit. In the morning her picture would be in all the papers, the event described on every radio station.

People from the Virtue Party told me repeatedly that because Merve Kavakci was allowed to pick up her documents, they felt that the swearing-in ceremony would not be that big a deal. They expected some objections and perhaps demonstrations, but believed that would be it.

The same day that she picked up her permit, Ecevit suddenly left for a brief stay in Cyprus, just seventy miles off the coast of Turkey. He said, 'I have come on a definitely private basis. I need to stay away from public attention for a few days, to rest and to think.'[13]

Having received no guidance from her party, Merve called on the one person whom she had come to admire most, Tayyip Erdogan. He was now in Pinarhisar Prison, sentenced to ten months (he would serve four) ostensibly for reading a poem, as noted earlier. He would emerge as a national figure after the election and, four years later, as the leader of Turkey and one of the foremost leaders in the Middle East.

Merve made two trips to visit him, one with Erdogan's wife, Emine, and the other with her sister Ravza. Both times she asked him for advice and perhaps intervention regarding the oath ceremony. She remembers quite vividly a phrase he used: 'Let us see whose hand is in whose pocket.' Erdogan had a contact on the 'other side', Husamettin Ozkan, who would soon become Deputy Prime Minister and the right-hand man of Ecevit for both the government and the DSP party. Ozkan may have felt some loyalty to Erdogan because he too was an Imam Hatip graduate. In fact, Ozkan was from the same province as Abdullah Gul and had a good relationship with the Virtue Party. He was even being considered as President of the party at one point. Erdogan warned Merve about her constituents' support, which was very strong at the time. He said, 'You can't count on this; one day they support you but the day might come when they forget about you and you end up in jail.' Erdogan, as noted by Merve earlier, did not support her election to Parliament. It is likely he realized that the timing was bad, given his own imprisonment after the 1997 coup, which was a result of his political charisma and popularity rather than his preferences for poetry. He seemed to have a good grasp of what was permissible and what was not. In a few years he would form the moderate AK Party, focused not on ideology but on issues, resulting in Erdogan becoming Prime Minister.

The Virtue Party's executive board held a meeting on 28 April and, according to *Hurriyet*, sent a message to Ecevit offering to form a government with the DSP. Aydin Menderes urged the party to make things easier for Ecevit and not require any conditions for Virtue's support.

The pressure builds

But the following day, back from Cyprus, Ecevit demanded his own conditions from the Virtue Party. A 'headscarf summit' was reported to have taken place between Husamettin Ozkan, representing Ecevit, and Abdullah Gul, Deputy Chairman of the Virtue Party. Ecevit expected understanding from the party regarding Merve Kavakci, but Gul's response, reported by *Hurriyet*, was, 'She presented a picture showing her wearing a headscarf to the Supreme Elections Board. The board did not object, it's up to her.' Gul allegedly had two phone conversations with Kavakci warning her not to 'take an ideological stance'.[14] However, according to Merve that never happened.

The next day, Ecevit himself applied more pressure. He issued the following statement on 29 April 1999:

> In Turkey, anyone who wishes to cover her hair can do so in her private life; however, every institution has its own regulations and traditions. My advice is that this particular female deputy can arrive in Parliament with her headscarf and work in her private office wearing her headscarf, but in the General Assembly Hall and during the Parliamentary commission meetings, I hope that she conforms fully with the traditional dress code for Parliament.[15]

In an interview with *Sabah*, Septioglu then seemed to have changed his tune, implying that he would not swear in Merve wearing a headscarf. He noted that the National Order Party had been closed down, then the Welfare Party. 'One must learn a lesson from the past,' he said. 'If one fails to do that, one will come to harm.' Given Septioglu's subsequent actions, as will be seen, this interview seems to lack credibility, but, then again, his advanced age likely did not lend itself to consistency. *Hurriyet* reported that the VP leadership said that if Merve were prevented from taking her oath they would not make it into an issue for the party.[16] Who exactly said that in the 'VP leadership' is unknown. *Radikal,* in a bold headline, declared: 'You Were the Last Thing We Needed' next to a picture of Merve, and argued in the article that her insistence on wearing a headscarf 'has caused a crisis'.[17] Once again, it was Merve who was viewed as causing the crisis, already typecast as the provocateur. This unfair label would stick to this day, and will persist until the secular bloc realizes that the real culprit is not Merve Kavakci but the chasm between aggressive Kemalist restrictions on Islamic dress and the reality that the majority of the population of Turkey are practising Muslims.

Meanwhile, Merve rejected Prime Minister Ecevit's proposal. She was not about to accept being allocated a room in Parliament that would justify her being treated as a second-class citizen. She noted years later that 'his rationale conflicted with democracy, a lawful state and all talks of modernization'. More importantly, in the moment when pressure was put upn her by the Prime Minister of Turkey, Merve Kavakci did not budge from her principles and beliefs. As all her family gathered in Ankara, including her father, who came across from America, she jokingly asked him if he would be watching his daughter's first day at work in Parliament.

On Monday, she needed to go to Parliament with her permit to register. She had been watching other newly elected members do the same on television. After completing some of these procedures beforehand, she had to complete the remaining tasks, get her fingerprints taken and receive an insignia pin. Upon her arrival she first went upstairs to Kutan's office but it was too crowded for much of a meeting. Kutan, Mustafa Bas, Salih Kapusuz, and Abdullah Gul were all there. They sat for a while and made small talk, then proposed going downstairs for registration. As soon as they were seen, the press charged towards them, too many for her guard, Osman, to fend off. The Parliament security guards came to help. All together, without knowing where to step next, they were swept along downstairs. First an officer took her fingerprints and handed Merve a Parliament sign for her car. Then she picked out an insignia and the lady officer present helped her put it on. They sat at a table that had been prepared for them with Mustafa Bas in the middle of the room. Immediately a question came: 'Are you going to uncover your hair this Sunday during the Parliament ceremony?' Her answer was clear and straight: 'Whatever the rules require, I will follow!' Inside she laughed at the notion of her uncovering. Her election filled her with pride. The more pressure she received, the more she clung to her headscarf. Every day she increasingly viewed her wearing it as a way to combat all the injustice that covered women had endured over the years. The more pressure she received, the more determined she became. This same factor – the oppressive and pushed-aside treatment of women, daughters, wives and mothers – was also what generated some of the support she received. Merve was in the middle of a maelstrom.

The entire country was now on the alert for a possible incident at the swearing-in ceremony. On the front page of *Gunes*, a Kemalist newspaper, was the headline: 'There Will Be an Incident on Sunday' over a picture of Merve Kavakci and Nazli Ilicak getting their licences. The article stated, 'Eighteen Virtue Party Parliamentarians have taken their licences. Merve Safa Kavakci has stated once again that she won't take her headscarf off. Meanwhile, Nazli Ilicak told the press, "We expect a Parliament which is respectful of everyone."'

It was widely reported that two days before the swearing-in ceremony, on Friday 30 April, the monthly meeting of the National Security Council (MGK) convened and 'indicated that it "would not remain quiet in the face of a challenge to the secular republic".'[18] The MGK had been the initial vehicle used by the military to carry out their intervention two years earlier, handing a list of demands to then Prime Minister Erbakan without firing a shot or even holding a weapon. Now the generals voiced their concerns to President Demirel, Prime Minister Ecevit and Defence Minister Hikment Sami Turk, who all attended the meeting.

On 1 May 1999, the day before the oath-taking ceremony, every newspaper in Turkey featured multiple headlines about the crisis that was about to unfold in the Parliament. The 1 May issue of *Milliyet* is typical. There were two articles about Merve on the front page, including a picture of her wearing a silver-coloured headscarf completing the necessary paperwork for a new deputy at the Parliament Building. The headline ran 'Merve in the Parliament'. There were five more articles about Merve inside the paper.

Another example:

National Security Council Warning on Turban

In a meeting of the National Security Council (MGK) yesterday, members announced that taking the oath in the Parliament under a turban is against the Parliamentary bylaws and constitutional decisions.

Fazilet's new MP Merve Kavakci's attempt to take the oath with her headscarf in the Parliament has been discussed by the MGK members yesterday. After a five-hour meeting, they decided that it's against both constitutional and Parliamentary bylaws. The chair of the MGK, President Suleyman Demirel, has explained the decision: 'It's true that there is no article that prevents taking the oath with a turban. But Parliamentary bylaws are not about what is prohibited in the Parliament, it's actually about what is allowed in the Parliament. The law says that, "The head of the Parliamentarian wears a tie, and black jacket. Women MPs have to wear a skirt and jacket." In the history of the Turkish Republic, no woman MP has worn the *hijab* (headscarf). Also, the turban is contradictory to the MP's oath because it is a secular swearing. In fact, the Constitutional Court has pointed out that the turban is contrary to secularism as well.'

In the notice, it's been emphasized that the MGK believes that the new Parliament will do its best to protect citizen's security and will fight illegal attempts against secularism. It's been heard that the MGK is also working on a new regulation similar to the dismissed article 163 to fight against individuals and institutions that might be fundamentalist.[19]

Dr Esra Arsan, a communication's expert, noted that the MGK is not the law-making institution in Turkey but an anti-democratic power centre supported by the establishment, which views the military as the protector of secularism. 'By publishing this story on the front page, with big letters, *Hurriyet* defines its own position against Merve Kavakci,' said Arsan. She added, 'Although journalists have to be fair and balance their coverage, this particular news is not balanced.'

And so on 1 May 1999 the pressure was building against Merve and her party, from the military, from the mainstream press, and from the government. However, of the five political parties represented in Parliament only Ecevit's Democratic Left Party (DSP) had voiced opposition to Merve. The Nationalist Movement Party (MHP), Motherland Party (ANAP) and True Path Party (DYP) had all been silent until this point. The Republican People's Party (CHP), the first political party created by Ataturk, was feared to be the one most likely to make a protest over Merve Kavakci, but they were not in the Parliament due to failing to meet the 10 per cent minimum for representation. The Virtue Party had defended Merve's right to enter the Parliament but when pressed on what their position would be stated that it was up to her to decide, rather than insisting that she should enter. Note that 'leaving it up to her to decide' is a far different stance from standing behind Merve and supporting her rights. By taking the former position the party shifted responsibility to Merve while looking like her supporter.

Merve had still been unable to secure a private meeting with Recai Kutan. Along with the intense pressure coming from the government and now the military, she was left out of conversations and meetings; in fact, she was left completely in the dark until the day before her entrance into Parliament, when she was visited by Turkey's future President, Abdullah Gul.

Gul's visit

On Saturday morning, the day before the swearing-in ceremony, Merve Kavakci awoke to find every single media outlet transfixed by the question of her wearing her headscarf in Parliament. The phone calls began early with the same question. She felt insulted but answered, along with Ravza, the definitive 'yes, of course!' It seemed to her that the content of her campaign had been tossed aside and forgotten by her constituents. Meanwhile, there was no communication coming from the party, which was acting like a closed box. Its silence was unsettling.

Finally, Abdullah Gul phoned at around noon and asked to visit. About two hours later he arrived at Merve's house in the Mebusevleri area of Ankara, along with Salih Kapusuz and Lutfu Esengun. As Gul handed her a box of *baklava* (Turks do not arrive at a house empty-handed), he congratulated her father with an anxious smile, trying to hide the worry on his face. Together they moved into the living room and sat down. Gul and Kapusuz did the talking, saying that there had been a meeting in the Administrative Council that morning with lengthy discussions over the next day's oath-taking ceremony. Kapusuz told Merve of the party's decision: 'You will be going to Septioglu tomorrow morning to pay your respects and seek his consent to take the oath. If he approves, then you will come to the Parliament and into the General Assembly Hall. If he does not, then you shall not enter the Parliament but conduct a press conference to say you have decided not to be in the Parliament.'

Merve froze, in shock, then turned to her father, whose face registered her feelings of intense disappointment. She immediately questioned in her mind what kind of deal this was. Was this the 'advice' they were bringing to her? Who made this decision? How? She pulled herself together and asked why a visit to Mr Septioglu was required. She then said, 'I have infinite respect for Mr Septioglu, who is the oldest Member of the Parliament. Of course I will be honoured to visit him as a young Parliamentarian, but it is meaningless to conduct this visit as if to ask for his approval. As a matter of fact, my visit to him would not affect his perspective in this regard. And as for the press conference, I cannot say that I have decided not to go to Parliament before even entering it. This is impossible. If I don't go to the Parliament tomorrow but announce that I decided not to go, then how will it look to those who voted for me and the millions who tied their hopes to me? Only if I am barred from entering Parliament, after having tried, will I conduct such a press conference!'

Her voice was quivering, getting louder and louder; then she pulled back and forced a smile. She felt that the Administrative Council had treated her like a child and wondered how it would be as a Parliamentarian with this party. Kapusuz spoke up, 'No, no, you should definitely visit Mr Septioglu tomorrow.' After tea and a bit of small talk, the three left.

Her apartment became silent. She tried to rid herself of the initial shock and think about what to do. She could see now why, two weeks earlier, her efforts to meet with Recai Kutan had been fruitless, and thought of what her mother, half jokingly, had said, 'What if they disowned you!' It was a joke no more. They sat in silence and absorbed the disappearance of support from her party.

After a while, Merve suddenly grabbed the phone and called Gul, who was still in the car, on his mobile. She told him she had thought about what he said and reiterated that it was impossible for her to act accordingly. She insisted that, together, they find a solution to this, adding that she wished she had been present in their morning meeting. Gul responded that she was not a member of the Administration. 'True,' she said, 'but the decisions made at that meeting would be affecting my life.' He responded that she should meet with Kutan at the dinner for the party's Parliamentary members to be held that night, although he could not attend himself. She agreed and ended the call. Her mother had said that this would be the most troublesome day of her life. She thought how right she had been. Now, nothing was certain.

Towards evening, her close women friends from the Istanbul branch of the party came to visit her. They immediately could see that something had happened, and they wanted to know what. She could only tell them that she was worried that she would not be allowed to take her oath, but could not tell them who or what was worrying her. Among the guests that day was Nevin Gokce, head of the women's division of the party's Istanbul branch, a woman with exceptional organizational skills, and Muzeyyen Tasci, her press advisor, who was consistently supportive of her. Soon women from the DSP party would be calling her day and night, swearing, yelling, and threatening her on the phone.

Change of heart

Based on my informed sources, what appears to have happened is this: Necmettin Erbakan had a change of heart. The threats and warnings from the military and the government were clear and public. We do not know what Recai Kutan was telling him, nor all of the informal pressures Erbakan and Kutan were receiving from the state, though many of them were publicized, nor how the 'reformers' of the party were afraid of what might happen and were communicating that fear to Kutan and objecting to Erbakan's directions. But it is certain that this change of heart came directly from Necmettin Erbakan; it was not a decision of the Virtue Party. In fact, at a party leadership meeting on 1 May 1999, Merve Kavakci was not even discussed.

Also, it appears that an informal word got out to the government and the military that the Virtue Party would not dare bring Merve Kavakci into the Grand National Assembly. This conclusion is based on an incident that took place on the morning of May 2, as we shall see. Did Erbakan or others give the impression to the government and the military that Merve Kavakci would not be coming to the Parliament?

Finally, it appears that the so-called 'provocative' Necmettin Erbakan actually came up with a conflict-avoiding solution: Merve Kavakci would be sworn in late at night, when most of the deputies in the Great Hall would be absent. We can call this the 'stealth' swearing-in ceremony. Whatever we call it, it certainly was not provocative, not a so-called 'time bomb' on Erbakan's part.

The night before

Perturbed about Gul's visit, Merve went to a pre-Parliament dinner to press Kutan – whom she had yet to meet with – for a strategy and to convey what Gul had said to her. However, it became clear that she was on her own and thus she began, in her words, 'reprioritizing' what to do. She prided herself on being a person who always kept her promises and there was no way that she was going to hang her head in the eyes of her friends and constituents. It was not so much a matter of courage, but of honour.

The dinner was at the ASKI complex in Ankara. She sat at a table with Nazli Ilicak and told her what had happened. Nazli told her that she would go and talk to Septioglu after the dinner. Merve told her that she would meet with Kutan after the dinner also.

Nazli Ilicak met with Ali Reza Septioglu. He was Kurdish, with a headscarved wife and daughters and knew all about repression. Although he had vacillated over the last couple of weeks, he told Nazli he would announce Merve Kavakci's name and call her to take her oath of office. This was important because Merve could not be sworn in unless her name was called.

At about the same time, Merve Kavakci walked over to Kutan's table. The light from the cameras of the press members positioned in the complex garden lit the little hall on the upper floor where they went to meet. Kutan, Zeki Unal, Temel Karamollaoglu, Cemil Cicek, Salih

Kapusuz and Merve sat at a round table in the middle of the hall. She told Kutan what had happened, how she felt it was unnecessary for her to pay her respects to Septioglu at this time and of the impossibility of her announcing that she would give up her seat in Parliament in case his answer was no. She added that this would be horrible for the people who had voted for her and that she could only hold such a press conference after having tried unsuccessfully to enter the Parliament. Kutan was contemplative and worried. He didn't object, but didn't say much either.

The discussion then shifted to when she was to arrive at the Parliament complex. Merve thought that was simple, that she should arrive with everyone else at 3 p.m. Zeki Unal agreed with her, but Cemil Cicek objected. Unal insisted on an explanation for this objection, saying that if they all believed that Ms Kavakci is a Parliamentarian then she should be present with her peers. Cicek replied, 'We know of indications of which you are not aware.' Cemil Cicek would go on to become a member of Erdogan's cabinet of ministers. The 'indications' were likely coming from the military; two years later Merve was told of the rumours that the military would have engineered an intervention, taking over the political process completely, had she been sworn in. In addition, she was told by a VP deputy that Kutan had been receiving several threatening calls from General Cevik Bir, who was deputy Chief of General Staff of the Turkish Armed Forces. These threats were confirmed to me by another VP deputy, as noted above. In 1997 General Bir had received the Secularism and Democracy award in Washington, DC from the Ataturk Society of America. Given the other statements by Demirel even before the election, and threats published in the press coming from the military, as well as the presence of key generals observing the oath ceremony in the Parliament, the idea of a threatened intervention was probable.

However, Kutan denied this when I interviewed him and said there was no contact between him and anyone in the military, or with anyone in the government for that matter, during this time, in spite of statements by others to the contrary. Moreover, on the eve of the big day, there was no indication that the Virtue Party would do anything to support Merve in taking her seat in Parliament. Contrary to her being manipulated, the opposite was true. The Party seems to have been manipulated itself by the pressure.

Notes

1   *Sabah*, 20 April 1999.
2   M. Hakan Yavuz, *Islamic Political Identity in Turkey*, Oxford University Press, 2003, p. 250.
3   Yavuz, p. 251.
4   *Sabah*, 26 April 1999
5   *Turkish Daily News*, 21 April 1999.
6   *Turkish Daily News*, 23 April 1999.
7   *Ibid.*
8   See Esra Erduran, 'Virtue at the Crossroads', *Turkish Daily News*, 20 April 1999.
9   *Sabah*, 22 April 1999.
10 *Milliyet*, 22 April 1999.
11 *Turkish Daily News*, 22 April 1999.
12 *The Star*, 23 April 1999.
13 *Hurriyet*, 28 April 1999.
14 *Hurriyet*, 29 April 1999.
15 *Turkish Daily News*, 1 May 1999.
16 *Hurriyet*, 29 April 1999.
17 *Radikal*, 29 April 1999.
18 'Military Reaction Feared', *Turkish Daily News*, 4 May 1999.
19 *Hurriyet*, 1 May 1999.

FIGURE 1
Ethem Gungen, Merve's maternal grandfather, spent thirty years in the Turkish military and was wounded during the War of Independence. Photo courtesy of Kavakci family.

FIGURE 2
Merve's parents, Yusuf Kavakci and Gulhan Gungen, taken during Yusuf's military service in 1968. Photo courtesy of the Kavakci family.

FIGURE 3
Merve, aged two, with her father, Yusuf Kavakci.
Photo courtesy of the Kavakci family.

FIGURE 4
Merve (centre, holding the flute) participating in Children's Day
celebrations, 23 April 1978. Photo courtesy of the Kavakci family.

FIGURE 5
Merve, centre, aged sixteen, with sisters Elif, left and Ravza,
right, on a family vacation in Tripoli, Libya, 1984.
Photo courtesy of the Kavakci family.

FIGURE 6
Merve with Fatima and Mariam at her graduation from the
University of Texas at Dallas, 1993. Photo courtesy of the
Kavakci family.

FIGURE 7
Merve Kavakci's grandmother, Kadriye Gungen, who helped care for her children
when she returned to Turkey, Ankara, 1994. Photo courtesy of the Kavakci family.

FIGURE 8
Merve's daughters, Mariam and Fatima, at Anittepe School in 1999, the
same year that demonstrations were orchestrated against them by the
television media. Photo courtesy of the Kavakci family.

FIGURE 9
Merve speaking in Pretoria, 1997. She gave speeches in several countries for the
Welfare and Virtue Parties. Photo courtesy of the Kavakci family.

FIGURE 10
Merve campaigning for Parliament in Istanbul, March, 1999.
Photo courtesy of the Kavakci family.

FIGURE 11
Merve campaigning with Recai Kutan and Nazli Ilicak, 19 March 1999.
Photo by *Anadolu Ajansi*.

FIGURE 12

Merve (centre) campaigning with Tayyip Erdogan and Ali Mufit Gurtana (back row),
Nevin Gokce (left) and Mrs Erdogan (right), 23 March 1999 in Istanbul.
Photo by *Anadolu Ajansi*.

FIGURE 13
Nazli Ilicak and Merve Kavakci pick up their election certificates, 28 April 1999.
This image was shown in the media throughout Turkey prior to Merve's scheduled
oath-taking ceremony. Photo by *Anadolu Ajansi*.

FIGURE 14

Merve Kavakci completed registration forms, was fingerprinted and received a pin as a Member of Parliament, 30 April 1999; another widely distributed image in Turkey before her entrance into Parliament. Photo by *Anadolu Ajansi*.

FIGURE 15
Nazli Ilicak and Merve Kavakci walk into the Turkish Parliament, 2 May 1999.
Photo by *Anadolu Ajansi*.

FIGURE 16

Pandemonium breaks out in the Grand National Assembly as DSP party members
protest against Merve Kavakci's presence in the Parliament wearing a headscarf.
Merve and Nazli Ilicak are seen trying to calm members of the Virtue Party, one of
whom yelled that he had a gun. Photo by *Anadolu Ajansi*.

FIGURE 17

Women DSP members trying to block Merve Kavakci from approaching the podium are directed back to their seats. Photo by *Anadolu Ajansi*.

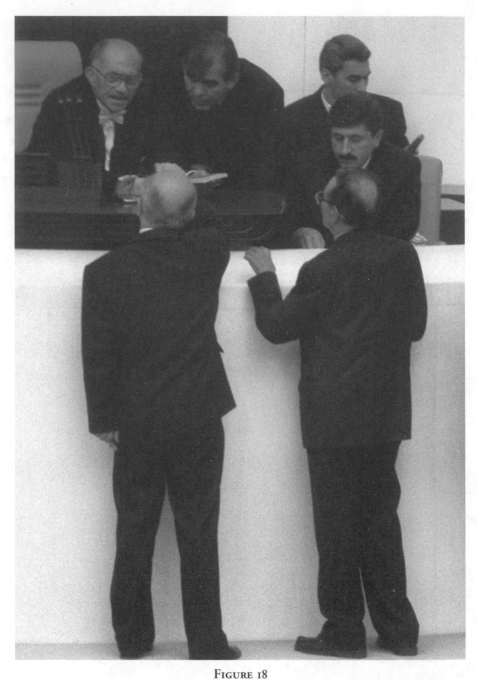

FIGURE 18

DSP leader and Prime Minister Bulent Ecevit (standing right) and Hikmet Sami
Turk (left) argue for Merve's ejection with Acting Speaker of the Parliament Ali Riza
Septioglu, which he refused, 2 May 1999. Photo by *Anadolu Ajansi*.

FIGURE 19
Prime Minister Ecevit took the podium and shouted, 'Put this woman in her place',
2 May 1999. DSP members cheered while all other parties remained silent.
Photo by *Anadolu Ajansi*.

FIGURE 20
The wives and friends of DSP deputies protest against Merve Kavakci in the grounds
of the Parliament complex, holding pictures of Ataturk, 2 May 1999.
Photo by *Anadolu Ajansi*.

FIGURE 21
Virtue Party members, including Merve Kavakci, leave the Parliament hall during the
dinner recess, 2 May 1999. Photo by *Anadolu Ajansi*.

FIGURE 22
Merve Kavakci during her press conference on 3 May 1999, showing her
certification as a Member of Parliament. Photo by *Anadolu Ajansi*.

FIGURE 23

An example of biased media coverage. The headline is 'Militant Merve' and the
subhead above it reads: 'Nesrin of MHP behaved like a Member of Parliament,
Kavakci of FP declared war.'

FIGURE 24

A typical cartoon of Merve Kavakci during
this time. Translation – Merve: We'll try
to make Shariah the law. It should be
applied to families and schools. Nazli:
Merve's opinions are not binding on
me. Illustration courtesy of *Cumhuriyet*
newspaper, 8 May 1999.

FIGURE 25
The sign reads: 'Merve we are behind you' at a National View conference in Koln, Germany, attended by many Turks, on 22 May 1999. Photo by *Anadolu Ajansi*.

FIGURE 26
The day after a raid on Merve's apartment, 19 October 1999. Behind her to the left is Zeki Unal, and to the right is Nazli Ilicak, both of whom continually supported her. Photo by *Anadolu Ajansi*.

FOREIGN POLICY

SUMMER 1999   US $7.95/CAN $10.50

WHO IS EUROPE?

**Making Sense of
the New Europe**

Articles by Felipe González, Dominique Moïsi,
Bruce Hoffman, and Franco Amatori

PLUS, Tina Rosenberg on 1989 and Emma
Rothschild on Globalization, 18th-Century Style

9 2>

0 73361 64794 8

FIGURE 27
Merve on the cover of *Foreign Policy*, Summer 1999.
Photo courtesy of the Kavakci family.

FIGURE 28

Merve with her two daughters, Mariam and Fatima, at their college graduation, May 2010. Photo courtesy of the Kavakci family.

FIGURE 29
Sibel Eraslan and Yildiz Ramazanoglu. Photo by Richard Peres.

FIGURE 30
Osman Ulusoy, Merve's bodyguard in 1999. Photo by Richard Peres.

FIGURE 31

Abdullah Gul, President of Turkey, and Tayyip Erdogan, Prime Minister, October, 2010. Mr Erdogan was re-elected in June of 2011 for a third term. Photo by Richard Peres at the inauguration of Sehir Istanbul University.

FIGURE 32

Dr Cihangir Islam and Merve Kavakci Islam, 2010, Istanbul, shortly after their wedding. Photo by Richard Peres.

FIGURE 33
Another 'Merve' attends the wedding party for Merve Kavakci Islam, June 2010,
Istanbul. Photo courtesy of the Kavakci family.

FIGURE 34
Merve with her two sisters, Ravza and Elif. Photo courtesy of the Kavakci family.

FIGURE 35

The Kavakci family. Top, left to right: Bekir Tanriover, MD (Elif's husband); Elif Kavakci Tanriover; Cihangir Islam MD; Merve; Mariam; Erva (Ravza's daughter); Osman Kan MD (Ravza's husband); Ravza; Fatima. Bottom row: Janna (Elif's daughter); Yusuf; Sidra (Elif's daughter); Gulhan. Photo by Muhammed Ismail, courtesy of the Kavakci family.

5

2 May 1999

Merve's apartment

Merve awoke in great excitement still believing that on this day the Virtue Party would make Turkish history with the first headscarved Member of Parliament, but uncertainty clouded the morning, and as the day progressed that uncertainty gained momentum. In addition to Gul's statements of the day before and Kutan's nebulousness, no arrangements were made to bring Merve to Parliament – no plans, nothing. She was due to be present at 3 p.m. along with all the other 549 members for the official ceremonies, yet there was no indication that the party supported the idea.

Gul had told her early on in the campaign that she was now one of them, someone on the inside of the party workings, but then revealed that inside was nothing, a vacuum, with few if any concrete plans. Moreover, she was left out of key meetings in which decisions were made about her, and had little idea of what was happening. Journalists seemed to know more. She had had no contact with Kutan, despite her attempts, until the previous evening's dinner, which was a let-down. It was like that scene in the *Wizard of Oz* when Dorothy goes behind the curtain and finds out that the wizard, after all, is just a timid man with a microphone and sound effects.

A phone call from Kutan this fateful morning seemed to support the notion that the party was not functioning. The discussion revolved around whether she should go in at 3 p.m. or at night, and Kutan's decision was 'We will call you.' As Merve told me years later from her Washington, DC office, 'It was already clear to me that probably these guys were just going to avoid the situation because of the pressure they were under.' The party was obviously fearful and indecisive; regardless of the importance of the day to Merve, they were not going to make a principled stand.

This invisible force of fear in a country that has frequently experienced military interventions and violations of civil rights can actually be quite physical. I have seen it in the eyes of my colleagues at McGraw-Hill in Brazil when Joan Baez was tossed out of the country by military escort for pro-democracy statements while 100,000 fans waited for her to perform in a stadium. 'They must have had a good reason to send her home,' was the typical response from my colleagues in the McGraw-Hill office. Threats do not need to be continually made for the state, or nefarious doings of the 'deep state', to have an impact. In Turkey, four coups in forty years took its toll on the nation's psyche. Images of a hanged Prime Minister, tortured journalists, murdered academics and missing persons last seen in the custody of the police don't easily fade away. I saw it in the face of Merve's mother when she described for me what it was like to attend Istanbul University in the 1960s, penetrating its invisible walls before headscarf bans were formally imposed.

Even when the military is not overtly in power, even when they seem to be quiet and are not critical of the government, the power of fear is there. Military might is evident in what journalists do not write and how they censor themselves, in what academics do not say when questioned by students, or discuss openly on university campuses or in conferences. The innocuous topics of academic papers avoid important issues and current political topics. To compound that fear, in Turkey the military has its friends, in the judiciary at various local and state levels, in the rector offices of state and even private universities, in the state bureaucracy, in certain political parties, in secular business groups and media cartels. This secular bloc, cultivated by the military, although a historical phenomenon, has intensified and closed ranks since the 28 February intervention, which was in full bloom during Merve's run for Parliament.

Merve could perceive this fear among the leaders of the Virtue Party with the exception of one man, Tayyip Erdogan, sitting in jail for reading a poem, the person she admired the most and whom she mentioned in her interviews. Years later Bono, of the rock band U2, gave concerts in Istanbul; he visited Prime Minister Erdogan and asked him why he was put in jail. When Erdogan told him it was for reading a poem, Bono roared with laughter. Erdogan told of Bono's laughter in a speech the following day to 100,000 people in support of constitutional changes, citing it as an example of Turkey's biased judiciary.[1]

If Merve felt any fear, she did not show it. Perhaps it was because she had no job to protect, no future political career to think about, because she was at the beginning of everything. Or perhaps it was because fear was a matter of course, something that was overcome each day she ventured out of her house or into an unfriendly neighbourhood. It was dealt with like any other constant but annoying problem, with familiarity and resigned resoluteness. It was something to be overcome, not succumbed to, like the guards at the gates of Ankara Medical School, who had altered her life. Ironically, she thought of those guards on the morning of the oath ceremony too. How was she going to get to Parliament? What if the guards stopped her?

What Merve did understand was the importance of this day to some people, many people, the people who had cheered her during the campaign, and the crowds of headscarved women who shouted in unison, 'We are women, we are strong and we exist' at VP rallies. Those people, her constituents, were busy calling her on one of her three cell phones and two landlines on 2 May. Those calls represented the reality of representative democracy, not an ideology or attitude. All of those phones started to ring almost at once, a torrent of calls, as the day began. Some were from family and friends; many were not. The overriding comments were the same questions she had heard for weeks, 'You're going to go in, right? You are not going to take it off and you will go into the Parliament, right?'

It seemed that all of Turkey – family, friends and strangers – seemed to be trying to reach her. Ravza, Merve and even Merve's mother all worked to answer the calls, Merve focusing on those coming from her constituents. Merve asked each and every one of them for their prayers, which they promised to do. Or she would say, 'We are all together on this road, this is our struggle.' Merve felt that if they saw her in Parliament, they would see themselves, their daughters, sisters, nieces and wives. She lost her identity in them and became one with them. Merve: 'This event had become the response to their unanswered prayers, the long-awaited realization of their hopes for the future.'

The Kavakci family ate breakfast together. The children were running around and playing – Fatima, Mariam and Merve's niece, Erva. Their innocence, joy, and smiling faces were an antidote to the cruel reality that was creeping into the apartment. Merve's mother and father sat quietly, contemplative, thinking again about Gul's comments. But Merve had already made up her mind. She was not going to kiss the hand of Septioglu and ask to be sworn in, nor was she going to sneak into the Parliament late at night when the hall would be empty. She too thought of the conversations from the day before and her mother saying that they might not let her in. With no plan coming from the party, she made up her own mind, 'shifting responsibility from the party to my own shoulders', as she told me several times in interviews, and 'reprioritizing' her plans. It is one of those defining moments in a person's life, a moment of decision, of clarity and, as is often the case, a moment of greatness and character. The thirty-year-old novice politician, formerly a medical student, then a party worker, thrown into a campaign in which she connected with thousands of people, could have listened to her party, sat at home, and waited, letting others direct her fate, especially in a male-dominated country and a male-directed party in which she was one of the few female candidates. Left isolated by her party, pressured by her government, Merve relied on the strength of her faith and constituent support to ignore her party's wishes and even the directives of the country's Prime Minister, and the shadow government that is the Turkish armed forces.

She spoke with Nazli Ilicak several times that morning, as well as Nazli's husband, whose opinion she valued, and they realized that it was very possible that night would come and nobody would call her. Nazli told her, 'Whatever you decide, I am with you.'

She then called Zeki Unal, an experienced Member of Parliament, who happened to be a distant relative, her cousin's father-in-law, and who was also very supportive. His help was important because it was Merve's first election to Parliament; she had not taken the oath yet and thus had no office to go to. Zeki Unal did have an office and knew the underground system in the building.

Nazli's support, during the campaign and through to the upcoming crisis in the Parliament, was extraordinary and Merve realized it:

> She is a great woman. She is brave and truthful, says whatever is right, and is behind every word she speaks until the end. She paid a big price for sticking by me and was banned from politics for five years. She is a secular woman, with a secular life style, yet supported me to do what was right. It is so sad how everyone turned against her, even the party.

Salih Kapusuz called Merve and said there was no reason to visit Septioglu, which Merve had already decided against. Then, around noon, Kutan called again and told her to come only after they called her. Kutan told me that he thought Merve was probably not trusting the party leadership at this point and may have thought that the call at night would never have come. (He was correct.)

Seeing that things were in disarray and that she was truly on her own, Merve thought about what would happen if the party actually prevented her from taking her oath, and what she would say to the public who had elected her and 'placed their hopes on my shoulders'. So with great foresight, she asked Ravza to help her write a speech on her behalf in case it were needed. Merve:

> I sat in my favourite corner of the house by the kitchen window that overlooks Ankara. Ravza wrote down my words as I spoke. She added some more to its content, which resulted in a finished product that became the recipient of much speculation the next day as to who had come up with it. How amusing! I placed the text into my briefcase not exactly knowing when I might need it.

She then spoke to Zeki Unal again on the phone. He remained supportive and felt that she should be present in the Parliament with all the other party members, as their names were going to be called in alphabetical order. Meanwhile a large group of media people were waiting downstairs outside her apartment. She felt a sense of pride and heartache for her children, who had seen little of her during the campaign. As the clock approached 3 p.m. everyone in the apartment became tense and lost the strength to answer the phones. In Parliament, when the public didn't see her, the frequency of the calls increased. The oath-taking ceremony had begun right after President Demirel's speech.

Precedence had it that the Parliamentarians would come to the stage one by one and take their oath in accordance with the alphabetic order of the cities from which they were elected. When it came to Antalya, Nesrin Unal appeared uncovered and with a strange look on her face, wearing a white dress, a colour opposite to the other female Parliamentarians' attire, she approached the podium. Merve:

> The hands that voted for her in Antalya were symbolically broken by their owners. Their eyes became wet, and their lips quivered.

And amidst the applause of her newfound supporters, Nesrin Unal took her oath in the Parliament Hall and then disappeared from view as if to escape her guilt. Simultaneously, as the media deemed her the 'good girl' that had obeyed the non-existent laws, she repeatedly answered a journalist about how she felt today with a chilling answer that she felt naked.

The applause that greeted her in Parliament included some of the top generals of the Turkish Armed Forces who were observing from the balcony in a section reserved for them, which was widely reported by the press. Although expected, Nesrin Unal's succumbing to the pressure was a big blow to Merve Kavakci, who had hoped that having more than one covered Member of Parliament would have lasting benefits for the future of pluralism and tolerance in Turkey and the development of women's liberties and solidarity.

Merve decided, after watching Nesrin Unal be sworn in, uncovered, and after all of the calls, that she should go to the Parliament now; she could not wait any longer. As the afternoon approached, she started to get ready to leave the house. She put on the suit that she had especially bought for this day and neatly covered her hair. She had decided on a navy blue suit that seemed appropriate for the seriousness of Parliament and a navy blue head cover with red and blue stripes on its sides. Her heart was already pounding. She was going to the Parliament building and would await Kutan's directives. Her distrust of the party management had been reduced; but on the other hand, she still could not erase the question of the party's real plans. First she kissed the hands of her grandmother, the eldest of her family. After that she received her prayers and hugged her children, and, with her mother and father's eyes wet with tears and their lips moving with prayers, she left the house. As she descended to the ground floor, she was greeted by a few friendly neighbours, then she got into the car with Zeki Unal. Ravza and her husband, Osman, followed. An army of media followed them to the Parliament.

As they arrived at the Grand National Parliament of Turkey, they entered via the main gates and then made their way to the underground parking garage. With that, for a short time, they were safe from the media's attention. But after passing through a labyrinth of hallways, just before arriving at Unal's office, a journalist from the *Star* newspaper caught them.

At the Parliament
Meanwhile, that morning at the Parliament, an interesting thing occurred. Nazli Ilicak met Bulent Ecevit in the corridors of the Parliament. She had heard that Ecevit's Democratic Leftist Party had planned an incident in which the women of his party were going to rip off Merve's headscarf should she approach the front of the Assembly Hall to be sworn in. Nazli had known Ecevit for a long time, as they had been together during the 1980 coup. She told him about this rumour and asked him to please tell his people not to do such a thing, warning that it would result in a major scandal that would not be supported by anyone. Ecevit just looked at her, then went to his office and wrote the speech he would give later in the Parliament. It occurred to Nazli later that Ecevit had likely thought that Merve Kavakci would not be coming to the Parliament and that she inadvertently informed him she would. It was not done on purpose. Ironically, everyone in the Virtue Party thought that Merve was coming, but the military and government did not think the VP would dare to let it happen, after all the warnings in the press and conversations with people in the party.

***

Later, the word spread quickly that Merve had arrived at Parliament. They went to the office of Zeki Unal; shortly afterwards, Nazli also came into the room. Merve could see that Nazli was very worried and tense. She couldn't sit still. Merve was reviewing the text of the oath while drinking a cup of tea. After a while, the door opened and Temel Karamollaoglu entered. He was one of her father's oldest friends, and Merve was friends with his daughter and daughter-in-law, so she initially was happy to see a familiar face. After welcoming her to Parliament, she asked him whether he knew when she was supposed to enter into the Parliament Hall. When he told her, 'a little later', she realized that there was another mix-up in the recent 'plans' that were never really made and 'strategies' that never really existed.

She began to worry yet again, wondering if the party leaders would even let her take her oath. Erdogan's warnings regarding them leaving her alone and unprotected in the middle of a crisis and Gul's complaints about the party not having a strategy were both ringing in her ears. Zeki Unal's small office room now seemed cramped with the onset of her inner distress. She turned to the only window in the room and looked outside in order to collect her thoughts.

She had thought that today she should be treated like the other Parliamentarians, that the forces aligned against her should not succeed. The party people should do what is right and not forget whom they represented. She believed that Ecevit's earlier proposal to the Fazilet Party for Merve Kavakci to not enter the Parliament Hall but sit in her office with her headscarf, get her pay cheque, not be a Parliamentarian, should not find any favour in the name of womanhood, humanity and the nation today. Today the people needed to rule their Parliament, not those conformists who claimed to be pro-Western.

She would hold fast to her promise to the people; do everything in her hands to keep her promise to the 70 per cent of Turkish women she represented with her dress and all those men, women, religious, non-religious, young and old who had voted for her, and take her place in the Parliament. She felt that with her experience, education tolerant attitude and desire to serve her people, she should take her first step to fulfil her duty with pride and keep her head high. There was no reason to feel any other way. She should take on this public responsibility bestowed upon her knowing that she had not committed any crime or sin.

So why was there so much fear in the air and who was instigating it? After brainstorming for a couple of minutes, she collected herself and turned her eyes from the window to Temel. She told him, 'When my turn comes, I should take my oath. I promised the people, and I have to keep my promise,' adding, 'I shouldn't leave this place without taking the oath.' Now, suddenly, Temel became more specific. Merve saw that the party had obviously sent a friendly face to be the bearer of bad news. He informed her that the timing of her entrance into the Parliament had been discussed the previous evening, and it had been concluded that she would enter at night. According to my contacts in the VP, this instruction came from Erbakan, who asked Temel Karamollaoglu to pass it on to Merve. The rank and file of the Virtue Party were not aware of this new tactic, but the leadership likely was. Merve immediately responded. 'No, I don't agree. I should take my oath when my turn comes, along with the other Parliamentarians from Istanbul, as it was decided before.' She was adamant that the 'plan', the so-called plan, should not have continually changed at the last minute.

Merve thought that instead of channelling their energy against the opposing powers in the Parliament, the Virtue Party spent its time fighting itself, delaying and not acting. The memory of how Kutan had made her wait for three days and ultimately refused to meet with her when she arrived in Ankara after the elections came to her mind again and bothered her. She realized just how ineffective and almost helpless the party was now and she had no idea whom to trust, if anyone.

Twelve years later, Merve Kavakci Islam visited the home of Nevzat Yalcintas, a VP deputy who attended the Administrative Council's meeting on 1 May. He revealed that their decision that day for Merve not to take her oath was to ward off the military, opposition parties and the media. Yalcintas suggested that there was a person appointed by the Council to deliver this message to Merve, but did not say who it was. At the same time, Yalcintas told Merve that he had never heard of the 'plan' relating to Septioglu. This makes sense; Kutan told me of it in my interview with him, but the rest of the leadership of the party may not have known it. It was not a group decision, nor was it an official party move. It was from Erbakan who, at this point, seems to have been the only person still pushing for Merve Kavakci to take her oath in Parliament.

In Merve's eyes the Virtue Party was not supporting her. Temel left Zeki Unal's office, then Ravza, her husband and Osman were escorted to the observation balcony. Merve remained with Nazil Ilicak and Zeki in his office. 'What should I do, Nazli?' asked Merve. Nazli said that she would support whatever Merve wanted to do but that she, Merve, had to make the decision herself. They talked about it briefly and whilst Nazli reiterated that Merve had to make the ultimate decision, she stated that in her opinion the approach of entering late at night, when the hall was almost empty, was not right, and that it made the swearing-in look as if it were illegal; that it was somehow a compromising act. Merve agreed with Nazli and was concerned that they would prevent her from taking her oath, perhaps permanently, if she did not finish it now. Merve told Nazli, 'Okay, let's go' and the three of them, led by Zeki Unal, began walking towards the Great Hall.

As they walked, she recited a prayer of the Prophet: 'My Lord, let me enter through a proper entrance and leave by an honest exit! Grant me supporting authority from Your presence' (Qur'an 17:80).

They descended to the red-carpeted corridors underneath the Parliament next to the underground garage, which seemed like never-ending halls, with several ninety-degree turns. Her anxiety increased. Not knowing her surroundings made it even worse. While Zeki took long strides in front to lead the way, she and Nazli were rushing to keep up. Suddenly they found themselves in a crowded corridor with lots of cigarette smoke, gloomy lights and excessive noise. Nazli informed her that they had arrived at the lobby of the Grand National Assembly's meeting hall. Merve was startled by the staring looks of the crowd and felt very uncomfortable as the group of three walked through them towards the door. She thought about what she would do if someone tried to stop her. Would she resist? With quick steps, they made their entrance into the main hall, using the huge door on the right.

Eleven years later, almost to the day, Dr Mehmet Silay, who had been a member of the Virtue Party at the time in question, took me down the same tunnel where Merve Kavakci walked. It is plush red with many show cases of Turkish crafts and artefacts. He was proud and excited to show me, explaining how Merve avoided the press coverage outside by using the tunnel, and allowed me to quickly take a picture when no one was looking. He was nervous as we entered the hallway where Merve had emerged and told me not to speak in English, and to make believe I understood what he was saying in Turkish! He pointed out silently one of the two big doors, on the right, where Merve entered, and we walked quickly past it without lingering. Dr Mehmet Silay was in the balcony when Merve entered that day and watched events unfolding live, while most of Turkey watched on television.

Pandemonium

At 6.20 p.m. local time, Merve Kavakci, along with Nazli Ilicak, entered Parliament, walking down the aisle. The reddish leather seats seemed to overwhelm her senses, as if she could not see anybody else in the hall, just bright reddish leather seats. Finally, here she was, in the Parliament, she thought, and felt her heart would explode.

Merve:

> The Anatolian women who have been pushed around and discriminated against for over two decades due to defending their religious right to wear a headscarf with pride and honour regardless

of all the tears and heartache were now in the Parliament ... the Parliament of the People. Also my mother who had to resign from her university teaching position because of her scarf when I was just a child now had a representative inside the Parliament Hall. And finally, that young medical student, me, who was attacked at the gate of the university by its employees for wearing a scarf, was now in the Parliament.

It was but one brief moment of triumph.

Then she noticed a loud noise as she walked with Nazli towards the front rows. It was more of a banging really. At that instant, she realized that those whose hands pounded on the representatives' desks were enraged, raised voices protesting her presence in their sacred realm. No matter what, she thought, as a Parliamentary representative, she felt she had to hold her head up and keep smiling for the sake of her people. She struggled to appear calm as she walked in. She wondered which members of Parliament were the source of this loud noise and banging? Who could prevent someone who was elected by the people from entering the Parliament? Who could have such audacity?

Some of the people were just staring at her in astonishment while she walked, and some colleagues like Aslan Polat and Mustafa Kamalak, as well as others from her party, were applauding in encouragement as she took a seat in the second row.

Aslan Polat, a friend of the family and Member of Parliament, knew Merve's father from Erzurum, the district that elected him, and gave up his seat to Merve when she entered. He told me about yet another VP 'plan' – that the party had decided that five Parliamentarians were to take their oath around midnight when the atmosphere was calmer, and that Salih Kapusuz, elected from Kayseri (Abdullah Gul's district), was to create the list of the five. Merve was not told of these plans, as she was not told of other discussions about her, or that representatives of the government had met with Gul a few days earlier. Whatever 'plans' were in place, entering the Parliament at this time was not one of them. Thus her sudden entrance with Nazli surprised her party colleagues in the Grand National Assembly.

Merve tried her best not to show the intense anxiety building inside her. Simultaneously, the intensity of the climate came to its breaking point: chaos broke out in the hall. To her right, the DSP (Democratic

Leftist Party) burst into even more intense protest, jumping to their feet while she sat, beating on their desks, banging their hands together, and bellowing, 'GET OUT! GET OUT!' Between her and them, to her immediate right, the MHP (Nationalist Movement Party) sat without obvious emotion as if frozen by their confusion as to how they should respond. Merve was completely astonished by their behaviour, keenly aware of what was happening, but forced herself to calm down, suddenly feeling at peace with what she and those whom she represented were accomplishing, while at the same time feeling the pain of this rejection. She kept a bittersweet smile on her lips as she strove to repeat a prayer, making an extra effort not to move her lips:

> We have placed a barrier before them and another barrier behind
> them, and have covered them up so they do not notice anything.
> (Qur'an 36:9)

Merve remembers that she felt not only bewildered and astonished at their reactions towards her, but also embarrassed for them, and for Turkey. She thought about the possibility that among those people who were protesting against her presence with taunting claps and shouting, there might have even been some religious families or ones who had relatives who wore headscarves, or perhaps among the women were those who had lectured about women's rights. She looked at the female Parliamentarians, some of whom had received their education in the West trying their best to fit into the modern world, and thought that they had obviously not absorbed Western beliefs concerning pluralism and democracy. She thought of how Anatolian women were not being represented here. She could not believe the hatred in their eyes.

At this point, a group of women deputies, not well rehearsed apparently, surrounded the podium to prevent Merve from taking her oath, but they got their signals crossed. Almost ten of them occupied the floor at the wrong moment to block the podium, forming a circle around it. They had 'jumped the gun', apparently, and should have waited until Merve Kavakci had walked towards the podium to take her oath. Then two male deputies herded them back to their seats. Some of these women had campaigned for votes wearing headscarves, distributing these very scarves as campaign mementos, kissing the Qur'an and touching it to their forehead as a sign of respect for its contents.

While Hikmet Ulugbay (DSP deputy and party leader) and Hikmet Sami Turk (DSP deputy) were clamouring inside the hall for Merve Kavakci to get out, their wives were occupying the Parliament's courtyard in protest, in violation of laws that forbid protests in the vicinity of Parliament.

Three people approached Speaker Ali Riza Septioglu – Ecevit; DSP Deputy and Defence Minister Hikmet Sami Turk; and DSP Deputy and Minister of Education Metin Bostancioglu – and asked that Merve Kavakci be removed from the premises. Septioglu, a member of the True Path Party (DYP), refused their request. At the same time, Kamer Genc of Septioglu's party stood up and started to scream, 'Mr Speaker, Mr Speaker, please tell this woman to leave the hall! She has to remove her headscarf ... it is a treason against secularism! Throw her out! Throw her out!' (This lone outburst by a non-DSP deputy earned Genc a congratulatory call later from Air Force Commander General Ilhan Kilic.) But Septioglu was shaking the *Code of Governing by Law* book in his hand and responded, 'What is wrong with you! Of course Kavakci is going to take her oath. Where is it written in this Code that her dress is against the bylaws?' They withdrew. It seemed that Septioglu had finally found his position on the headscarf controversy.

It was reported by the *Turkish Daily News* that Ecevit, Husamettin Ozkan (Deputy Prime Minister) and Hikmet Sami Turk asked Septioglu a second time to remove Merve from the hall and he refused.[2] Some Parliamentarians from the Virtue Party began shouting aggressively to show their support. Mr Kahraman, who had been sitting behind them, stood up suddenly, taking a belligerent posture. While continuing to smile, Merve turned to him and begged him to take his seat. Nazli too was indicating to the others to please take their places. After a moment, they concurred and sat down.

Merve also heard one of the VP deputies shout, 'I have a gun.' One of the perks of being a Member of Parliament is the opportunity to purchase a specially made hand gun. Some deputies ceremonially display theirs in their offices or homes, while others actually carry one with them and are, in fact, allowed to do so in the hall. While she tried to calm her outwardly aggressive colleagues down, Merve was also warmed by the support of these men with whom she did not directly work, as close interaction between the men and woman of the party was discouraged.

The session was forced into recess but few deputies left the hall. Mr Septioglu, along with Parliamentarians from the Democratic Leftist Party and Virtue party, exited through the back door and remained out of sight while the demonstration continued. The DSP deputies were still screaming, 'Get out! Get out!' and clapping their hands in protest.

Merve looked in awe at the rest of the deputies, who remained quiet. Merve:

> As if some invisible chain was binding their mouths and minds, they were just watching in a deep silence. Amazingly, the ones from MHP had campaigned against the Welfare Party proclaiming that 'they would be the ones who were man enough' to restore women's rights to wear headscarves as required by God in Islam. Weren't they the ones who proclaimed that their wives, sisters, nieces and even their own daughters wear a scarf? Some of the female deputies even campaigned with scarves, either covering their head or wearing it over their shoulders, in search of votes, telling the people, 'We are your mothers. We are your sisters.' Now what were they doing? In spite of such loud shouting, they were sinking into their chairs. They were sinking in their silence.

Merve's cell phone was switched off, so Nazli took the calls from Channel 6. Later on, other media sources, in an attempt to sensationalize or distort things, implied that this call was actually coaching from the previous Welfare Party head, Mr Erbakan.

Suddenly there was complete silence. Merve turned to Nazli, who was boiling with emotion, and said, 'It's over.' At this moment, Bulent Ecevit, head of the DSP and soon to be Prime Minister, got up from his seat and walked to the podium. He reached into his pocket and took out a prepared speech, then shouted, 'No one in Turkey can interfere with the dress code or the headscarf or the private life of a woman; however, this is not a private abode. This is the highest institution of the state. Those who work here have to abide by the laws and customs of the state. This is not a place to challenge the state. Please put this woman in her place!'

Merve sat, alone, and watched the soon-to-be Prime Minister of the country attack her. Merve:

> I was saddened as I listened to this speech full of hatred. I was saddened for the sake of my country. I was saddened for the

portrayal of Turkey under such sad circumstances in the world media. I was saddened to see these narrow-minded people thinking they were being 'modern'.

Septioglu announced a dinner break until 8 p.m. At this point neither Merve nor other members of the party seemed to know what to do.

Merve turned to Nazli and asked, 'What do you think we should do now?' She asked the same of the others. Even with the members of the Virtue Party all around her, Merve could not decide if it would be better to go out during the break or remain seated, so she sat and waited. She felt that even if she left, she would have to be back at 8 p.m. Her father was trying to call her on her cell phone to encourage her to remain seated no matter what.

Septioglu meeting
One of the insiders to what happened at this time was Mustafa Kamalak,[3] Virtue Party Deputy from the Kahramanmaras district, constitutional law professor and respected attorney. Kamalak was also surprised by Merve's entrance with Nazli. After the break he and other deputies from both parties began to argue among themselves and Ali Riza Septioglu in the lobby. One deputy yelled at Septioglu, 'You ruined the Parliament traditions.' Kamalak argued with him, stating that if law and tradition conflict, you should obviously rely on the law; he then proceeded to show him section 56 of the law regarding female Parliamentarians wearing suits with no other requirements. A DSP deputy argued that there was no clause regarding headscarves, to which Kamalak replied, 'Honourable Parliamentarian, you are a jurist. Freedom is fundamental in the law. If legislation does not prohibit something, it means it's allowed.'

At this point Septioglu cleared his office of others and asked Kamalak, Salih Kapusuz, Abdullatif Sener and Abdullah Gul to stay for a meeting. Before Kamalak entered the meeting, he went to the general hall, where Nazli and Merve were still sitting. According to Kamalak, he told Merve not to leave the hall and then entered Septioglu's office. However, Merve has no recollection of this.

Here is a direct translation of what Mustafa Kamalak told me about the meeting with Septioglu after the recess.

Abdullah Gul said, 'Let us make Merve leave the hall so the other representatives may continue to take the oath.' I said, 'If you make Merve leave, you cannot bring her in again. Let us open a discussion on the issue and then vote on it. I mean, is the headscarf an obstacle to take the oath of a female representative? Let us open a discussion on it, vote on it and accept what the Parliament decides.' Gul said, 'That might create tension.' And I said, 'It might, but everything has a time, everything has a reward. If you make her leave, you cannot bring her back in. Let us open a discussion on it. Now MHP has a headscarved representative, willingly or unwillingly MHP has to support us. The DYP already acts with us, we were ruling together in the former cabinet so they are with us. ANAP always spoke about the [Turgut] Ozal [former liberal President] mission during the campaign and talked about freedom. They can't take a position that is opposite of what they promised. In this case, DSP will be left alone. I think they have only 136 or 137 representatives. We can vote after all. And the majority of the Parliament will come up with the decision that there is no prohibition in the law regarding wearing a headscarf as an obstacle to taking the oath.'

Unfortunately, Mr Gul said it might create tension and our friends supported him. I mean Abdullatif Sener and Salih Kapusuz supported Abdullah Gul. Then Gul said, 'Let's have the other representatives continue to take their oaths, and we may bring Merve at the end, and she could take her oath then.' I repeated, 'Mr Chairman, once you take her out you cannot bring her in.'

There was no chance. At the end, Merve was made to leave the hall after that discussion. I emphasized with great persistence what a wrong decision was being made, but I could not make them listen. Although I was trying hopelessly to control the group and was saying to them, 'Do not fall apart! Merve will come later around midnight; a swearing-in takes only 53 to 55 seconds; we can do it and move on', it was a hopeless expectation of course.

Septioglu also told Kamalak that he would support whatever the party decided regarding Merve Kavakci. He said, 'I believe what the law says. And most important, according to my faith, the headscarf comes from Islamic belief and tomorrow at the Day of Judgement I worry about what I will explain to Allah and His Messenger about it.' After much wavering, Septioglu would not be the one stopping Merve from being sworn in. Years later when Merve's sister Ravza visited me in Istanbul, along with her parents, I reminded her of Septioglu's role in what happened. She told me that the family remembers him in their prayers.

At the time of writing, Mustafa Kamalak is leader of the Felicity (Saadet) Party which, not surprisingly, nominated headscarved women for the 12 June 2011 elections. However, Felicity's votes did not pass the 10 per cent vote threshold for representation in the Turkish Parliament.

At this point, everyone was giving Merve different advice. Seref Malkoc, deputy from Trabzon, told her, 'Let us go out.' Some others were thinking differently. Merve thought that if she left now she would return later, although she was concerned that she might be prevented from doing so. Merve: 'But like an innocent child, I followed the majority, and we left the General Assembly Hall. I now look back and believe that this was a major mistake. I should have stayed there no matter what.'

She walked to Kutan's office with Nazli Ilicak and Zeki Unal. Other party members who were sitting there said that it would not be appropriate to go back to the General Assembly Hall immediately. Meanwhile, Kamalak called Erbakan and explained the situation to him. Kamalak said that Erbakan's response was, 'Our friends did wrong. Say my greetings to Mr Recai Kutan, and have her take the oath today.' Kamalak passed the message to Kutan and was told, 'Our programme is to do so.' Kamalak then returned to the General Assembly. However, Erbakan's plan to have Merve slip in at night as a stealth swearing-in seemed doomed at this point, given that it would no longer be a surprise move, and that the reaction had been close to violent.

Merve sat in Kutan's office and followed the proceedings on television. One by one the members came up to take the oath of office. It was painful for her to watch, especially when a deputy repeated the phrase 'human rights' and 'I swear with honour and dignity'. When the turn came for the delegates of Istanbul, they announced her name after all, 'Merve Safa Kavakci – absent.' Perhaps it was only announced because she was absent. Her heart burned. She felt the crushing weight of the votes on her shoulders but could do nothing.

The deputies in the office told Merve that they would have the opportunity to try once again to have her take the oath close to the end of the ceremony. The Erbakan plan had apparently now been conveyed to others. They continued by saying to Merve, 'You go home now. Rest a little bit. After everything settles down, you can come and take your oath.' Merve: 'Again with the innocence and naivety of a little child, I obeyed them and left the office.' So she left the meeting and was once again on her own. However, this so-called meeting, with Merve present, was not what it seemed.

According to Aslan Polat, before Merve got to the office a meeting took place in which members of the party did not want her to take the oath. One of those opposed was Aydin Menderes; another was Salih Kapusuz. Some in that meeting blamed Nazli for bringing her into the Parliament. Several mentioned the closure of the Welfare Party and feared the same for Virtue. The sudden move by Nazli and Merve exacerbated the split within the party and showed that Kutan lacked authority to take any decisive actions. At this point, after the harsh reaction downstairs, the split in the party became a deep fracture and almost a revolt against Erbakan, who was already out of politics (at least officially) and had a lot less to lose from another party closure.

It was reported later in the press that 'Ozkan [Ecevit's deputy] had spoken with VP executives and persuaded them to keep Kavakci from entering the General Assembly after the recess.'[4] In an editorial of the same paper, Ilnur Cevik wrote, 'Amid protests, the plenary session was delayed for an hour while veteran deputy Kamran Inan worked out a compromise in which Kavakci would not return to the plenary session for the day, and thus the oath-taking session in Parliament would continue. So the crisis was defused for the time being.'[5]

After the meeting, Merve was downcast and exhausted; she did not want to face the media downstairs and give the impression that she had lost. She felt a dark shadow cast over the future of headscarved women in Turkey, a future that she felt she was carrying on her shoulders. She thought of the young girls in their last year of completing a university degree being forced to leave school, the teachers whose careers were ended, including her mother's, the degradation of brainwashing in 'Persuasion Rooms' at Istanbul university, the army officers thrown out of the military because their wives wore headscarves, the headscarved demonstrators trying to enter universities whose wrists were bleeding from handcuffs.

Her close friends came to the rescue. Zeki Unal provided his car, and Osman Ulusoy, her driver and bodyguard, drove her to Aslan Polat's house, which was located in the Parliamentarian housing complex secured by guards in the Oran neighbourhood in the south of Ankara. Bahar Polat, his wife, and Latife Ozbek, another close friend, met her at the door, which she could hardly walk through. After resting a bit she thought that only a group effort from her party could break through the injustice that was being done to her, and that they were more frightened and hesitant to take action than she was. It had to be a group effort; they had to have a sense of pride. She called Nazli, but her phone was off. She remembered the number of Mr Kahraman, who told her that the Chairman's Committee of the party was in session. This angered her, their once again making decisions without her even though she was the one in the line of fire from Ecevit, the press and the opposition. She had no idea who was there and what they were talking about. Then she called Ravza, not telling her where she was, hearing the tell-tale static of wire-tapping on the line.

The President speaks

Meanwhile, later that evening, President Suleyman Demirel appeared live on TRT-1, one of Turkey's state-owned television stations, on the *Pulse of the Politics* programme and responded to questions about the incident in Parliament. He said: 'If you say I am Muslim because I cover my head, and the ones who do not cover their heads are not Muslims, then you are committing a sin. This is contrary to Islam, this is separatism.' To the casual Western observer, this may seem to make no sense. The millions of women who wear headscarves in Turkey are not saying anything about those who do not. Moreover it is difficult to comprehend that Demirel would take on the role of religious interpreter for Turkey, claiming that wearing a headscarf is contrary to Islam. On the other hand, President Demirel was basically making a political statement, rather than a religious interpretation, at the height of the coup process. He was putting forth the secularist argument that views 'secular, so-called modern' Turks as the victim in the public sphere, instead of the reverse; that secular Turks are made to feel bad by religious Turks, and that wearing a headscarf is not modern, but backward. Forget that covered women were suffering from not being able to work for the state, nor teach in a university, nor, at this time, attend universities in Turkey. The reversal of victimization argument portrays women as making a political statement, bringing religion to the public space for political reasons, and goes even further and defines what is and is not Islamic and a sin. Remember, in Turkey the Directorate of Religious Affairs controls what imams say in mosques so it's not a big step to give this power to the President of the Republic. No matter that surveys do not support these political motives on the part of covered women in Turkey.

Demirel portrayed Merve's entrance into the Parliament as a provocation that was planned for days, claiming that he knew about it and issued warnings about it. He pointed out that twenty-six of twenty-seven women deputies in the Parliament abided by the rules, that Merve's act was 'contrary to Islam' and that 'the initiative to enter the Parliament with a headscarf was something that happens against a "democratic republic"'. This definition of democracy is compliant with the Turkish view of a secular democratic republic originating with the new republic and Kemalism.

Demirel went on to say that Parliament, which accounted for Turkey's salvation in the past, should not be a stage for such incidents, adding that, 'Everybody condemned this incident.' He asked, 'Why do they make people uneasy? It is impossible to understand.' He noted that the Parliamentarians were elected with the free will of the people and 'all of them take the oath there with determination and excitement. They take the oath on the inseparable integrity, Ataturk's reforms, secularism and secular democratic Turkey. When this is happening, a blotch of ink is dropped at the scene, which people cover with pleasure. I advise calmness to my people.'

Demirel called the headscarf incident an act of 'extremism'. He went on:

> This has a base in Turkey and Turkey has struggled with this base for some time. This is what we call fundamentalism. This means to found a state based on religion. Yet, Turkey showed with the seventy-fifth anniversary of the foundation of the Turkish Republic and with general elections that it is faithful to the Republic founded by Mustafa Kemal Ataturk. The things they do are in vain and it makes people unhappy.

He added that the act was a tool of a movement in Turkey and abroad and pointed out that 'this is to announce their name by causing chaos and some of them are provocateurs'.[6]

Merve watched in horror from the Polat's residence. Demirel was from the same hometown as both of her uncles and used to know her family well, and even invited her father to the President's Palace once a year when Yusuf was a university dean of Islamic Studies. Merve heard Demirel, from Islamkoy (literally translated, Islamic village) without blinking his eyes state that Merve Kavakci was an 'agent provocateur'. She felt slandered and could not believe the attack so soon on her by the President of her country who knew her family. The next day one of the most respected professors of constitutional law, Dr Mustafa Erdogan, made clear in an interview on Kanal 7 that there was nothing in the law to prevent Merve Kavakci from being sworn in. Regardless, the President had not made a legal argument but rather the customary one of disingenuousness about anything that combined Islam with politics.

The Executive Council of the Virtue Party met after Demirel's speech at around 10 p.m. according to Kamalak. When Seref Malkoc heard about a meeting taking place, he ran upstairs but it was already over and its members dispersed. That speech was obviously the final blow.

Merve had not given up, however. While no one from the party was calling her, and Merve couldn't reach anybody, she thought she should go back to the Parliament again around midnight. On television she could see that Nazli was still in the main hall. They had discussed meeting at around midnight, but that was before Demirel's speech. She wanted to avoid the media, who would tip off the Democratic Leftist Party. The fact that she was alone without any party assistance did not give her much encouragement. Through a friend she managed to have a car with tinted windows sent to pick her up. Undetected, she made her way into the Parliament complex. When she stepped into Zeki Unal's office, Nazli showed up. It seemed that only a short time remained in the ceremony. Parliamentarians who were absent at the first announcement were going to be invited to the podium one more time to take their oath. In fact, some of her colleagues from the Fazilet Party were waiting for her in the General Assembly Hall. They had decided to form a human barricade around her to allow for her safe and easy passage to the podium to take her oath. Suddenly the phone rang and Zeki Unal answered it. Kapusuz was calling from Kutan's office saying, 'Before you go down to the hall, please come here.' 'If that's the case, let's go,' said Merve, and they walked with long strides to the office. As they walked in the corridor, Nazli said, 'Merve, these people are not going to let you take your oath.' In shock, Merve kept walking, almost running to Kutan's office.

Kutan's office

They walked in and found Kutan, Kapusuz and Ms Akgonenc all with long faces. One of them spoke: 'Ms Kavakci, the board had a meeting and decided that you should not go to the General Assembly.' Astonished, Merve yelled 'WHAT?!' She was tortured to know what was happening, who was making these decisions and why everyone was afraid. Just then, Ravza called her on her cell. 'Sis, where are you? Your turn is coming,' said Ravza in a worried and exhausted tone. 'Ravza, they are not going to let me in,' said Merve, then hung up. She immediately turned around and yelled again, 'I believe it's my sole right to know what's going on here!' Kutan said, 'Mr Menderes has threatened that he will reveal Erbakan's connection to the party. He said he would resign. In addition, Demirel's allegation affected our decision.' Merve remained outraged. They all knew that Demirel's accusations were false, but their fear was obvious. Ignoring that Kutan was a family friend and an elder, she looked at Kutan and shouted: 'Mr Kutan, you are a coward!'

Sometime after, Mustafa Kamalak returned to the hall, after speaking by phone with Erbakan. He was approached by Seref Malkoc, who came to the hall to tell him, 'Dear Professor, you try to control and calm the group here but probably Merve will not have her oath done today.' Asked why, Malkoc said that he had better go up to see Kutan, and that Demirel had been on television accusing Merve of being an 'agent provocateur'. Kamalak asked Malkoc to stay in the hall and control the other VP deputies, then went upstairs.

Kamalak arrived in Kutan's office and found Nazli, Merve and Kapusuz sitting with Kutan. He told Kutan what he had heard and Kutan confirmed it, telling Kamalak that the party did not plan to have Merve take her oath that day. Kamalak argued that if not now, there would never be another opportunity. Kapusuz argued back that she could take the oath when the environment calmed down. Kamalak pressed him for a date, and he responded, 'in two or three months'. Kamalak reminded Kapusuz of their discussion earlier in Septioglu's office and informed him that Law 84 of the Constitution required a Member of Parliament to attend at least five times a month or risk losing his or her membership, so his view was not feasible. Finally Kutan spoke: 'Professor, the Party Executive Council made the decision about not having her swear in today so these discussions do not make any sense now.' Kamalak yet again argued that this was a mistake, and then left the meeting.

Merve thought how ironic it was that she was not fighting Kemalists, but her own party. Kutan sat without saying another word on the couch. Ravza called again, 'Sister, what is going on? Just now someone … she … called … it was Nermin (Erbakan) conveying the message from her husband, "No matter what, you have to enter and take the oath." So what is happening, Sis?' Merve replied, 'Ravza, that's it. The leaders of the party are frightened.'

The next day, Ravza's hesitation to say Erbakan's wife's name would be seen as proof that Merve was but a tool of Erbakan, since the newspapers were given the wire-tapped conversation between Ravza and Erbakan's wife by the Ministry of State (which obviously had access to the calls to Merve's house), declaring, 'Yesterday, a call was made to Kavakci's home that was received by either Kavakci's mother or sister from Erbakan.' This phone conversation was also mentioned by Husamettin Ozkan to a VP official, indicating that if made public it would mean trouble for the VP. Ravza confirmed to me that Nermin Erbakan was conveying her husband's instructions but they were not heeded by the Virtue Party by this point.

Ravza was shouting from the other end of the line, 'My sister, how can you do that? You have to try one more time!' With raised voice, she was demanding that Merve remember the promise she'd made. She was disheartened, like millions of others, devastated by what they were observing on TV.

Later on, Merve found out that security staff had been standing outside waiting for her, wanting her to come out from behind those shut doors so that they might carry her on their shoulders and place her unharmed where she belonged at the podium in the Parliamentary Hall to take her oath. But those doors never opened. Outside of Kutan's office Osman Ulusoy, her loyal driver and bodyguard, was waiting with policemen when they got the message from Septioglu at five minutes before midnight that she could come to the Parliament to take her oath. The DSP deputies did not know about the meeting upstairs and had left already, so it would now have been possible to go downstairs and have Merve sworn in. Ulusoy told me:

> We got the call from downstairs that it was time, she was called by Septioglu and I knocked on the door. No one answered. Then I realized it was locked. Then another man came upstairs and said it's

Merve's turn to come downstairs. One of the policemen said let's knock the door down and take her out. We were talking outside about what to do. It wasn't a strong door; they could easily hear us outside. When we saw that the door was not opening everyone started to cry, including me, the police and administrative people working inside the Parliament.

Mustafa Kamalak and Osman Ulusoy both support the notion that Septioglu would have facilitated swearing-in Merve just before midnight. But it was Merve's own party that prevented it from happening, rejecting Erbakan's wishes, and those of Merve Kavakci, who was hardly his 'tool' but simply wanted to take her seat in Parliament. In the General Assembly Hall, as the end approached, the VP Parliamentarians were turning their heads in wonder thinking, 'Where is Kavakci? Why is she not here?' The Speaker of the Parliament was calling 'Merve Kavakci, Merve Kavakci', and 'Absent' was the answer he received. At the same moment, Merve was following everything in Kutan's office from the television trying to contain the fire raging within her and to muffle her silent screams. Merve:

> I wished I hadn't agreed to come to the office when Kapusuz called us to come. I wish I had gone directly to the General Assembly Hall. I felt it was the end of everything. Only then did I fully understand what my party was, as one of the 200,000 volunteer women for so many years.

'Yes, I am expecting an explanation,' Merve insisted of Kutan as he sat there still silent. The oath ceremony was over, and the TV was turned off. Instead, Kapusuz spoke, explaining about his visit with Gul the day before to Merve's house, but Merve corrected him about what was actually said. After a while, Abdullah Gul arrived. He didn't speak. Mustafa Kamalak arrived and also appeared devastated. Two months later, Merve had her first meeting with Mrs Erbakan after the incident in Parliament. She found out that Erbakan had designated Kamalak with responsibility for facilitating the taking of her oath. Obviously, she was not aware of it until that day, nor had she and Kamalak ever met regarding this matter. The plan to come late had been communicated to her by Temel, whom she did not trust, and thus she rejected it.

Merve left the room and made it back to the Parliament Residences. She called Mrs Erbakan and relayed all that had happened.

Merve wanted to go home to see her children but was reluctant to do so, knowing the media would be waiting for her.

Home

Ulusoy drove Merve home, to Mebusevleri, where she rushed into the house. It was 2 a.m. and she could hardly climb the stairs to the apartment. Her mother was waiting at the door. Her father looked sad. Her grandmother was on the verge of tears. The children were already in bed. Her sister, Ravza, was worried and anxious. 'Can you make a good tea for me, Ravza?' she asked.

Tea is the national drink of Turkey, which produces its own version – hot and dark and drunk at any time of the day or night. It is especially popular in Erzurum, where Merve grew up, where there is snow almost eight months a year. People from Erzurum have a special way of using the sugar. Instead of putting it in those precious, clear, hourglass-shaped teacups, they hold these special cubes of sugar in their mouths letting them slowly dissolve as they sip their tea. Through those elegant, petite glasses the rich, shining amber colour of the tea can be seen inviting one to savour its flavour. The need for tea gets worse during the days of the Holy Month of Ramadan because Islamic people must refrain from eating or drinking anything from dawn to dusk. They can hardly function. Today Merve drinks tea with several cubes of sugar, not uncommon in Erzurum.

She sat in the living room and was distressed by the look on her father's face, deep in thought. She was too exhausted to discuss much then because she and Ravza had to continue working on a speech they had prepared earlier just in case she was prevented from taking her oath, and because it was decided that tomorrow at 10 a.m. she would meet with Kutan in his office and then hold a press conference. Afterwards, around 3 a.m., she filled in the details for her parents about what had happened. At one point her father said she should not have left the General Assembly Hall but Merve could not see there had been any alternative, and it made no sense anyway to look back. She observed his disappointment. Her father had dedicated everything to his children, and for Merve there had been no limits: educating her in languages, sports, music, sending her to private schools, ordering ice skates for her from England when the first skating rink opened in Turkey, taking her to academic seminars, teaching her to drive at the age of twelve, and developing a great sense of pride in her achievements. Noticing what kind of difference it was making in the character of all his daughters to have the freedom of thought at home, he had striven to improve their skills in defending their beliefs and developing proper decision-making techniques from a very young age. In spite of Merve's youth, seeing her political articles published in foreign newspapers and reading her Turkish translations of stories originally written in English in some Turkish magazines bolstered his hopes for her future. He wanted her to be enlightened. He exposed her to the environment of intellectual scholars like professors Muhammed Hamidullah, Tayyip Okic, Anne Marie Schimel and Kaya Bilgegil. But he was crushed that on one day, on that day ... some people filled with hatred, grudges and opposition to what they considered to be unsecular and unmodern signs of her religious outfit showed up to lynch his child ... his beloved daughter ... regardless of her modern qualities, brilliant mind, education and character.

Her father and the rest of the family were amazed that her party had not supported her. Eventually, close to sunrise, she went to bed, completely restless, not able to sleep, her mind racing like an endless nightmare, questions entering her mind until daybreak.

And so 2 May 1999 came to an end. The threats from the secular bloc had been successful.

The Welfare Party came to power because of the hard work of women who wore headscarves, but they had no women candidates. Women's studies programmes had rightly criticized the party. The closure of the Welfare Party because of 'anti-secular' activities brought about a successor, the Virtue Party, which voiced a new identity, had women candidates for the first time, like Nazli Ilicak, and logically favoured headscarved candidates. Merve Kavakci was the result, but in the end her party lost its nerve, lost its heart and gave in to those who held power in Turkey.

Notes

1. *Sabah*, 6 September 2010.
2. 'DSP Lone Voice in Parliament', *Turkish Daily News*, 4 May 1999.
3. Information here is based on my interview, with an interpreter, of Mustafa Kamalak at his law office in Ankara on 23 April 2010.
4. *Ibid.*
5. *Ibid.*
6. *Anadolu News Agency*, 3 May 1999.

6

The Bright Future Darkens

A campaign flyer for Merve Safa Kavakci shows the candidate wearing a pure white headscarf next to the logo of the Fazilet Partisi, which includes the tagline: 'Turkiye'nin Aydinlik Gelecegi' (which translates as 'Turkey's Bright Future'). In big letters at the bottom of flyer is, 'fark bizde' ('the difference is us'). As reaction from the press and the public came into focus, that bright future had darkened considerably by the following day.

Merve Kavakci had tried to strategize with Kutan from the beginning of the campaign but was unable to see him until the night before the oath ceremony. Perhaps it was because, as Merve explained, the leadership did not know how to deal with a bright and educated headscarved woman – an unfamiliar fixture in white-collared jobs, front-office positions, and in the party – unlike Nazli Ilicak and other uncovered, secular women. Grandmothers from the countryside were different, respected in a special way, but young religious women, as an equal partner in the party, seemed to have made the party leaders uncomfortable. At any rate, the child who tugged on the parent's jacket to no avail, pointing skyward to the falling sky, could no longer be ignored. Indeed, the sky fell and destroyed the party in the process.

Eleven years later I asked both Kutan and Temel Karamollaoglu if Merve Kavakci had brought about the closure of the Virtue Party. They both quickly answered 'no', adding that there were many factors, and Merve was just one of them. But evidence to the contrary is everywhere, including the charges from the prosecutor and decisions of the court.

There were only meagre attempts by the party leadership to resuscitate Merve's efforts to take her seat in Parliament after 2 May. There were no second thoughts to possibly repair what had happened the night before. The entire effort for Merve's swear-in crashed mercilessly and irreparably. The decision to back down due to the torrent of opposition stuck. From this point on it mattered little what the players in the party did; their half-hearted plans, strategies, legal tactics, speeches and appeals were carried out with little energy and anyway fell on plugged ears, rendered deaf by the ultimate need for the Turkish secular state to prevail. Its rulers had spoken and every component of the state would now fall in line: bureaucrats, judges, prosecutors, the so-called modern Turks of the cities, non-Islamic business organizations, bar associations, an army of journalists controlled by the two newspaper cartels, the television stations and the mainstream press.

Turkey's Kemalist establishment convulsed at the sight of Merve Kavakci on the hallowed ground of the Grand National Assembly, in spite of Merve's courage and attempts to take matters into her own hands. She was stamped in perpetuity as a person who caused a crisis. The 'other' Turkey dared to cross the line. It was acceptable to see headscarved women in the street, or working as domestic servants, or as 'irrelevant peasants' in the countryside. It was tolerable to be awoken at 5.30 each morning with the call to prayer in Arabic that emanated via loudspeakers from thousands of mosques throughout Turkey. It was barely tolerable to see covered women dare to enter a new, super-modern shopping mall or restaurant. It was unacceptable to see them compete in classrooms at elite high schools and universities – a decade would pass before this would begin to change. And it was not possible to allow them into the halls of Parliament in violation of 'unwritten' laws and customs.

One might think that Merve's education and background would make a difference, that she exemplified the kind of modern women who secularists would aspire to: fluent in English, educated in America, from an educated, middle-class family. But Turkish modernization under the new republic began as the antithesis of Islam, the presence of which was repressed in public soon after the Republic was founded, based on the assumption that Islam had brought backwardness to Turkey. The plan seemed to work. Turkey grew and expanded. But Merve was different, she was the other 'other'. She was religious *and* highly educated, trying to enter the public sphere of 'white' Turks. Because Turkish modernization was aggressively secular and a variant of the French laicism model it adopted, education would not be the 'great leveller' for a new Islam-friendly generation, in particular women who wore headscarves tightly around their head, covering their hair, the symbol of political Islam for the Kemalist establishment. Merve was not to be the first one of this new generation, knocking at the door of equality. She was not to be the Rosa

Parks or James Meredith of Turkey. She did not have the political clout in Parliament, nor, more importantly, a political movement behind her. Even if she did, the military would see to it that she would not succeed. Demirel and Ecevit would not risk their positions to fight the military, just two years after the post-modern coup. Demirel had been victimized by the military more than once in his long career and knew its power – first on 12 March 1971, when the Chief of the General Staff handed him an ultimatum that resulted in his resignation three hours later, and then his banishment from politics for six years after the 12 September 1980 military intervention. And it was Demirel's support of the military that ended Erbakan's tenuous rule in 1997, allowing for an extension of his career.

A Turkish American I met in 2010 inadvertently exposed the paradox of Turkish modernism when I asked him why the crowd at the finals of the 2010 World Basketball Championships in Istanbul booed President Gul and Prime Minister Erdogan when they handed out medals to the one of the teams. 'You don't understand,' he told me. 'The people who go to basketball games are educated.' I reminded my friend that Gul received his PhD from the University of Istanbul in 1983, and that Erdogan studied Business Administration at Marmara University. Never having questioned Kemalist assumptions, he looked puzzled. He was educated to view these religious men as the 'other' Turkey, even if they were educated, the opposite of Turkish modernism because they infringed upon the Turkish identity that Merve refers to as 'uniformist'. There is hostility towards those not fitting the mould.

Similarly, the following year I met a well-known past leader of TUSIAD, the non-Islamic business association, and asked him if TUSIAD ever collaborated with MUSIAD, its Islamic counterpart, for the promotion of business-oriented legislation for Turkey. He replied, 'Why should we work with them?' In Western eyes Merve Kavakci may have been seen as a 'modern Islamic woman', but in Turkey she was, and remains, part of the 'other' – there would be no room for a so-called 'modern' Merve Kavakci in the Turkish Parliament.

***

The next day, Monday 3 May, the fracture between the secular bloc and the majority Islamic population exposed itself. Ecevit's party had succeeded in rolling over the other parties, who were actually criticized by the mainstream press for being neutral and not reacting vociferously against Merve's entrance into the Parliament. It is the fracture that millions of adoring tourists fail to see when they visit Turkey as they shop in awe at the Grand Bazaar, marvel at the Haghia Sophia, or take pictures of whirling dervishes performing just for them. On 3 May the fracture was brought to the surface and exposed, fault lines that had a long background existing since the reformist era of the Ottoman Empire and intensified since the imposition of Ataturk's reforms in the early 1920s. These deep fractures would surface periodically during the young republic's history, in spite of crackdowns.

To make matters worse, the failure to seat Merve would have broad negative implications for headscarved women in Turkey for a long time. For, knowing the consequences and seeing the reaction, what party would dare enfranchise this beleaguered group of women now? The fact that Tayyip Erdogan in 2011 as two-term-serving Prime Minister since 2002 and head of the ruling AK Party did not nominate any headscarved women for the Parliamentary elections, even though he is viewed as a friend of the Kavakci family, demonstrates the lasting impact of the incident in Parliament that day and his understanding of Turkey's fault lines.

There was not a bit of empathy expressed openly from the secular establishment for what seemed like a simple act of democracy and the right for people to vote for their own representatives in a decision-making body. The Turkish secular state had come to power by providing a limited, one-party version of democracy with limits on the rights of others, including Kurds and religious people, viewed by some as in-country Orientalism. The new republic originated as a product of an independence movement against occupying foreign powers and a puppet Ottoman state, a movement for freedom of the state. In the Turkish Constitution the right of the people is subjugated to the right of the secular state to prevail. The concept of democracy was not an underlying, expressed tenet for the establishment of the state, as in those Western countries Turkey sought to emulate. If it had succeeded it might have provided freedoms for the 'other' Turkey, which was viewed as having ruined Turkey in the past because of its backwardness. The remedy to that backwardness emerged after the independence movement of Mustafa Kemal and the subsequent reforms he single-handedly implemented. Perhaps understandably (just think of rising fascism in nearby Europe), the concept of democracy was secondary in 1923.

Lost in this momentous clash of the two Turkeys was the persona of Merve Kavakci. The young, energetic, intelligent, hard-working, single mother, committed to her family and her faith, stopped at the gates of medical school because of her headscarf and who had to journey 6,000 miles to get an education, yet who wanted to return to *her country* to raise her children, was made irrelevant by the onslaught that had just begun. Few secularists wanted to know anything good about her and, apart from the 'other' Turkey, few cared. She would be put in the same category as Ocalan, the Kurdish terrorist recently captured and brought to Turkey for justice, whom Turks wanted executed regardless of world opinion to the contrary. Beginning on 3 May, Merve's vilification would be accelerated in extremely de-humanized, objectified and marginalized ways. The 'good' persona was known to her constituents, but the overwhelming portrait promoted by the press was ugly, insulting and bigoted, damaging her in the eyes of Turks perhaps forever. Even today when she visits with Prime Minister Erdogan and his family she does so at his home and under cover of darkness. There are no official visits for Merve Kavakci in Turkey, no association with the ruling Islamic-friendly party, no photo opportunities. Merve's persona would suffer for future generations as well, including the eleven-year-olds at that time who would grow up to be my students at Bilkent University and looked at me quizzically when I mentioned that I was writing a book about her. When I inadvertently brought up the subject of my book to others I would invariably see the same expressions of disappointment in their faces regardless of educational background or age.

Her vilification was easy, a 'no brainer'. The Erbakan-led government had been essentially overthrown two years earlier by the military, its party closed and its leader banned from politics for five years. Erbakan's support for a headscarved woman to be nominated for the Parliament was misperceived as simply a provocation to get back at the state, sitting in the background and orchestrating Merve's entrance into the Great Hall. This was a clear opportunity for the state, and particularly the military, to strike back to keep Islamic parties outside of the political sphere. It mattered little that the Virtue Party had a different platform and consisted in part of reform-minded leaders, like Erdogan and Gul. The state did not view them any differently from the Welfare Party and did not believe its new rhetoric. The proof was clear: Merve's headscarf, completely covering the hair and tightly pinned beneath the chin, a powerful political Islamist symbol ... full stop.

As luck would have it, two key reformers within the party were protected from association with her. Erdogan was locked away in prison, out of the limelight and association with Merve, whose candidacy he did not favour anyway, but whom he liked, respected and tried to help.

And Abdullah Gul, as we have seen, played a cautious hand throughout, seemingly her friend, perhaps wanting her to succeed, but in actuality not supporting her when it counted in executive meetings, with Septioglu, or when challenged by Ecevit's emissary a few days before the oath-taking ceremonies. He knew what could happen if he promoted and supported Merve. Although he got her some interviews on television on 3 May, he managed to avoid being photographed with her and speaking on her behalf, as did most of the leadership. That avoidance worked, or something else had, because he and Kutan were, incredibly, not banned when the Virtue Party was closed, a matter that will be discussed later. His being banned would have been a disaster for his ambitions. The future President of Turkey was making all the right moves for his career, even telling Merve's uncle years later that the reason Merve was unable to take her oath was Merve's fault, that she did not listen to the party by her decision to come early to the Parliament. He was defending a party that was criticized now for leaving Merve 'out to dry'. The facts clearly show that it was not Merve Kavakci who was at fault for her party's lack of strategy, direction and more importantly 'will' in enabling her to take her oath. The party did not truly support her from the beginning because it was too risky, and because its leaders were motivated by their own preservation during the coup process, not democratic ideals for others.

Moreover, Gul had been through this all before with the Welfare Party. In 1998 he had come to the support of another headscarved woman, his wife, whose application to Ankara University was rejected because of her attached photograph which showed her wearing a headscarf. As a Member of Parliament with the Welfare Party he accompanied his wife to the university with television cameras rolling, then gave a speech on the campus with his wife at his side protesting against the violation of democracy and religious freedom. It was one of the reasons the Welfare Party was subsequently shut down by the courts.

He was not about to repeat this behaviour with Merve Kavakci at his side two years after the coup. Hayrunnisa Gul filed an action with the European Court of Human Rights after her appeals in Turkey failed, but later withdrew the case because of her husband's position as Foreign Minister in the AK Party government.

None of us who go about our jobs, manage risks and avoid stringent conflicts in our daily lives can adequately imagine what it was like for Merve at this time, falling into the vortex of an entire nation's negative powers, its mean side, a massive tidal wave of limitless enmity in the face of her morality, her decent behaviour, her hard work and trying to do what was right and legal. She was not an experienced political leader used to such abuse and treatment, but rather shocked by the response of her country. More than simply an enormous let-down, the cataclysmic reaction of the nation to her swung the massive proverbial pendulum in the opposite direction. She did not simply suffer the disappointment of being elected and not taking her seat. Not only had her nation let her down and changed the rules in the middle of the game, and not only had her party failed to support her. Now the nation started to attack her relentlessly.

Dr Thomas Stockmann, in *An Enemy of the People*, said 'the strongest man in the world is the man who stands most alone' and 'the majority is always wrong'. However, though outnumbered Merve was not completely alone. First and foremost she had her faith from an early age. She was a *hafiz*, an exalted title in the Muslim world, someone who could recite the Qur'an during Ramadan in mosques for others, and who would, according to her faith, go to Heaven. Second, she had her family, who supported her unquestionably and who acted in unison throughout her life – her children, her parents, grandparents, aunts and uncles and cousins, her steadfast, unofficial bodyguard sister, Ravza, and some close friends. Finally, she had her connection with the 'other' Turkey, the often silent majority whom she truly represented, whether in the Parliament or not, who loved her and named their children after her, even today. Yet, for a young entrant into politics, this maelstrom was difficult to take.

The press attacks

On 3 May 1999 Turkey's establishment papers exploded with the news, and the news was overwhelmingly bad. It was only the first day of a relentless attack against Merve Kavakci and the Virtue Party, one that turned into a tsunami of condemnation, bias and intrusive 'investigative' reporting aimed at vilification in the extreme. Some of this coverage began after the election and before the swearing-in ceremony when the spectre of a covered woman entering Parliament came into focus. The secular establishment in Turkey did, indeed, feel provoked, just as Demirel had portrayed it. It was as if you had pricked the foot of a giant dragon, which then turned around, swung its enormous tail and fought back with every resource and fire-breathing weapon in its arsenal. However, The Turkish press irresponsibly fuelled the flames of public opinion and began a campaign against Merve Kavakci unlike any other.

A comprehensive study of the press coverage on Merve Kavakci from 2 to 20 May 1999 was undertaken by Dr Esra Arsan, comparing the coverage of *Hurriyet*, an establishment paper, with *Yeni Safak*, an Islamic one. She analysed the words they selected in their reporting, the arguments they made and the sources they used.[1] Arsan found that *Hurriyet* did not critically discuss anything that Ecevit said because they agreed with him. Their sources were always 'official' – such as the ministries, military staff, Kemalist members of Parliament, the state security courts and Kemalist non-governmental organizations. They promoted the view of the state and tried to manufacture an official ideology of the state and laicism. They denied that Merve Kavakci had any supporters and did not write about them in any of their news coverage, even though there were demonstrations in support of Merve in Turkey and elsewhere in the world. *Hurriyet* was like the other mainstream media in Turkey at the time: it represented the interests and ideology of the state.

On the other hand, *Yeni Safak*, an Islamic-friendly paper, clearly supported Merve and viewed her as a victim of Ecevit. Arsan cites several articles and headlines in which Yeni Safak shows its subjective view, including headlines like 'You are Our Queen' and 'This Kind of Behavior Does Not Suit the Republic'.

However, Arsan goes further and blames *Hurriyet* and the other establishment papers as responsible for Merve's eventual loss of citizenship and the closure of the Virtue Party. She notes that Prosecutor Savas used news coverage of *Hurriyet* as proof in his case against her party. She admonishes *Hurriyet* for not adhering to the basics of objective journalism, for simply representing the state's views and for marginalizing any reports that disagreed with their positions.

In examples noted by Arsan, on 3 May *Hurriyet*'s headline was, 'Erbakan, This Is Your Work.' The text inside included: 'Erbakan this is your contribution to the Parliament. You caused this crisis. This kind of behaviour does not suit the Republic. The Parliament is not a place to challenge the principles of the state.' Citing Ecevit's speech, another *Hurriyet* banner headline declared 'Historical Warning', while yet another article showed Ecevit with the headline, 'Parliament is Not a Place to Challenge the State'. An excerpt from one of the articles:

> Nazli Ilicak was the person behind this, she provided all the tactics.
> Merve Kavakci, who became a candidate with the encouragement of Erbakan, entered the Parliament with a headscarf. Nesrin Unal also wore a headscarf but she took it off because she was respectful of the Republic. Kavakci, on the other hand, was so stubborn that she continued to wear her headscarf. The deputies of the DSP told her to get out and, after this event, Parliament took a break.

The common word for headscarf in Turkish is *basortusu*, but those who interpret it in a negative way as a political statement use the word '*turban*'. On 3 May the banner headline in *Milliyet* was 'Turban Sabotage'. *Sabah*'s was 'Provocation and Common Sense' – common sense being Ecevit's harsh reaction to Kavakci. The *Star*'s top headline over a picture of the protesters in Parliament showed great respect to them, 'Gentlemen' accompanied by a prominent quote from Ataturk, along with his picture: 'You know very well that the Republic of Turkey cannot be the land of dervishes and sheiks. The righteous path is the path of civilization.'

Arsan analysed two national newspapers, *Hurriyet* and *Milliyet*, as representative of dominant, Kemalist ideology in their representation of Merve Kavakci. This is not to say that the Islamist press is immune to analysis – she views the Kemalist–Islamist conflict in similar terms, as 'between two political forces both of which are modernist-conservative'. As the power holders, however, supported by a strong military, the Kemalist control of the media provided damaging social power. She focused on the structure of the news – its persuasive content, organization, eyewitness descriptions and use of sources – and rhetoric or language, as well as terminologies used.

Dr Arsan described how *Hurriyet*'s coverage of 3 May was clearly biased:

> In this news, key words are 'crisis,' 'stubborn,' 'work of art,' 'chaos,'
> 'challenge,' and of course 'planned action.' First, *Hurriyet* newspaper
> represents the situation as a Parliamentary crisis. We have a woman
> MP who was voted by the public, but under turban. She was
> actually under turban before the election, and everybody knew that
> she would enter the Parliament if she won the election. Maybe she's
> got her seat just because she's under turban. She is more educated
> than many other women in Turkey; but because of her belief, she
> wears a headscarf. She is also a member of a religious party; so
> there is actually no crisis in this situation caused by Merve Kavakci.
> There is only one crisis, which is created by so-called 'laicist' MPs
> who don't want to see a woman under cover in their territory
> (Parliament) as a representative of ordinary religious citizens.
>
> Also *Hurriyet* thinks that she is a kind of 'public enemy,' a
> stubborn person who doesn't want to understand her own country's
> sensitivities. Although it's straight news, rather than a commentary,
> the newspaper puts its opinion and claim that she is 'stubborn.'
> *Hurriyet* thinks that Merve Kavakci is a product of former Islamist
> Party leader Necmettin Erbakan who wants to create chaos in
> Turkey's public sphere. They argue that if she gets rid of her turban,
> everything will be fine, and there won't be any problem, crisis or
> chaos in Turkey. *Hurriyet* also thinks that, by challenging the rules
> and regulations, Merve Kavakci made herself 'public enemy.' So,
> who is public, and who is the enemy? Did the public who voted for
> Kavakci think that she is the enemy? Are the people who voted for
> her during the election the enemy? If she is the enemy, why did the
> public vote for her? Without answering these questions, *Hurriyet*
> sets its opinion instead of public opinion, and decided that Kavakci
> is an enemy. The newspaper represent her as a product of an illegal
> attempt (work of art of fundamentalist Islam), a stubborn 'other'
> who doesn't want to be a part of Kemalist 'us.' The discourse of the
> news such as a 'planned action' seems like the newspaper is trying
> to accuse the Fazilet Party as a whole of being a part of an illegal
> attempt.[2]

On the same day, *Milliyet*'s article, under the banner headline, 'Turban
Sabotage,' appeared. It stated that 'the 21st term of the Turkish
Parliament has begun with a shocking turban event. It happened when
Merve Kavakci entered the assembly with her turban during the oath-
taking ceremony.' Dr Arsan asks, 'Sabotage against what? Probably it's
against democracy. How does one think that a woman MP can damage

democracy with her turban? In fact, one can easily argue that *Hurriyet* daily is damaging democracy by insulting, and accusing, an elected MP.' She points out that events on their own need to be made intelligible, by translating real events into symbolic form, a process of discourse that analysts call *encoding*:

> The selection of codes, those which are preferred codes in the different domains, and which appear to embody the 'natural' explanations which most members of society would accept ... casts these problematic events, consensually, somewhere within the repertoire of the dominant ideologies. The word, sabotage, is a symbolic form of representation of the religious 'other' as a threat to democracy.

As Dr Arsan explained to me, 'There are journalistic standards and professionalization in the Western media, but not in Turkey, which also lacks ethics codes, journalistic honesty and unions to protect your rights. You are basically tied to your bosses and editors and have to do what they say. If you are a regular reporter trying to uncover reality you are in big trouble.'

That 'big trouble' could also mean prison. Freedom of the press has always been tenuous in Turkey. Repression of an independent press dates to the Ottoman Empire with a law in 1857 that required printing houses to get permission from the sultan before books were published. Censorship of newspapers continued in 1909. After the birth of the Republic, newspapers were closed and journalists jailed by the Independence Courts. During the Second World War, newspapers were also shut down, then fines and sentences increased under Adnan Menderes in the 1950s, with more restrictions after the 1980 coup. Article 8 of the Anti-Terror Law was used in the 1990s to punish 'separatist propaganda', including non-violent offences. 'Article 312 of the criminal code imposes three-year prison sentences for incitement to commit an offence and incitement to religious or racial hatred',[3] and was used to imprison Tayyip Erdogan for reading a poem. At the time of this writing forty-eight journalists are currently in prison in Turkey with seven hundred facing cases – some, like that of Helin Sahin, for reporting on information presented in court in public trials.[4]

The mainstream press attacked Merve Kavakci mercilessly and those journalists who objected to such attacks could find themselves not only without a job, but also in jail. This type of an environment smothers objectivity and stifles independent thought:

> It's not about trying to write the truth. It's about a power struggle between political Islam and Kemalists. In 1999 it was about the power struggle between the military and political Islam with political and journalist actors creating realities, not trying to tell the truth, not trying to do investigative reporting contrary to these power struggles.[5]

So as the days progressed more stories came out, a powerful wall of repression that smothered Merve and frustrated her and her family, signs of a deluge in the making, one that would ultimately convince her to leave Turkey again.

On 3 May it was also reported that the Chief Prosecutor of the Supreme Court, Vural Savas, said: 'I am personally covering the incidents. Nobody should have doubts; I will do what is required by the Constitution and laws.' He added that he would seek the videotape of the session and the names of deputies who registered with the Virtue Party after the closure of the Welfare Party. Also, it was reported that a group of about 150 people had gathered in the park in front of the Parliament protesting against Kavakci, led by the wives of two government ministers, the Ataturk Association and the Turkish Women's Union, singing the national anthem and chanting slogans such as 'Turkey is secular and she will remain secular'. The head of the CHP (Republican People's Party) led another demonstration, yelling that 'the secularism principle is the main element of internal peace in Turkey'. General Rasim Betir, Head of the Gendarmerie, was quoted as saying, 'This even shouldn't have taken place in the Parliament, but it happened, but the necessary reaction was shown against it', referring to the DSP's demonstration.

The *Star* reported that Merve Kavakci confessed in a speech at a meeting of Hamas in 1997 that 'with our Sudanese brothers and Dr Turabi, we established El Islami El Alemi two years ago' – a fiction, yet a first attempt to make Merve look like a terrorist.

There were also pictures of Merve in various outfits under the headline: 'MERVESSACE – Merve who is changing her dresses like models every day prefers the brand Versace, which is also preferred by Erbakan, who is the advisor of Merve.'

Meanwhile, President Demirel issued a mandate to Ecevit to form a new and harmonious government, one that 'won't give concessions from the basic principles of the secular and democratic state'. Ecevit himself said he hoped 'this problem would be overcome by our understanding of the secular republic soon and I trust our people's common sense'. He noted that the demonstrators against Kavakci understood this and that his party did not want to 'implement secularism in a way that doesn't put the real believers, who don't manipulate religion, into a difficult position'. Needless to say, the Virtue Party would not be part of any coalition government.

Merve's press briefing

Within this context, Merve and her sister Ravza left her home in Ankara and made the short trip to the Virtue Party's headquarters, arriving at around ten in the morning. Merve did not have time to look at the morning's newspapers.

However, this morning it was easier for Merve to get her meeting with Kutan because her entrance in the Parliament grabbed the entire attention of the country and became 'the day that Turkey stood still'. Had she bothered to take a look at the papers that morning she would have noticed there was no other news in Turkey. The country had stopped to see what would happen next.

As Merve and Ravza entered the meeting room they once again found long faces sitting around the table: Recai Kutan, Cemil Cicek, Ali Coskun, Ismail Alptekin, Salih Kapusuz, Abdullah Gul and Mustafa Kamalak, all members of the party and Parliament.

Kutan looked exhausted. According to Merve, he and Erbakan had spent many hours during the night on the phone. Certainly Kutan was placed in a difficult position as leader of this party. Sometimes his mild and gentle character allowed others to take advantage of him.

When Merve entered they had been talking about what was written in the newspapers. She asked about the press coverage and Kapusuz responded that it might be better if she didn't read the reports to avoid getting upset. She now saw that everything was worse than she ever imagined. Kutan exclaimed: 'Tonight the President is giving a dinner. I should not go.' Picking up the phone he said, 'Call the President's office and tell them that I am not able to attend the dinner and find an excuse.' After hanging up the phone, he thought for a moment and then picked it up again. The distress was evident on his face as he spoke to his special assistant, 'Don't give any excuse. Just tell them I am not going to attend the dinner!'

Merve and Ravza quickly realized on this morning that the party had made no preparation for the press conference and that no one seemed concerned about what needed to be said. The sisters were young, not part of the party hierarchy, and expected the party to take control of the situation. However, it was obvious that the party's leadership had no such plans. Merve and Ravza started getting upset at their lack of direction and preparation. Trying to be calm and collect herself, Merve got up and approached Kutan. 'Sir, I scratched out a draft, but it needs to be reviewed. If you like, I can read it, and you can give me your feedback.' According to Merve, 'Everybody in the room jumped at this proposal as if it were a lifesaver. They made some important points, and I took notes.'

As the discussion continued, Cicek insisted that Merve add a line about a scandal involving Ecevit, 'We did not forget what happened at the Gunes Motel.' Kutan also suggested that Merve criticize Ecevit's behaviour in various areas and issues that occurred twenty years earlier. Merve refused both of these suggestions, telling them that such insinuations did not suit her character. She realized that they were attempting to use her as their mouthpiece to say things that they themselves would not say. How could this possibly help Merve's cause?

More importantly, the group insisted that Merve add a statement that it was she who decided not to return to the Parliament after the recess. Merve went along with it. She was not about to break from her party, and not in public.

Zeki Unal, who consistently supported Merve, accompanied her for the short trip by car from the party's offices to the Parliament for the press conference. In the Parliament they first walked to Kutan's office to rest a bit and were joined by Abdullatif Sener. But where were the others? Merve was shocked to see that those who had been in the party headquarters discussing her speech with her were now gone. They had abandoned her. She was now a pariah; being photographed for all memoriam could be damaging for those who valued their careers. This was confirmed to me by party insiders. As they went downstairs Gul was paying special attention to staying away from the line of sight of the cameras. Later Ravza asked him, 'Mr Gul, as a vice-chairman are you not going to sit next to my sister?' His answer was, 'I will stay on that side,' pointing to a position behind the cameras.' On this subject, Ravza recalls:

> After a while we were on our way to the press conference, and as everybody was going in Abdullah Gul suggested that I do not go in with her, and he took me to a room for the reporters. He introduced me to them and told me to wait there until the press conference was over. At that point I kept asking him over and over again: 'Are you not going into the press conference?' He made a gesture that he would. I remember that he was at the conference but behind all the cameras.

The key party leaders were not standing or sitting with Merve as she spoke. Kutan was in his office; Gul was out of view. The next day *Milliyet* reported that Salih Kapusuz, Lutfu Esengun, Genel Baskan Yardimcilari, Cemil Cicek and Abdullah Gul were there, but a picture clearly shows that, except for Esengun, they were not there at all. Shown in the photo were Mehmet Ergun Dagcioglu, Mehmet Aydinbas, Zeki Unal and Abdulkadir Aksu (now a prominent AKP member) and in the front row Lutfu Esengul (who came to her house the day before the oath ceremony with Gul and Kapusuz), Abdullatif Sener, the Deputy Head of the VP in the Parliament and the one chairing the conference, Merve Kavakci, Mehmet Ali Sahin (who was later speaker of the Parliament) and an unidentified member.

Merve was startled when she entered the room. Not yet recovered from the shock of the day before, she was now in front of the entire Turkish press, those who had attacked her for weeks. She was trying to concentrate on controlling her expressions and gestures, and to smile regardless of how difficult representing the honour of headscarved women had become. Abdullatif Sener politely pulled out her chair to help her be seated. She announced that she would not take any questions. She silently recited the prayer of the Prophet Moses in her head:

> Oh my Lord, ease my chest for me! Make my affair easier for me,
>   And allow me to speak so they may understand whatever I say. (Qur'an 20:25–28)

Distinguished members of the press, respectfully I greet you all. I am grateful for your interest and taking the time to join us today. Yesterday, in this very Parliament a sad and thought-provoking event occurred that would not have taken place in any democratic country according to its rules and regulations. In the National Assembly, a representative of the nation was denied the ability to represent those who elected her. The will of the people was neglected in the 'People's Assembly'.

Yesterday, in the Turkish National Assembly the Constitution and the Code of Law were violated. There is no decree in the Constitution, Code of Law, or any other law to prevent me from taking my oath in this attire. I applied to the High Election Committee as I now appear. My nomination was approved and confirmed by the High Election Committee as you see me now. The people came to know me in this way, and I campaigned as such. My nation showed me kindness. Like any other Parliamentarian, they gave me the right to go to their Assembly to represent them. According to the procedure, I received my licence registering me like all the others at the Assembly. I also received the Certificate of Approval from the Parliament and entered the General Assembly Hall to take my oath like all the others who had acquired the same status as me.

Respected press, the certificate that I now hold was prepared by the Director of the Personnel and Treasury Department of the General Secretary of the Turkish National Assembly and written on it is, 'Ms Merve Kavakci was elected on April 18, 1999, for the twenty-first session of the Parliamentary Election from Istanbul and her Parliamentary position is valid.'

Like the other Parliamentarians, I went to the National Assembly yesterday. What happened here? Our nation has watched with contemplation. I am a child of the Republic. Today I stand before you with the authority of my nation, the authority to represent them in their own Assembly, but the forceful mentality present at this level demanding conformity to their uniform frame of mind prevented me from taking my oath according to the Secular Republic of Turkey. They hindered the authority of the nation from exercising its rights. They denied 'sovereignty without any conditions belongs to the nation' as its founder, Ataturk, expressed so long ago. This scarf that also covers the heads of the mothers and wives whose children or husbands lost their lives in defence of this land is used today as an obstacle for Merve Kavakci's taking her place in the National Assembly. The scarf was labelled as a political symbol. I want to make it very clear. My head is covered because of my faith. It is my personal choice to wear a scarf. Assuredly, this is under the protection of international law and the Constitution.

My desire is simply for the application of the Second Article of the Constitution. Additionally, I call for the fulfilment of the numerous international agreements regarding democracy and human rights approved of and signed by the Republic of Turkey. This topic is also covered in the Nineteenth Article of the Constitution. Had I been given the opportunity to read the text of the oath, which is found in the Eighty-First Article of the Constitution, we could see what has happened is even against the contents of the oath itself that states: 'Everyone has the right to the benefits of human rights and freedom.' Yesterday, with a democratic perspective I conducted myself according to the international laws, the Constitution, and the Turkish Code of Law. They labelled me a 'provoker'. If they could look at this matter without bias, they would see that this word better suits those who prevented me from taking my oath. As a daughter of an academic mother and father whose motto was to 'seek knowledge from the cradle to the grave' and as a granddaughter of a military officer who fought with his blood and soul on two different fronts in the War of Independence, with my education and collected potential, I am here in order to serve this nation in the best way.

My nation should know that on the campaign trail those who claimed to be the defenders of democracy, who used to use the headscarf as material for their campaign, left Merve Kavakci by herself today in the democratic movement as they cowered in the presence of injustice. Ironically in a country where 75 per cent of the ladies wear the headscarf and each of whom voted for different parties, their own Parliamentarians couldn't accept Merve Kavakci, one person from among themselves to represent the nation wearing a headscarf. How sad it is that they don't give me the opportunity to serve my country although wearing this same attire I obtained my education in the United States, the cradle of democracy and human rights and modern thought. Yesterday in the National Assembly, a picture of Turkey was exhibited which contradicts our country's efforts to be democratic and contemporary while this injustice and unlawful act was carried out in the name of democracy and modern thought. In addition, the National Assembly of Turkey took a step backwards in the democratic struggle.

It seems to me that our democratic and reconciliatory demeanour in striving for the right to wear the headscarf because of our faith is going to be like the struggle of the blacks for human rights and freedom years back in the United States. As a Parliamentarian, I am only accountable to the people of my nation.

Honourable press members, I would like you to know that I will defend to the end the duty and honourable right of representing my people in democratic arenas adhering to the laws in a style suitable to a woman. Last evening, although my turn came to take my oath, I decided for the following reasons not to take my oath.

To avoid straining the environment.

To prevent the opportunists and exploiters from having the chance to take advantage of the situation.

I am thankful to my people who gave their support with calls and faxes since my nomination was announced. I am going to try my best to deserve their trust. I have a request for my honourable nation … I invite you to act according to common sense not to lend your ear to the provokers who want to set us against each other. Respectfully, I bid you all a good day. Thank you very much.

This is a remarkable document that Merve and Ravza managed to put together over twenty-four hours, despite exhaustion, with just some minor editing by the party. It sets forth a clear case for adherence to legal and democratic principles. Note that Merve did not blame her own party for preventing her from returning to the Parliament around midnight and, at their direction, added that she decided on her own to not take her oath, even though she could have rightfully placed the blame where it belonged. In view of the political crisis in the nation, one would think that this document deserved to be typeset word for word and placed on the front page of all the establishment papers and be a focus for discussion by the country. However, it did not seem to appear anywhere. What was quoted the most from her speech was the phrase, 'I am a daughter of the Republic'.

The Virtue Party compounded its missed opportunity of the previous night of not having Merve Kavakci sworn in with yet another one, perhaps even more damaging, at the press conference. Incredibly they not only left it for Merve herself to write her speech – had she not, it seems unlikely there would even have been a press conference that day – but they also did not even consider responding to questions and making their case to the nation. Their leadership was absent. No one spoke for her; they did not take responsibility for their actions. The party that had spent countless hours talking about democracy during the election seemed to give up on the issue on the evening of 2 May after Demirel's speech, if not before, so impactful was the fear instilled by the government and the military. In front of enormous press coverage, they surrendered without any argument whatsoever and let Merve Kavakci take sole responsibility for not being sworn in, when in fact it was ultimately the party that had blocked her from taking the oath. In Mafia talk, she 'took the hit' for them.

Why had the party acted so badly? It should be recalled that it was not the party leadership that had favoured her nomination, in spite of its importance to the VP's female membership and to the party's democratic ethos. It came from Erbakan and was supported by some others, notably Nazli Ilicak and Mustafa Kamalak, but the reformist wing and most of the leadership was apprehensive about covered candidates. Now the party was in damage mode and were not about to battle for Merve Kavakci. Erbakan, in those lengthy conversations with Kutan before Merve arrived at party headquarters, probably gave up, knowing that he could be prosecuted further for violating his ban from politics with a more aggressive stance by the Virtue Party. Or perhaps Kutan received a call from a general, or Ecevit's right-hand man …

Let us remember again that just over two years earlier, during a National Security Council meeting, the military issued its demands to Erbakan, demands that he ignored for as long as he could until he eventually resigned. Among the eighteen directives issued by the NSC were these.[6]

- 'The principle of secularism should be strictly enforced and laws should be modified for that purpose, if necessary.'
- 'Media groups that oppose the military and depict is members as inimical to religion should be brought under control.'
- 'Practices that violate the attire law and that may give Turkey a backward image must be prevented.'
- 'Measures taken … to prevent infiltration … by the extremist religious sector.'

Demirel and Erbakan certainly had fresh memories of what was possible on the part of the Turkish military. Subsequent to the NSC's 1997 intervention, as the generals briefed the parties, press, judiciary and others on the need to fight *irtica* (reactionism), as they purged almost one thousand military officers and key bureaucrats because of their Islamic lifestyle,[7] the two would go in different directions. Demirel knew what was coming and his party supported the military intervention. He had aligned himself with the military before and would do it again. Erbakan would end up resigning from office and be banned from politics. He would not implement their directives no matter what. He had supported Merve taking her oath. But now it seemed that he too had given up, or reformers in the party now held sway.

Another factor that needs to be mentioned: the patriarchal character of Islamic men and ambivalence towards the Islamic women who worked for the party and who were left out of the decision-making process. In Merve's case these men were particularly Janus-faced. After all, the lineage of the Virtue Party can be traced back to Erbakan's Milli Gorus (National Outlook) movement, whose first party began in 1969, only to close a year later. After thirty years Merve was the first covered female candidate in Turkey's history. During the campaign, when pressed about Merve's keeping her headscarf the party spoke of democracy in vague terms and proclaimed 'the choice is hers' argument, a way to avoid their responsibility. In Kutan's offices they did not, in fact, leave it up to her. Instead they made her take responsibility for their actions, transferring it to her. Had the party truly supported women's empowerment they would have spoken for Merve at the press conference and taken responsibility for their actions. Ultimately, after all the rhetoric about democracy, they treated her as less-than-equal. The male leadership of the VP occasionally engaged the rhetoric of the women within their party – 'we are women, we are strong and we exist' – because of the pressures they received from the Islamic women's political support that helped to bring Erdogan into the Istanbul mayor's office and Erbakan to power. But they did not fully adopt the construct of equality, and no party has done so in Turkey to this day. Notwithstanding the many passages of the Qur'an that support women, the patriarchal attitude of men in Turkey is contrary to the Western notion of women's rights, coming from both Islamic and secular men, and remains so today.

The 2010 issue of the Gender Gap Report, produced by the World Economic Forum, ranked Turkey 126th among 134 countries. Its political empowerment ranking was ninety-ninth. Its women's labour force participation was 26 per cent, the lowest in Europe. Despite Mustafa Kemal Ataturk's uniquely progressive views and policies towards women's equality in the areas of employment and politics – far ahead of his contemporaries – Turkey's record in this area is 'appalling'.[8]

Regardless, the Virtue Party, at this important event, was a 'no-show', doing nothing to either repair or explain what had happened, nothing to fight back or make its case with the public and the nation when it had an opportunity to do so. From a modern public relations perspective, their performance was incompetent. They left it to a thirty-year-old novice to handle the press conference, did not issue a policy statement and did not use the opportunity to answer questions soon after the incident. It was a continuation of their general abandonment of Merve that began at the start of the campaign when the media started to pressure her.

Merve finished her speech, ignoring all questions from the media as she said she would, and left with those few who stood by her. Perhaps it would have been better for her to take questions and dispel the misinformation that was brewing in the press, but this was not done and no preparation was made for her to handle questions anyway. Merve had done what she could. She had expressed herself articulately, made history that could not be ignored, and thus walked out with some satisfaction. We can only imagine what would have occurred had the party backed her and taken a stand on 3 May 1999 and the impact it would have had in Turkey today.

Television interviews

After the press conference, Abdullatif Sener invited Merve and Ravza for lunch at the restaurant on the ground floor of the Parliament. Sener earned his PhD in Political Science from Gazi University in Ankara and would later become a co-founder of the AK Party and Deputy Prime Minister in the Erdogan government; he later quit that post and formed his own party.

After lunch, they went up to a meeting room to discuss what to do next. Mustafa Bas, Abdullah Gul and Mehmet Sahin were there, as well as Orhan Ugurluoglu from Star TV, whom Merve did not recognize at first. Several ideas were thrown out for discussion but it seemed to Merve that the discussion was not serious given the gravity of the situation. Bas proposed that Kavakci be sent to Istanbul to rally the people so that she could take her oath in their presence, but that idea was opposed and cast aside. Sahin, who had a legal background, suggested some legal steps to be taken. Someone recommended seeking a new election because a Member of Parliament had been illegally stopped from taking office, but that did not find support either.

Meanwhile, Gul was on the phone lining up interviews for Merve on various television stations. He had already scheduled her to appear on Kanal 7, an Islamic-friendly station owned by the Yimpas conglomerate, at 9 p.m. He then introduced Merve to Orhan and said they were discussing Merve's appearance on his show. Because she was extremely sleep-deprived she was apprehensive of appearing on multiple shows late at night. Anyway, Orhan declined when he found out that Merve would be appearing first on Kanal 7.

Merve's supporters had joined those in the room, including Mehmet Aksay, a close family friend, who had just arrived from Istanbul. It became so overcrowded that it was decided to move down the hall to a larger meeting room. This proved difficult because of the swarms of media waiting at the door, crowding in on them as they filtered out from one room to the other, pointing their television cameras and glaring lights. Merve was one of the first to arrive in the new room. She looked out to a view of the front courtyard of the National Assembly building and then rested her head on her arm for a few moments until Gul and Kapusuz arrived.

The discussion continued about the cancellation of Star TV and the need for a replacement. Merve protested due to her exhaustion but the group insisted that they had to present some explanation of the matter although for some reason that need had not compelled them to use the press conference held that morning for that very purpose in which every television station was present, nor to place themselves on television as her representative. Instead, they left if to Merve to fight her own battles on television. The corridors were filled with stations wanting interviews. Gul had a good relationship with the ATV station and favoured Merve being on the ATV Evening News with Ali Kirca, a well-known anchor-man who heads up the news division for that station today. He suggested that she interview first with ATV, at 7 p.m. Kanal 7's show was at 9 p.m. Merve and Ravza were uncomfortable with this because not only had Kanal 7 been promised the first interview, but Ahmet Hakan Coskun was already flying in from Istanbul to do it. Merve argued for Kanal 7 that it would be sufficient to 'give our message to the Turkish nation' and because the station was Islamic friendly and she was sure they would be friendly to her. Gul said no, that ATV had a larger audience. Merve proposed to do the ATV interview the next day but that idea was also turned down by the group. She argued again, insisting, but was ignored. The party members paid no attention to her concerns because they couldn't find any other solution.

The time for *zhuhr* – the midday prayer – had arrived. Gul stepped out of the room to talk to ATV while Merve and Ravza put some paper on the floor to serve as their prayer rug and performed their prayer. It was a rare peaceful moment in what would be a horrific week, one that would try her strength and patience, but not her faith. She looked out of the window again at the garden and was captivated by the peaceful view, which for some reason saddened her. A couple of minutes later Gul popped in with the reporter from ATV and she came back to reality. He was excited about the interview to come and relayed instructions about the questions that should not be asked. 'Yes sir!' said the reporter, but those instructions evaporated by the time Ali Kirca started the show.

As the sun was setting Merve, Ravza, Gul and Kutan's press assistant made their way to the Karum Shopping Centre by car, where ATV was located, followed by what seemed like the entire Turkish media. As their car approached the station and slowed because of the traffic, all the reporters and journalists began running alongside and in front of their car. A mob of other reporters and numerous live cameras were waiting for them as well, plus a small group of protestors, as they proceeded into the underground parking garage. Some of the protestors waited for Merve by the elevator and began taunting her. She thought, oh my Lord, please give me patience and strength.

Gul did not accompany Merve and Ravza when they exited the cars and entered the studio, avoiding the reporters and cameramen.

When they arrived at ATV, the producer welcomed them. They passed Ali Kirca, who was having make-up applied. He did not get up and hardly said hello. After a tea break in the producer's office, Merve wanted to wash her face. With the station's cameraman on her heels, she went to the washroom. He waited by the door and took her picture when she emerged. She struggled inwardly not to show her anger, which she felt was contrary to the character of a believer, who did not succumb to pressure or allow circumstances to be devastating. The believer is hopeful. The believer must always cheerfully endure, she thought.

Ali Kirca attacked Merve Kavakci for an hour. Ravza was watching in the waiting room with Kutan's press secretary and Abdullah Gul. Ravza's recollections:

> Ali Kirca was at this time a very experienced and popular news anchor and he was shocked and paralyzed to see that his harsh attacks were not strong enough for beating Merve Kavakci up. Ali Kirca continued firing questions without waiting for any answers and each time Merve would calmly say, 'But Ali Bey, you need to let me speak, so that I can answer all your questions', and continue to answer them.
>
> The waiting room had many screens displaying the news on different channels. As the programme started, all the screens were displaying views of my sister, interviews with distant relatives in Adapazari, pictures of our family members, etc. I remember being devastated realizing that we were going into a severe political tornado. Meanwhile, Abdullah Gul and Kutan's press secretary were watching the interview with great excitement and enthusiasm. They looked exactly as if they were watching a national soccer game. At one point Abdullah Gul yelled out 'bu kizi basbakan yapalim' ('let's make this girl the Prime Minister'). I was so surprised at their attitude and their lack of comprehension of the fact that a huge political lynching campaign was underway against my sister.

The Ali Kirca interview is instructive for us for it conveys the attitude of the mainstream media toward Merve, her party and Islamic people during this time, and for this reason I have included a somewhat lengthy encapsulation of the complete 'interview', written and translated by an independent observer:

> Introduction, welcome: Ali Kirca points out that Kavakci shakes hands with him despite the fact that it is said that many headscarved women do not shake hands with men. Merve explains that according to Western rules of etiquette a gentleman does not extend his hand unless a lady does, however because he did she responded in the same way to be polite.
>
> Ali Kirca continues to discuss the rules of hand-shaking, but Merve indicates that she is finished with this subject.
>
> Ali Kirca introduces the topic of the headscarf as being highly important and declares that the public eagerly awaits Kavakci's statements. He asks her to give a brief biography before delving into the topic. She explains that she was born in Ankara in 1968, her parents' occupations, that she graduated from Ankara College,

then she got her second choice in university preferences, which was Ankara University's Faculty of Medicine. Because of the laws concerning headscarves in the university, her family went to America.

Ali Kirca asks for clarification on her parents' professions. Merve explains that her father was Turkey's first professor of Islamic law. At the same time, he was a practising lawyer. Her mother taught on the Faculty of German Language and Literature. Then Ali Kirca points out that they both worked at the same university.

Ali Kirca asks if her mother was forced to retire. She replies that she was not forced to retire. She offers to explain the situation. Ali Kirca says that for the sake of chronology, the public should get to know her parents before getting to know her. He recounts the claims that Merve's father gave a talk in Iran about Turkish secularism and the Turkish regime. Ali Kirca invites Merve to explain the story in her own words.

Merve explains that her father was a very well-connected, international and scholarly person. He had participated in conferences in his fields of law and Islamic law in many locations throughout the world. She explains that at the conference that Ali Kirca is referring to, many professors were alongside him.

Ali Kirca interrupts to ask if that meeting was not important – that it was in 1982, about the third anniversary of the Islamic Republic of Iran. He reads from his notes that her father gave a talk concerning secularism in Turkey and the Turkish regime. Merve denies that this was the topic and tries to change the subject to talk about her mother.

Ali Kirca cuts her off to ask why her father left the university. In her reply, she trips over her words, blurting out that her father resigned and corrects herself, saying that he retired. She explains that she and her younger sister were studying at Ankara College, that her mother grew up in Istanbul, and graduated from an Austrian high school and later continued her studies in German Language and Literature at Istanbul University. And in Erzurum she found a job as a lecturer.

Ali Kirca interrupts her to ask if it was true that her mother had to leave the university during that time because of her headscarf. Merve confirms that this is true – that during this period it was necessary. Her parents had to make a decision, and they wanted their children to study at Ankara College and be near the rest of the family. From there her mother went to work privately.

Ali Kirca points out that her family then went to America. She explains that after her father left the university he served as a consultant for a legal organization and then their family went to America.

Ali Kirca asks how many years her family has been in America. She replies that they have been there since 1988. Ali Kirca points out that that makes eleven years and she confirms. She explains that they went at the beginning of 1988. She continues, describing how she used to go visit them on her breaks from studying medicine at Ankara University. She states that because of some problems related to her headscarf, she chose to complete her studies in America.

Ali Kirca interrupts her to point out that not everyone is lucky enough to study in America, but that she of course had such an opportunity because her family was there. She says that she considers herself lucky that she was able to study software engineering in America. She explains that in her heart she desired that there should be such an opportunity in Turkey, because she knows that not everyone has had the chance that she did. She goes on to acknowledge that there are many Turks who have found opportunities and chosen to stay in America. She says that she would like to work towards having such opportunities available in her own country.

Ali Kirca changes the topic to her life while studying in America and Merve offers to continue. She explains that she got married around the time that she started studying software engineering at The University of Texas. Her husband was an American and a Muslim. She explains that they couldn't agree on some things and they got divorced.

Ali Kirca asks if she got married to someone else after her divorce, and she denies this. She says that she returned to Turkey after completing her education.

Ali Kirca continues on the topic of Merve Kavakci's life in America. He reads from his notes that Merve's father was part of an Islamic organization. She confirms that he was the director of that organization.

Ali Kirca says that there are claims she gave a talk at a meeting of an Islamic organization. This information has appeared on the Internet and, according to certain sources, the organization supports Hamas. Ali Kirca points out that this organization has been accused of terrorism by the American government. He asks Kavakci to confirm whether or not she participated in such a meeting. She explains that she may have participated in the conferences of several different types of Islamic organizations in a variety of capacities both during her time in America and afterward.

Ali Kirca asks if she participated in a conference 1999 [sic] concerning the Islamic Association of Palestine. As she hesitates, he reads the English name of the organization from his notes and turns back to her. She says that she may have participated in the meeting.

After confirming, Ali Kirca points out that this is group classified as a terrorist organization by the US government. He continues to explain that a report has been submitted on this group and that it is said that this foundation supports Hamas. It is therefore considered to be quite a radical organization and, he insists, her participation in this organization puts her name on the list of shadow cabinet members of the Refah Party.

Kavakci furrows her brow momentarily and cuts in to say that she would like to explain.

Ali Kirca presses on by pulling out the Senate Judiciary Committee's report on the Islamic Association of Palestine and pointing out to her that her participation at that conference was documented in this report and then jumps to a sentence that declares that this organization supports Hamas.

Kavakci defends her participation on the grounds that it was of a purely religious nature, and Ali Kirca cuts her off to point out that she participated in a meeting of the most radical group's most radical meeting.

Kavakci jumps in to say that she needs to make an important distinction: she is a very active person and has participated in conferences of many types of organizations. As she tries to explain that this organization is legal (as in, not criminal) in America, she has to raise her voice to try to talk over Ali Kirca. She is unable to explain herself, as he interrupts her to insist that she doesn't know which organizations are or aren't legal in America. He claims that his information has come from his report, which he holds up and reiterates that it is a report from the US Congress. As Kavakci begins her explanation, Ali Kirca focuses on organizing his notes and says 'yes' to himself. She says that the American government works very diligently on these matters and would never sanction the meeting of any illegal organization.

Ali Kirca acknowledges that the meeting was not illegal, and Kavakci insists over him that the organization was also not illegal. He continues, backpedalling, saying that Congress became concerned over a later meeting of the organization in which support was declared by Hamas. He raises his voice and nods his head during this statement.

Ali Kirca shuffles his papers as Kavakci begins to explain that such things were part of the group's later activities and insists with a smile that the meeting she attended was one in which many prominent scholarly and political figures participated.

Ali Kirca changes the subject to Kavakci's transition to Turkey. She confirms that she decided to go right into politics. She explains that she is very sensitive to what is going on around her so politics suits her personality. She expresses her desire that every person should be involved in politics and that Turkey should have an active civil society.

Ali Kirca asks who offered her the position as MP for the Virtue Party. She explains that she was working as the assistant to the president of the women's association of the Virtue Party. She recounts that the Virtue Party had seventeen candidates. Friends in the association recommended that she be a candidate for office.

Ali Kirca asks if Erbakan supported her in her nomination. She claims that she did not know of any support from him to become a candidate for the Virtue Party.

Ali Kirca says that she must have met with Erbakan at some point. Merve claims that they had no private meeting. He presses, asking if at any point either before her nomination or during the campaign she had a meeting with Erbakan. Kavakci replies that Erbakan is a political figure whom she respects, but insists that he had nothing to do with her nomination.

Ali Kirca lets Kavakci know that before switching to the topic of her swearing-in ceremony, he would like to ask one more personal question. He points out that she is dressed in a very chic manner. He asks if she keeps up with fashion and who dresses her. Kavacki gives out a nervous laugh and explains that she thinks people should wear what makes them look attractive. She explains that while some women like jewellery or shoes, she likes clothes. She confesses that she likes shopping and she likes to dress nicely. The interviewer seems to slip in a comment about her having money and being able to wear what she wants.

Ali Kirca asks if Kavacki selects her own outfits or if someone helps her co-ordinate them. Kavacki replies that she chooses her outfits herself. She says that she likes pastels, generally, and that she prefers plain outfits.

Ali Kirca transitions to 2 May. He recounts Merve's entrance into the hall of Turkey's Grand National Assembly. He explained that Anahaber [his TV show] was there before the building opened at 3 p.m., and that they were waiting anxiously to see her. He points out that she was not in line with the other Parliament members, but that she made her entrance later. He asks why she was not present at the beginning of the ceremony and whether her late entrance was co-ordinated by the Virtue Party leadership. [Just as she begins to speak, a recording of the Parliamentary proceedings in which Kavakci is wearing her headscarf begins to roll.] She explains that it was just a personal preference of hers.

The interviewer asks if she expected to attract attention by coming into the hall late. She denies that she had any such intention. [The footage from the Parliament shows Kavakci in her seat wearing her headscarf as other Parliament members bustle around her.]

The interviewer points out that Kavacki must have known that the public had been waiting eagerly to see how she would present herself at Parliament and that people were very sensitive about this issue. For this, he explains, a reaction to her lateness could not have been avoided. Kavakci responds that it is natural that the public, which has been whipped into fervour over this issue, would feel this way. She goes on to state that the hall holds 550 MPs, and it was a 'first' for the Parliament to have a headscarved woman in its midst, so of course people would take notice. And, she says, she believes that her presence was appropriate for a democratic environment.

Ali Kirca recounts a previous female Parliament member, Nesrin Unal, who normally wears a headscarf, but chose to remove her headscarf when taking the oath of office. Kavakci responds her choice to remove her headscarf was a personal one. The interviewer talks over Kavakci and repeats that Unal, as a person of faith, chose to remove her headscarf when taking the oath of office. He takes an accusatory tone, declaring that it didn't kill her [Unal]. Kavakci insists that for Unal, that was personally the correct decision, but that it has nothing to do with her own decision. Kavakci objects to the idea that there is a 'sore spot' among the public over the headscarf. She points to the rise of Islamic fashion within the district where she has been elected – a district that she claims is composed of people of a wide variety of socioeconomic backgrounds. She also notes that both men and women from outside of the Virtue Party supported her as a young, female candidate.

Ali Kirca jumps in to say that all people are happy to support the election of a woman to Parliament. Furthermore, he says that no one will bother her as she walks about in public wearing a headscarf. He recounts that even Bulent Ecevit made a speech following the incident at the swearing-in ceremony saying that women have the right to wear the headscarf without harassment. He acknowledges that the propaganda used during the campaign was very different. 'Nevertheless,' he continues, 'you came to the Parliament wearing the headscarf, knowing how sensitive the public is about it.' He recalls that the Welfare Party has been closed for four years, and he claims that the headscarf has become the flag of the previous tension over that party that is being re-embodied in the campaigns of the Virtue Party. He asks Kavakci if she believes the public wants that kind of renewed tension. She responds that she does not believe that there is a tension within the public, but that it is being created by certain parties. She insists that the Virtue Party is young, progressive and open to people of all cultural, economic and social backgrounds.

Ali Kirca jumps in, talking over her, acknowledging that at its base the Virtue Party is very young, but insists that the people at the top are the same as the Welfare Party. Kavakci elaborates [with a triumphant tone] that the Virtue Party even at the candidate level is composed of a wide variety of people – men, women, covered, uncovered – all brought together with a common sense of joy. She acknowledges a female writer who helped guide her decision to run in the election. Kavakci goes on to say that among the youth, the women …

Ali Kirca interrupts her and jumps in to say that no one doubts that these people are living freely in Turkey. However, he claims, the rules of the Parliament, posted in the building, generally state that women cannot enter the Parliament building wearing a headscarf. Kavakci responds [despite the interviewer repeatedly jumping in to talk over her] that the Constitution supersedes the rules of the Parliament. [Meanwhile the tape of her in the Parliament hall plays in the background.]

Ali Kirca goes on to make a distinction between the traditional headscarf that many a Turkish mother or grandmother would wear, and the outfit that Kavakci is wearing during the interview [he points to her] as well as the one that she wore at the swearing-in ceremony. He says that she came in wearing the version that has come to be a political symbol. Kavakci laughs as she replies that this is his interpretation. She points out that the style of her headscarf is the same as many women who do working-class jobs like cleaning, etc.

Ali Kirca talks over her, insisting that he respects her decision to wear the headscarf and that he has no problem with her wearing it in the TV studio. He uses his hands to emphasize his next point, which is that 'a seventy-five-word list of rules [for the Parliament] is one thing, but a seventy-five-year-old Republic – and within that time, not a single covered woman has entered that Parliament – furthermore in the last fifty years is another. Here Kavakci tries to jump in. Ali Kirca and Kavakci both raise their hands and voices and then Ali Kirca relents. Kavakci questions why her headscarf is a problem for a seventy-five-year-old Republic. She insists that she is exercising her rights as a citizen of a secular democracy. She says that there are many men and women from outside of the Virtue Party that support her in this area. She insists that the scarf on her head is completely a manifestation of her internal sense of conscience and freedom. She calls for her head covering not to be misunderstood. She insists that there is no greater importance for her headscarf than for those women working in the fields, etc. Just because she is educated, she says, does not mean that they are lower than her.

Ali Kirca talks over her, asking 'So, it's not a symbol?' She says, 'Excuse me', in order to be able to get her point across and asks that a distinction should not be made between the headscarves of 'educated' women and those of other women.

Ali Kirca again asks 'Is it not a symbol?' Kavakci responds that it is a way for her to express her religious faith. She insists that it is her right, and it is protected by the constitution. Ali Kirca says that no one has any objections to human rights in Turkey with regard to some matters, but that most people in Turkey know that in the last ten to fifteen years this type of headscarf has been used as the symbol of a political movement. He says that if you ask many of those who wear the headscarf, they will confirm that they do, in fact, wear it as a political symbol. He reiterates that Kavakci entered the Parliament wearing this symbol. Kavakci claims that those close to her will testify that she is honest and that her headscarf is a personal preference. Ali Kirca talks over her, saying that his words represent a large segment of public opinion. Kavakci says that the scarf had been politicized during the campaign, but that she has been covering her head since the age of eighteen and that it is a personal choice.

Ali Kirca talks over her, saying that Kavakci wore her headscarf to the swearing-in ceremony knowing what kind of response she would get. Kavakci says that there is no such sensitivity over the headscarf within the Turkish public.

The interviewer cuts her off; Kavakci clarifies that she was not trying to be a teacher, not trying to work as a doctor. She was going to serve as a Member of Parliament, believing in the supremacy of the law and knowing that the law was on her side.

As she tries to explain further Ali Kirca cuts her off by talking loudly over her saying that she believes there is no sensitivity over the headscarf in Turkish society and that she doesn't believe that this could have been a reason for the response to her headscarf in Parliament. But he points out, picking up a newspaper, reading a quote from Aydin Menderes, deputy leader of the Virtue Party, who made a statement saying that the headscarf has 'nothing to do with faith or religion … and is not in the service of democracy'. Kavakci says that she respects the opinions of Aydin Menderes but that there will be differences of opinion. She clarifies that she was acting with the authority given to her by the people.

The interviewer jumps in to suggest that she went in ignoring the Turkish regime. She denies this, explaining that they are all 'children of the Republic', living together. Her family lives here with many other types of people …

Here the interviewer cuts her off again. He then reiterates that Nesrin Unal, being sensitive to public opinion, took off her headscarf while taking the oath. Kavakci insists that this was Unal's personal preference and asks again why her headscarf is a problem. Ali Kirca explains [using his hand for emphasis] that it is the use of the headscarf as a political symbol and her bringing that symbol into the hall of the Parliament that is the problem and there is no other problem. Kavakci insists that she wears the headscarf not as a political symbol but as a requirement of her faith and a personal preference – that's it.

Ali Kirca reads a quotation from the newspaper from a high-ranking Virtue Party member saying that the headscarf has no connection with religion, faith or sexuality. Kavakci says that she is a software engineer, and acknowledges that there may be different views.

Ali Kirca reiterates that in spite of the fact that experienced politicians have predicted that the headscarf would create tension within Turkish society and that the deputy head of her party said that it was not a symbol of faith, she insisted on bringing that symbol into the Parliament. Kavakci responds that Menderes has his own views and she has hers. In the name of greater democratization, she says – the interviewer attempts to cut her off, but she asks him to let her speak – she insists that this is Aydin Menderes' own opinion.

Ali Kirca clarifies that it actually was the opinion of another well-informed Parliament member. Nevertheless, she insists, whether that statement was from someone within her own party, she is entitled to her own opinions. Just as she wore a white jacket and skirt to this interview, she explains, her headscarf is a personal preference related to her faith. While some may see it as too light or too extreme, she says, she has chosen her own (she claims 'moderate') path. She explains that she would like people to see her – not as a Parliamentarian with a headscarf – but as a dynamic young woman who is a software engineer, who has been educated abroad, who has experience and who wants to do things for her country. Kavakci recounts that she said several times before the cameras on the day that she entered the Parliament that – unfortunately many of things she does, such as going to mosque, are going to be broadcast …

At this point she and the interviewer are talking over one another so much that it is hard to tell what they are saying. In the end the interviewer's voice comes out stronger and he reiterates that Nesrin Unal, taking into consideration the feelings of the public, entered the Parliament hall without a headscarf. Kavakci states that she respects the decisions of others because she believes that her entrance into the Parliament building that day was a step forward for Turkey's democratization. She reminds Ali Kirca that democracy must include everyone within a society. So, she explains, she entered the Parliament as a true democrat, within the protection of the law.

She repeats that she was within the protection of the law as Ali Kirca talks over her to ask his next question: Was there any discussion or planning of these events within the Virtue Party? As he asks this, she talks over him to ask whether or not they will discuss what happened in the Parliament hall. She insists on discussing this before moving forward. She recounts that she entered the hall as a Member of Parliament and took her seat in a manner befitting a democracy.

At this point the interviewer interrupts her, asking: 'You knew you were going to get that reaction, didn't you?' Kavakci asks him not to interrupt and continues, saying that people can react in a way that befits a democracy.

Ali Kirca interjects that it was democratic and Kavakci disagrees. He blurts out something over her and she asks for him to please allow her to express her ideas. She explains that she does not believe that the reaction was very democratic because to her democracy means respecting the person across from you even if you have a difference of opinion or hold authority over him. For those reasons, she claims, she considered herself to be a true democrat and an enlightened individual.

Ali Kirca asks if she has entered the hall of Parliament again. She replies that she has. They talk over each other for a bit and then the interviewer asks if there were discussions within the Virtue Party about whether or not Kavakci should return to the hall of Parliament. Kavakci denies that there were such discussions. She explains that she returned to the Parliament hall again to take her oath, hoping that if people want to express their opinions, they would do it in a more democratic and humane fashion. She says that she didn't find any modernity, progressiveness or democracy in the reactions of the Democratic Left Party, which was present in the Parliament. She found their actions to be divisive, she says. The interviewer talks over her to acknowledge that the Democratic Left Party represents the views of its members.

Ali Kirca tries to change the subject to the fact that she made a late entrance and she fights to keep on the previous topic. She says that if she had responded with the same kind of behaviour with which she had been treated, it would not have been democratic because democracy means treating other people with respect even if they don't agree with you. She explains that she was not a random covered woman from off the street who entered the Parliament hall but a Member of Parliament.

Ali Kirca talks over her to change the topic to the second time that she entered the hall of Parliament. She explains that she did so in order to take her oath but she decided that the atmosphere was not one that supported her rights. He asks if it was she or the party that decided this. She responds that it was her decision. The interviewer asks if she had any contact with Erbakan during this time.

The interviewer asks if she will go back to the Parliament. She replies that she will. He asks when she will go to take her oath. She clarifies that the Prime Minister did not give her an ultimatum to either remove her headscarf or leave the Parliament hall. She says she hopes that she will make her oath in the Parliament hall using the right to cover her head that is granted to her in the constitution. The interviewer asks 'when?' and she says, 'In the days going forward.'

Ali Kirca asks what she will do if she gets the same reception. She replies that she will tell the Prime Minister that the law is on her side. If they agree, they will swear her in. She confesses meekly that she will not take the oath if they refuse to administer it and that she would not be a Member of Parliament. She says she is a person who obeys the rules. She begins to explain that the Parliament is not a place ruled by popular will when the interviewer begins to talk over her and she protests.

Ali Kirca says that there is a rumour that a member of the Virtue Party might take over leadership of the General Management Committee in the Parliament and will make the decision about whether or not she should be sworn in to Parliament. He asks if she is waiting for that to happen. Kavakci repeats that she is within her rights and she awaits permission to take her oath regardless of who is president.

The interviewer asks if she will try again if she receives the same response that she saw on 2 May. Kavakci says that no one can go up against the decision of the Prime Minister. She says that she expects everyone to act in a manner befitting a democracy. She expresses her opinion that the reaction of the other Parliamentarians was inappropriate given the fact that she wasn't bothering anyone. She is not the kind of person who would bother other people, she explains, and that she expects the same from others. She says she believes that whatever the Prime Minister decides, all Parliament members are obliged to adhere to that decision.

Ali Kirca asks what she thinks of the statement by the deputy head of her party that the headscarf is 'Neither being used, nor in the service of democracy ...' She asks what relevance a headscarf has to democracy. 'What relevance does my skirt have?' She repeats that it is a personal choice as someone who happens to be religious. She points to the article of the constitution that protects this freedom.

Ali Kirca mentions the protests held by the Democratic Left Party and other parties in response to Kavakci's action. He says that all parties except the Virtue Party came out against her. He asks what she expects will happen in Turkey in terms of social tension if she tries to take the oath. She responds that Turkey is in fact living in peace. He interrupts her to express his agreement and Kavakci points out that he is cutting her off. Kavakci describes close friends of hers whose social and religious views are quite different from her own. Despite this, she says, young people in Turkey are getting along fine.

At this point [again] they talk over each other and the dialogue is difficult to understand. Kavakci reiterates that her presence in the Parliament was a step forward for Turkish democracy. She expresses the hope that there will be more Parliamentarians from diverse cultural, religious and family backgrounds. Women especially, she hopes, will have a greater presence in Parliament. She says Turkey needs peace without any divisions.

Kavakci tries to reiterate that she took her seat in Parliament, not bothering anyone, while the interviewer talks over her saying that: 'It was done on purpose and it could have been done another way.' She insists that she doesn't understand how the scarf on her head makes her different from the other five hundred or so MPs in the room. He insists that there has been discussion of its use as a political symbol and is trying to get the questions of the public across to her.

Ali Kirca says that for the sake of Turkey's future, he hopes that there will be more good-natured feeling and behaviour within the Parliament. Kavakci smiles broadly and agrees. Thank-yous exchanged. Ali Kirca reiterates that Anahaber has tried to bring answers to the questions on their minds in Kavakci's own words. The questions are out there, the answers are out there, he asks the public to consider them for themselves.[9]

Once they were off the air, Ali Kirca was again impolite, not even saying 'good-bye' to Merve Kavakci when she left the studio. This is not acceptable behaviour in Turkey, where such pleasantries are expected by all, even when entering and leaving a taxi or store. Nonetheless, Merve felt as if she had been victorious, that Ali Kirca was surprised that his well-known tactic of bombarding his guests with words to leave them defenceless was not effective with her, and that is why he can be seen shuffling papers during the interview and ignoring her.

When they were leaving in the elevator a woman reporter asked Merve several times, 'Merve Hanim, it is said that you do not send your children to school; is this true?' At first Merve hadn't a clue what she was talking about. She responded that this was not the case; that she thought it better for the children to stay home a few days. Reporters had been harassing the students and the teachers at her children's school about whether Merve's children were covered or not. Their photos were stolen by reporters from the classroom bulletin board.

The group next went to Kanal 7, the Islamic-friendly station, where Merve would not be harangued, bombarded with multiple questions and comments at the same time, asked the same question a dozen times, and have each comment challenged. An indication of that friendliness was a phone call she received from Sefer Turan, the foreign affairs correspondent for Kanal 7, before the interview. Merve had been asked by Kirca about her association with Ishak al-Farhan, a Parliamentarian from Jordan who was known for his support of Palestine. The press was making a big deal about this speech, claiming that it was evidence that Merve supported terrorist groups. In fact, Turan contacted Ishak al-Farhan, who told him that in 1991 he had made a special trip to visit Demirel and Eceivit along with a group of other deputies from Jordan. If this showed that Merve were associating with terrorists, it follows logically that so were Demirel and Ecevit. Despite this fact, the press continued attacking her of guilt by association.

Ahmet Hakan Coskun was upset and offended that his show did not appear first as promised by Gul. Merve apologized, told him it was against her principles and that she was at the mercy of her party. As expected, the interview went well. After the programme she collapsed on the black couch in Zahit Akman's office, another news anchor. It had been a tortuously tiring two days and she needed sleep.

Afterwards, they dropped her at her modest walk-up apartment in the Mebusevleri district of Ankara where she and Ravza dragged themselves up the nine flights of stairs to their apartment on the top, fifth floor.

Then Merve, who had spent the day making a case to the people of Turkey, giving a press conference to the entire Turkish media, followed by two long interviews on television, finally looked at the day's papers. She was totally crushed at the negative attacks, the lies, the false accusations and the biased reporting. It seemed to come from everywhere and anyone.

This was only the beginning.

Notes

1 Esra Dogru Arsan, 'Medy-Guc Idelogoji Ekseninde Merve Kavakci Haberlerinin Iki Farkli Sunumu', in *Haber Hakikat ve Iktidar Iliskisi*, edited by Ciler Dursun, Kesit Tanitim Ltd, Ankara, Turkey, 2004.
2 Published with permission of the author, Dr Esra Arsan.
3 http://en.wikipedia.org/wiki/Censorship_in_Turkey.
4 *Turkish Daily News*, 5 October 2010.
5 Esra Dogru Arsan, 'Medy-Guc Idelogoji Ekseninde Merve Kavakci Haberlerinin Iki Farkli Sunumu'.
6 Yavuz, pp. 275–276.
7 Ahmet T. Kuru, *Secularism and State Policies Towards Religion: The United States, France and Turkey*, Cambridge University Press, 2009.
8 Nicole Pope, *Today's Zaman*, 15 October 2010.
9 Many thanks to Dayla Rogers for watching the video of Merve's interview with Ali Kirca and providing this somewhat detailed summary.

7

The Criminalization of Merve Kavakci

—

It is a sad irony that even if Merve Kavakci had managed to be sworn in as a Member of the Turkish Parliament, in all likelihood it would not have mattered. She would have been blocked from office anyway. It was not a matter of law at all, but the all-powerful forces aligned against her. Their power would have rendered insignificant the 'legal' impact of a one-minute oath-taking ceremony. She seemed at this time to have an unshakable belief in the law, as if somehow the law in Turkey in 1999 would have righted the wrong that was done to her.

Dr M. Hakan Yavuz, in his *Islamic Political Identity in Turkey* (Oxford University Press), in a chapter entitled 'The Securitization of Islam and the Triumph of the AKP', accurately summarized the progressive, distorted characterization of Merve Kavakci after her entrance into the Parliament:

> President Demirel accused Kavakcı of being an 'agent provocateur working for radical Islamic states,' and the chief prosecutor opened a case against the FP [Virtue Party] at the CC [Constitutional Court] on 7 May 1999. Since Kemalist state ideology criminalized all forms of identity claims, Kavakci was presented first as the 'other.' She then was portrayed not as a woman but as a militant, not as a politician but as a member of HAMAS, and even not as a Muslim but merely as an ideological symbol. This criminalization of opposition became the politics of the Turkish state in the late 1990s. The chief public prosecutor accused the 'FP of being vampires touring the country and gorging on ignorance.'[1]

The securitization of laws and regulations in Turkey, starting with the 1982 Constitution written by the 1980 coup government, followed by the implementation of the 28 February 1997 coup process, facilitated the prosecution of dissenters, the opposition and Islamic-friendly politicians and journalists, a process fully supported by an entrenched Kemalist judiciary. Tayyip Erdogan was but one example of someone who was prosecuted, as we know from above, for 'inciting hatred' by reading a poem found in textbooks, an easy way to put him aside during the 1999 elections.

The National Security Council, beginning 28 February, defined Islamic movements as internal enemies. Not only had the Welfare Party been shut down, but also the Islamic-oriented business association, MUSIAD, was charged with 'attempting to build a state on religious principles'. In 1999 the government continued to take steps to crack down on these 'internal enemies'. On 15 January the Council of Ministers set up a centre to better coordinate its 'measures against reaction'. Two weeks later, Prime Minister Ecevit concerned with 'reactionary, destructive and separatist activities against the regime' sent out a circular to provincial governors and prosecutors that included the following directives.

> Political exploitation of religion on politics, economy, trade, social life and mass support and activities to politicize religion will absolutely be prevented. To this end the Ministers in the capital and the governors in the countryside will take the legal precautions without hesitation. Necessary legal proceedings will be taken against those, who conduct reactionary, destructive and separatist activities, without hesitation.
>
> This is a duty for the protection of the Republic. The Republican prosecutors will show the same sensitivity. The governors and prosecutors of the Republic will lead the struggle jointly and in co-ordination. The basis of this activity is determination and stability.
>
> In particular all radio and TV stations broadcasting reactionary, destructive and separatist programmes will be supervised within the established system. Harmful programmes will be prevented and the responsible persons will be brought to justice.
>
> It has to be considered that those active for the destruction of the regime have developed new methods in order to make the measures ineffective. One has to be alert for cooperation, which those working for destruction and separatism have developed with those working for reactionism. All public personnel have to avoid appearing in a manner that weakens the struggle against reactionism. Particular sensitivity has to be shown in the implementation of the rules on dressing.[2]

In addition:

> On 5 February the BTK [Minister's Office] decided to establish close control for the sects and, if necessary, conduct raids on the centres. During the meeting the work on prevention of separatist and reactionary activities was evaluated and it was decided to be alert to reactionary activities during elections and control the speeches of representatives of political parties in line with the circular of the Prime Minister.[3]

The government's efforts to go after Merve Kavakci 'without hesitation' progressed within this background, an environment of broad-based violations of human rights that included extra-judicial executions, political killings, disappearances, torture, censorship, widespread wire-tapping, imprisoned journalists and repression of free speech. Details can be found in a 344-page report, *The Human Rights Foundation of Turkey's Report of 1999*. Some examples:

> In 1999 persons with dissident views on the State's politics and critics met with oppressive punishment. Trade unions, associations, political parties and similar organizations and those active in them in particular human rights activists faced detention, trials and imprisonment for such activities.
> 246 people were convicted of 'incitement to enmity and hatred'.
> 101 people were imprisoned for 'insult of state organs'.
> A total of 2,604 cases were launched against 3,174 defendants on charges of having violated the Press Law. 434 cases ended in acquittal and 1,911 cases resulted in convictions.
> There are a number of legal obstacles for the realization of the freedom of expression in Turkey. Frequently used Articles of the Turkish Penal Code (TPC) are Articles 159 and 312, but also Articles 155 and 311 TPC are used to punish certain opinions. The Law to Fight Terrorism and in particular Articles 6, 7 and 8 of this Law No. 3713 are used against the opposition. Law No. 5816 on Protection of Ataturk, the Press and the Law on Radio and TV broadcast (RTUK) are other laws restricting freedom of expression. A special law on the administration of provinces, martial law and the law on a state of emergency provide for additional measures against critical voices.[4]

The criminalization of Merve Kavakci was begun in earnest by the state and the new government when it became clear that she would not remove her headscarf in Parliament after her election. They started collecting and uncovering as much information as possible against her, without regard to any particular processes, rules of law, or fairness. The military initially threatened to get directly involved to stop her, from the days before her possible entrance into Parliament. Now, completely ignoring the legality of her election, the state went after her to invalidate her election and take her out of the political scene.

The President of Turkey launched her criminalization with warnings before the incident and only hours after it, making declarations without any adjudication whatsoever, accusing her of separatism and being an 'agent provocateur', a characterization that has been quoted in practically every book and news article on the subject, and is still used today in Turkey by secularists who continue to criticize positive articles about Merve Kavakci. The next day Demirel repeated his allegations (see later).

It is regrettable that in the internal-enemy-obsessed atmosphere of the day many academics and journalists have passed on without scrutiny, criticism, or qualification the pronouncements of the elected leaders, courts, prosecutors, and law-making bodies of Turkey regarding this incident, whose sole objective was ridding themselves of her.

Merve Kavakci struggled over the next six months to avoid the tortuous press, to avoid being imprisoned, to protect her family, to make her case, to uphold the law and to regain her seat in Parliament against a significant array of forces. She was trapped in a box but did not know how to stop fighting. It was not in her nature. Yet, she was also suffering, banging into one wall after another, taking the false accusations and tortured logic of those who opposed her at face value, and fighting back as if logical responses and a good legal defence would matter. They did not.

4 May

On 4 May 1999 at 3 a.m., a reporter for the *Hurriyet* newspaper rang the doorbell, awakening the Kavacki family. Her mother told the reporter that it was too early for questions. He persisted, ringing the bell until she had to pull it apart, basically breaking it. Osman Ulusoy came and kept guard outside their door until morning.

Merve performed the *fajr* (morning prayer) with the first light of day, then took a short nap, getting some much-needed rest. She felt good about her television interviews, especially her ability to deal with the aggressive Ali Kirca.

Calls began to come in from all over Turkey and the rest of the world offering support. The party's offices were besieged with faxes as well, almost all of them favourable, some saying 'we wish we didn't vote for CHP' and others stating, 'you are our dignity, our hero'. The (religiously) conservative media were publishing these faxes as full-page features and would do so for months. Internationally, opposition to her treatment came mainly from the Islamic world, however. In Jordan and Iran women organized protest marches in support of her. In Kuwait, members of Parliament were proposing a cut in trade with Turkey. A businessman from Qatar chose Merve as a role model for his daughter and offered to buy the scarf she wore that infamous day in the Parliament for US$500,000. Messages came from throughout the Muslim world.

In America, a delegation of leaders from several organizations, the Council of American Islamic Relations, Islamic Society of North America, Muslim Public Actions Committee, North American Council of Muslim Women and American-Arab Anti-Defamation Council, were meeting with President Clinton in Washington and Secretary of State Albright. In addition, an organization called SUM (Sisters United for Merve) led by a young American woman, Manal Omar, was demonstrating for days in front of the Turkish Embassy in Washington and the White House. In two American universities, student organizations led by their Muslim Student Association declared 'Support for the Head Cover Week' and distributed headscarves all week.

However, these were not mainstream American groups of any kind, nor was there any noticeable support for Merve from outside the Middle East. Thus, none of this mattered much in Turkey. If anything, women demonstrating in Iran hurt her, reaffirming the influence of those from outside of Turkey, from supporters of 'radical Islam'. From Paris, where he was on a state visit, President Demirel issued one salvo after another at Merve and was widely quoted in the press the following day:

> Today we – and the world – perceive the turban as the emblem of fundamentalism. And fundamentalism means moving away from a contemporary way of living. It means replacing the contemporary law with Shariah. Iran and Afghanistan have gone through this. And there are efforts to attempt that in Algeria – at the cost of the lives of over 100,000 people.[5]

I did not say that the deputy in question, Merve Kavakci, had external connections. But I used the word 'agent provocateur' deliberately. I think the state has information to that effect.[6]

You cannot make me say she should take the oath in that manner or she should not do it. I am asking you how can she take the oath while wearing a headscarf? I am saying no more than that.[7]

'Fundamentalism' is one of those words that is often at the centre of conflicts over Islam and its misconceptions, and is used extensively in a negative way in the West. Akbar S. Ahmed aptly clarified its meaning in *Islam Today: A Short Introduction to the Muslim World*:

Western commentators often use – or misuse – terms taken from Christianity and apply them to Islam. One of the most commonly used is fundamentalism. As we know, in its original application it means someone who believes in the fundamentals of religion, that in the Bible and the scriptures. In that sense every Muslim is a fundamentalist, believing in the Qur'an and the Prophet. However, in the manner that it is used in the media, to mean a fanatic or extremist, it does not illuminate either Muslim thought or Muslim society. In the Christian context it is a useful concept. In the Muslim context it simply confuses because by definition every Muslim believes in the fundamentals of Islam. But even Muslims differ in their ideas about how, and to what extent, to apply Islamic ideas to the modern world. These differences are noted from age to age country to country, indeed individual to individual. Yet a Muslim even talking of Islam will be quickly slapped with the label fundamentalist in the Western media.[8]

(Another excellent work on Islam, as well as this topic, is *Islam: A Short History* by Karen Armstrong).

As President Demirel and secularists in Turkey illustrated, the use, or misuse, of 'fundamentalism' as an accusation was not limited to the West. Other common words in their accusatory vocabulary were fanaticism and reactionism. For example, several women's organizations in Turkey also announced their opposition, including the Association for the Support and Training of Female Candidates (KADER), the one where Merve was given the cold shoulder. They expressed their pleasure with the twenty-three female deputies who were elected this time. However, 'KADER, espousing the principle of supporting women candidates who will work for the secular republic's being a total democracy and who will oppose all kinds of fanaticism, views with regret Kavakci being a "pawn" in the hands of fanatical politicians.'[9] Once again, Merve is viewed as being manipulated and is not acting on her own. KADER's opposition to Merve also illustrates the complete lack of solidarity among secular feminist groups with Muslim women. Driving home this point, the Kemalist view that Islamic women are not part of the 'legitimate' women's movement, Ecevit was reported as saying that he 'welcomed that there were some women wearing headscarves among the ones who criticized Merve Kavakci', although he did not mention who they were. And, as was noted before, the DSP had tried to engineer a demonstration of women deputies surrounding the podium in the Parliament to show that other women were against her. There were two separate women's movements in Turkey then, as now. In Turkey 'sisterhood' is also polarized.

The investigation, or rather collection of dirt, by the government and the press was yielding results. All kinds of other false accusations, assumptions and blatant lies began to be disseminated, similar to the ones raised exhaustingly and repeatedly by Ali Kirca, but worse. *Milliyet* reported that another deputy from ANAP, who met with Demirel before his trip to France, said on 4 May: 'I think the President has some information about Merve Kavakci, the VP deputy. If this is not true, the President wouldn't describe her as an agent and provocateur. We know that she has relations with other countries.' *Milliyet* reported the next day that 'her father has relations with the Palestinian Islamic Union (IAP) in the US. IAP is a supporter of the HAMAS (Islamic Resistance Organization), a terrorist organization.' *Hurriyet* said: 'Merve lied when she said she had to drop out of the medical faculty because of her headscarf ban. She was expelled because she failed her exams.' *Sabah* claimed: 'Merve's Hamas connection – a 1988 report presented to the US Congress refers to the meeting of an organization called the Palestine Islamic Union, which is pro-Hamas, a terrorist organization. Kavakci had made a speech at that meeting.' [In this case the 'Kavakci' referenced was actually Merve's father, who also gave speeches for the US State Department.] To add a mistruth to a lie, *Milliyet* quoted Kavakci as saying that she did take part in the meeting but that she did not know they were terrorists. An official of the union, Muhammed Usame, said Kavakci had attended the meeting but was not a member of the organization.[10]

Several people pushed for the punishment of those parties that did not join the attack against her in the Parliament. They questioned why they were so silent. For example, *Radikal* reported also that on 4 May there were 'harsh discussions' in the ANAP party because of their silence during the protest against Merve. Berna Ylmaz, the wife of the leader of the Motherland Party (ANAP), criticized the ANAP for their silence and a female ANAP member, Melike Hasefe, resigned. And *Sabah* reported that Aydin Menderes, the deputy leader of the Virtue Party (VP), 'harshly criticized the policy of his party in the headscarf crisis in the Parliament. Menderes said that the party was losing blood and that if they stretch the tread too much, it will break off.'

Even the Supreme Board of Elections (YSK) felt the need to be defensive. After all, they approved Merve to run for Parliament. On 4 May they stated that it was not their responsibility to get a photo from candidates or to get involved in the headscarf issue. However, Merve Kavakci did submit her photo and was investigated by them. The YSK also said that the behaviour and dress of candidates is the responsibility of the Office of the Parliament Speaker. It stated that 'the obstacles for being elected as a deputy are listed in the tenth and eleventh articles of the Deputy Election Law. The YSK requested the candidate deputy lists of the political parties for the 18 April elections, it carried out the necessary investigations within the framework of its investigation authority, completed the deficiencies and issued the definite candidate lists in the Official Gazette of March 9, 1999.' In other words, don't blame us. The YSK had announced the names of the elected candidates, including Merve Safa Kavakci, officially in the Official Gazette on 27 April 1999.

The refusal of Septioglu to throw Merve out of the Parliament, despite two requests to do so, also did not escape blame. *Sabah's* Gungor Mengi pointed out the need for the Parliament to 'take steps through legal channels' to immediately amend the bylaws to ban headscarves in the Parliament and to no longer let the first session of Parliament be chaired by the oldest deputy. As all this occurred before the press found out that Septioglu had attempted to let Merve be sworn in before midnight, one can easily speculate how the reaction would have escalated in the news if Septioglu's behaviour had leaked out.

In another *Sabah* article, under the headline 'Remove Your Hand, Fiend', Necmettin Erbakan was attacked for 'doing everything to punish the nation for refusing to fall into the trap you have laid out', once more pointing to Merve's manipulation.

In this overwhelmingly hostile environment, Recai Kutan held a press conference at the Parliament on 4 May, a day late, waiting until (he said) some of the tension had subsided. Instead, by the time of his press conference, it had accelerated. He accused the DSP of 'bullying' that was planned by Ecevit, proven by the prepared speech he pulled out of his pocket (on a scrap of paper). Although he asserted the continuance of the Virtue Party's struggle for democratic principles, he stated that Nazli Ilicak, in whose care Merve Kavakci had been entrusted, 'displayed her own stance and not that of the party'. This referred to Nazli bringing Merve into the Parliament. The *Turkish Daily News* reported, 'Kutan asserted that intra-party democracy works well in his party, that Kavakci had made her decision of her own free will and that no party officials had influenced her decision.' However, as we know, this was not true. Merve was not allowed to enter the Parliament by the party after the recess. Once again, the party was covering up its role in keeping her out and using the 'it's-her-choice' line to explain other actions, and claiming also that Nazli Ilicak acted on her own as well. Kutan denied that Merve was supported by outside powers and denied that she was a spy, in opposition to Demirel's claims dispersed throughout Turkey.

Was the 'it-was-her-choice' stance a way for the party to save face? Or does it reveal the red lines of women's rights that an Islamic-friendly party cannot cross, leaving it up to its covered women to make the decisions on their own? As Jenny White notes, even when activist women demonstrated at universities and marched on Ankara a year earlier to demand the right to wear headscarves in the university, they were not placed in an equal position with male activists. This led to dissension within the party:

> Dissonance within the party was controlled by populist rhetoric, the judicious use of unifying symbols in neutral contexts, and avoidance of language that would acknowledge cleavages. Party leaders deflected public statements on divisive issues, allowing differences in the lower ranks between men and women activists to be attributed to personal points of view.[11]

Even though the party in question here was Welfare, one wonders if the reliance on 'personal points of view' to explain Merve's activism was also the way Virtue's leaders were dealing with her and providing an explanation for her not cooperating with them.

Regardless, it's obvious that the party would not take responsibility for Merve's actions, nor defend her right to take her seat. I asked Kutan specifically whether the party ruled against her returning to the Parliament and he would only say, through a translator, 'it may not have been proper at that moment'.[12] On the day of Kutan's press conference, according to the *Turkish Daily News*, 'It was later reported that Ozkan [Deputy Prime Minister and Ecevit's right-hand man] had spoken with VP [Virtue Party] executives and persuaded them to keep Kavakci from entering the General Assembly after the recess.'[13] In the same paper on the same day in an editorial, Ilnur Cevik wrote that after the break 'veteran Deputy Kamran Inan worked out a compromise in which Kavakci would not return to the plenary session for the day ...' These pressures may have also played a part.

On this Tuesday morning, two days after the incident, Merve Kavakci awoke once again to a nightmare in the aftermath of her walk into the Parliament two days earlier. The constant news about her, on television, radio and in the papers, was overwhelming. For Merve it was something beyond comprehension, as if the country didn't have any other important issues to address. It would be repeated all day, every day, this 'news' about her, and each ensuing day she went from shock to amazement to a burning sensation. Even some of her neighbours began to cooperate with the media, giving interviews or providing their homes to reporters who ambushed her and her family.

Osman Ulusoy picked up Merve and Ravza and brought them to the Parliament, trailed by a convoy of the media, where Kutan and Salih Kapusuz waited for them in the party's office, which was so crowded that she was unable to talk to him about how to handle the media barrage. She then asked Kapusuz what could be done, but, annoyed, he told Merve to wait, that there were more important things to do at the moment. Ravza kept pressing him about the harassing phone calls day and night. She thought that their safety was being threatened and wanted to transfer to special residences for Parliament members in the Oran district of Ankara. Kapusuz told her to just turn their cell phones off and unplug the landlines.

On 4 May the *Turkish Daily News* reported that Merve Kavakci 'created havoc in Parliament by showing up with a headscarf', describing her as the provoker as opposed to the DSP deputies. However, they did present her views based on her press conference, quoting her: 'They say that my headscarf is a political symbol. But I wear this headscarf because of my faith, because of my personal choice.'[14] They repeated her argument that Article 2 of the Constitution should be implemented, and cited what that article says: 'The Republic of Turkey is a democratic, secular and social state governed by the rule of law: bearing in mind the concepts of public peace, national solidarity and justice; respecting human rights; loyal to the nationalism of Ataturk ...' And they repeated her claim that 'Yesterday [Sunday], democracy suffered a setback in Parliament.' Merve may not have seen this article because it was in English and likely not available in the news stands. As the time the *Turkish Daily News* was an independent daily and generally objective in its reporting.

This article also presented some bad news for her, repeated elsewhere, noting that Vural Savas, the Chief Prosecutor of the Court of Appeals in the Ankara State Security Court, was investigating the incident and that Savas had asked for videotapes showing her in the Parliament wearing a headscarf. 'The investigation will determine whether Kavakci violated Article 312 of the Turkish Penal Code, which stipulates penalties for actions of inciting hatred among people based on differences of class, race, religion and ethnicity.' The article stated that Savas 'only said that the authorities would do whatever the Constitution requires. He would have a lot more to say later in his filing.' Indeed, he did. On 7 May he filed a case with the Constitutional Court to outlaw the Virtue Party, charging that it was trying to put Turkey under Islamic law. In the indictment he called the Virtue Party a 'malignant tumour' and its members 'blood-sucking vampires'.[15] Separate charges were filed against Merve Kavakci for inciting hatred. Less than a week later the VP Deputy from Trabzon, Seref Malkoc, filed a complaint against Vural Savas stating that he had 'insulted his honour and dignity'. Mr Savas responded by explaining that a prosecutor has the right to make such characterizations for clarification purposes and that one needs to be sensitized to the issues of Turkey's integrity to protect the country and its Constitution.[16]

In summary, while Merve thought the law and Constitution were the reasons she should be seated in the Parliament, others felt her actions were unlawful and warranted a jail sentence. The prevailing Kemalist view in the press was articulated by Kemal Balci, ironically in this same issue of the *Turkish Daily News*:

Acceptance of women wearing headscarves, which is represented as a human rights issue and must for freedom of religion by the supporters of political Islam, has not been a serious problem among the public in the seventy-five-year history of the Republic. Political Islam supporters who are determined to re-organize the dress code at state offices according to the rules of Islam aim to escalate the problem via classes and mass demonstrations ...

The headscarf controversy in Turkey, an overwhelmingly Muslim country, is causing turmoil among the public as it paints a picture of women who don't wear headscarves as non-believers, thereby blocking the social tolerance that is needed for the solution. Supporters of political Islam who have shut their ears to comments that say civil servants wearing headscarves could increase polarization among citizens and could harm social peace are insistent on the issue. During this period of rapid and increasing polarization between secularists and anti-secularists, Kavakci's act caused a peak. This move, in which the headscarf that is viewed as the symbol of people supporting an Islamic Republic based on Shariah instead of a secular regime, has nearly destroyed the atmosphere of social tolerance. Entering Parliament with a headscarf, which is known as the uniform of Iran's Shiites, rather than wearing modern clothes was not an acceptable move that could easily be ventured.[17]

Merve decided not to give any more interviews to the Turkish media because she felt the newspapers were writing whatever they wanted regardless of what she said. Instead she spoke to the foreign press. That morning she was interviewed by Al-Jazeera television and the German *Der Spiegel* magazine. Although disheartened by the attacks in Turkey that made her country look bad, she wanted to use her exposure to help untold thousands of young girls who had suffered the oppression of the headscarf ban. She saw Ecevit as the guilty party, the person who created the tension, just the opposite of what Ali Kirca and the rest of the mainstream press repeatedly implied.

During one of her interviews, Abdullah Gul entered the room and asked her to sign a power of attorney for lawyers to file cases on her behalf. Merve signed the papers which, she says, resulted in damaging errors later on. She regretted not getting her own lawyer during her candidacy, something that was recommended to her. She maintains that if she had been more prepared before the elections, things might have turned out differently. Looking back on how the entire government and state apparatus were aligned against her, regardless of various laws, it's doubtful that different lawyers would have helped her. At this time all laws and, in particular, their administration by the courts, seemed to favour the interests of state preservation, secularism and Ataturkism.

Meanwhile, in the eastern province of Malatya, Merve's actions were supported by thousands of students who were already demonstrating against the local state university for denying entrance to headscarved students. About 160 were arrested.[18]

Merve returned home that evening but was no longer able to climb the stairs of her apartment building peacefully. A door suddenly opened on the third floor and a reporter lunged towards her, following her up the stairs with a camera. Osman stopped him and they were barely able to keep him out of their apartment. As noted above, some of Merve's neighbours were also out to 'get' her and were harbouring the media.

May 5: Ambush at Anittepe Elementary School

After two days of her children missing school, Merve decided to take them again, but she was unaware that the media were waiting for them. Only after this incident did she find out that reporters had been asking her children's teachers about whether they were headscarved, and took their pictures from the school bulletin board.

Fatima Kavakci, Merve's oldest daughter, was eight when this traumatic incident occurred. Today she is a young woman, college educated, bi-lingual and headscarved like her mother. Her memories of that day follow:

> I remember that day like it was yesterday. I even wrote an essay of that moment for my English class in eighth grade. I remember exactly how the day began and how the day ended for Mariam and I.
>
> We got up early around the usual time, 7 o'clock in the morning. We were getting ready for breakfast so I quickly put on my blue uniform with the detachable white collar buttoned around my neck. My grandmother was visiting from Dallas to help my mom and my great-grandmother had been taking care of us and giving moral support. So, my grandmother, whom I called 'Nenne' ever since I could speak, brushed my hair that morning and put my hair up in a beautiful bun. I told her I wanted it to be Cinderella style (in a bun). I didn't have a crown but she put two gold clips on both sides that pushed my hair back (I guess this would be the ideal Cinderella look for an elementary school student in Turkey).

I felt beautiful, confident, and poised just the way my mom and grandmother raised my sister and I to be.

That morning was not very different from other morning commotions since my mom's candidacy to the Turkish Parliament. The media was at the steps of our apartment's entrance 24/7. They were there when we would leave the house and return towards the end of the day. But, that particular morning, there was an atmosphere of unease that I sensed from my mom and grandma. They were talking with each other while Mariam and I had our breakfast. Someone had to take us to school soon before it was 8 o'clock. My mom was running late and she needed to get to the office at the headquarters of the Virtue Party. My mom said to my grandma, I'll drop-off the kids to school and head to work from there since it's on the way. My grandma held out our backpacks as we put our shoes on. We gave a big hug to her and my ninety-five-year-old great-grandma before heading out. Surprisingly, as we walked five floors down to the entrance of our apartment, there were not many reporters. We were quickly escorted to the car by my mom's bodyguards and we drove straight to school. Funny thing is, our school is only six blocks from our home. Mariam and I had been walking to school by ourselves since third grade. Even though we insisted on walking by ourselves as we had been doing for a year and a half, my mom didn't think it would be safe during this period.

As we pulled up to the front gate of the school we noticed some reporters standing around. Our driver, Osman Bey, said 'Merve Hanim, what should we do?' And my mom replied, 'Let's go, we're going to be late.' Mariam and I got down from the car first and my mother followed right behind us. For a moment I remember all three of us lingering at the corner of the gate with some hesitation thinking, 'Okay, what's this crowd all about?'

I thought to myself, is there a reason that reporters are at school and not in front of our apartment? Well, we were about to find out. So, as we walked in through the thin metal barred gate of the school, I noticed a man slouching against the handrail of the narrow pathway that led to the courtyard. He was looking around while a few other reporters ahead of him were talking to some of the students. My mom was in the middle with Mariam on her right side, and I was walking to her left. Interestingly, I came eye to eye with the slouching reporter. It took him a moment to realize that we had arrived. Immediately, almost with panic-like behaviour he straightened up, and looking directly and intently into my eyes, he said, 'Baslayin! Baslayin!' which means 'Start! Start!' Because he was looking so intently at my face, I thought, 'Start? What are we supposed to do? Did I miss something?' I glanced over to my mom for clarification as to 'what does he mean by "start"?'

It immediately hit me and there was no need for an explanation. There were four or five reporters and two of them that had cameras. The two cameramen were walking backwards a few feet ahead of us concentrating intently on not missing even a second of this staged verbal lynching ceremony. This may sound a bit funny, but the other three reporters were like goat-herders gathering the kids around and telling them to get louder and louder as they began yelling in chorus, 'Turkiye Laiktir Laik Kalacak!!!' ('Turkey is secular and it will remain secular!!!')

Of course, I immediately got goose bumps. I was scared, angry, upset, saddened all at once and in SHOCK. The experience is so vivid and clear in my recollection of that exact moment. My mom began to increase her pace as we crossed the narrow pathway into the courtyard and towards the entrance of the Anittepe school building. I remember not being able to see ahead, I couldn't see where I was walking. The bodyguards were carefully trying to make way for us to move forward. My mom's grip on my right hand got tighter and tighter. At one point I tugged at her arm telling her my hand hurts, but she didn't hear. I tried to pull my hand away from her grip, but there was no use. During these few minutes of trying to get through the crowd of yelling students, time seemed endless. I remember looking to the ground the whole time I was walking with my mom's tight grip of my hand. My head was held high, but I knew I did not want to look up, because if I did look up, and if I had seen the faces of those students, I knew I would hate them. I didn't want any enemies and did not want to be in conflict with anyone. In those minutes, anger and frustration was building up inside of me. After what seemed like two minutes of walking with eyes concentrated on my footsteps, I decided to look up at the crowd. I was hoping not to see a familiar face, but to my regret I did. I saw one kid from my classroom and I was going to question him later.

Finally, we were only a few steps away from the school building door. The student crowd had surrounded us all the way to the entrance. My mom, literally, pushed us through the doorway towards the Vice-Principal who was standing near the door. He immediately took us and in a rush let my mom know that it's all right and that we're safe in the school. I looked at my mom to say bye, I love you, or something but she didn't really see me. She was calm and cool, but I could tell she was furious at what had just happened to all three of us. Mariam and I went to our fourth-grade classroom and most of our classmates were there. Our teacher greeted us as she always did with a lovely smile. But it took a while for the shock to wear off. Before I took a seat, I went to the kid who I'd spotted when I looked up at the crowd of students. I knew I had to control myself and not get angry. I went up to him and in a loud tone said, 'Why did you all do that?' He said, 'They gave us money and told us we would be on TV.' I said, 'Who?' The kid said, 'Gazeteciler (the news reporters).'

When I heard that, I just walked away. What can you say to a person who does wrong in return for money? I thought. From that experience I learned many out there do unfortunately. That day Mariam and I only spent two class periods in school. We were picked up by bodyguards and taken home early. My mom returned home later in the afternoon. We sat down on the couch in the living room and she gave both of us a big tight hug. All she said was, 'This is a trial from God and whatever burden or challenge HE gives us in life, HE also gives us the strength to fight and overcome. This experience will make you stronger. In the future you will see that.' I looked up at her and said, 'Mom, I know and I believe that this will make us stronger, but right now, I feel so sad and upset. It was horrible.'

'I know,' she said.

Today, I look back and I remember that day like it was yesterday. It is very clear in my memory. And I remember my mom's words. It turned out exactly like she said. My mom's experience as the first headscarved Member of the Turkish Parliament had me step out of the shoes of a child's inexperienced view of life and face reality as a mature kid. Injustice is done all around the world. The discrimination and prejudice my mother, sister and I faced were a mere reflection of many injustices that continue around the world. Receiving that scar at a young age has become a reminder that I will fight to restore injustice whenever, wherever.

I am grateful to have shared a part of that pain with my mom. It made me grow and become wiser. And I thank ALLAH for giving me the guidance and strength to succeed in these trials.

For Merve the experience at Anittepe Elementary School was far worse than entering the Parliament because it had endangered her children and exposed them to the ugly, malicious torrent of feelings against her. By the time she entered the school she was shell-shocked. She called her father and told him of the taunting as she cried on the phone. Yusuf wanted to come right away but she told him not to.

That evening and the next day the media conveyed this event as if it were a legitimate expression of ten-year-olds and not a scene manipulated by them. On 6 May, *Hurriyet* published a picture of Merve and her children among the crowd that surrounded her upon entering the school grounds, with the following article:

Children Protest

After the crisis she caused at the Parliament, Merve Kavakci, who leaves her home only to go to the party headquarters and the Parliament was protested at her children's school when she dropped them there. The children, who recognized Merve Kavakci as soon as they saw her, chanted, 'Turkey is secular and will remain secular' and booed her. Merve Kavakci's children were surprised by the protests. Kavakci left for the party headquarters and then the Parliament without paying attention to the protests.[19]

Merve Kavakci had become an enemy of the state and *Hurriyet's* article was typical of the way the mainstream press joined the fray with no regard to the truth, portraying Merve as an inhuman agitator. After this incident, Fatima and Mariam had to be driven to and from school and were not able to play in the schoolyard during break times. From this point on, Merve needed a car with tinted windows and a driver and bodyguard at all times. Some reporters who witnessed the incident at Anittepe called Ravza to apologize for what happened. She listened in silence. Meanwhile, provocations at the children's school continued for about two weeks until the administration was able to quell them, but they then migrated to their home where Merve's children were taunted in front of the house and their doorbell rung for days. When asked about her children's experience later by reporters, she teared up – one of the rare times she did so in public.

Milliyet accusations

While Merve was trying to handle media harassment at her children's school, Demirel's widely reported statements labelling her as controlled by outside forces made its way to the US. The *Washington Post* published a short article on the incident in Parliament that relied completely on the *Milliyet* newspaper, which like other establishment papers supported the government and attacked Merve mercilessly:

The *Milliyet* newspaper quoted Turkish President Suleyman Demirel today as saying that Merve Kavakci, 31, a lawmaker with the pro-Islamic Virtue Party, had 'certain foreign connections.' 'We have established various things about her,' a characteristically enigmatic Demirel said Monday while en route to Paris. These allegedly include links with the US-based Islamic Association for Palestine and the militant Islamic group Hamas, the newspaper reported. It claimed that Kavakci had attended international 'anti-Semitic seminars.'[20]

That information came from a *Milliyet*-published article entitled 'Merve's Organization Connections' ['Merve'nin orgut baglantilari'] on 4 May 1999 written by Yasemin Congar, who today is a respected journalist for *Taraf*. The information in that article was widely quoted by the government and other newspapers as proof that Merve was an 'agent provocateur'. Here are the key excerpts and points from the article:

Merve has a connection to international Islamist organizations and a close relationship to the Islamic Association of Palestine (IAP). 'The fact that Merve Kavakci made a speech to the annual congress of the IAP in 1997 and the allegation that her father's mosque is being financed by IAP makes one think that the Kavakci family has an indirect connection with HAMAS.'

'Other activities of the IAP which is considered to be the chief propaganda institution of HAMAS in the US and Canada and has anti-Israeli broadcasts and campaigns to make anti-Jewish propaganda and to try to weaken the relationship between Israel and the US.'

At the 1997 Congress of the IAP Merve Kavakci made a speech with eight other executives of many organizations which are known to be pro-HAMAS.

Steven Emerson [terrorist expert] calls that meeting of the IAP 'undoubtedly the most radical meeting among ones organized by militant Islamic groups in the US that year'.

One of the people in attendance at the congress was Ishak Al Farhan, criticized by Steven Emerson. He was a Member of the Jordanian Parliament.

Papers were delivered on Palestine, Islam, Israel and Jews.

Merve Kavakci was in the shadow cabinet of the Welfare Party.

Some in the media have criticized Steve Emerson.

'Is is said that there is an "organic bond" between IAP and the North Texas Islamic Union to which Yusuf Kavakci's mosque is a member.'

'Yusuf Kavakci takes part in media broadcasts, writings and teachings; attention is drawn to the fact that an important part of these activities is organized by the IAP which is in the same vicinity.'

'On the other hand there are allegations that her formal Jordanian husband is a supporter of the Islamic Action Front.'

Merve gave a speech at Ohio State University in 1996 to the North American Islamic Union (ISNA), from 30 August to 1 September.

Voice of America Radio has reported that she said: 'We can divide the whole of humanity into two [sic: three]: those on the way to Islam, whose who have accepted Islam and those who are candidates for accepting Islam.'

Of the Welfare Party government in Turkey she said: 'All those domestic and external interests which did not want Muslims to unite tried to turn the Turkish nation and the world against us.'

'In her speech Merve Kavakci said it was important that the Welfare Party entered the government which was under the influence of Western countries and super powers and said "our aim is to stop or at least slow down the pressures on the Muslims, but we cannot do everything with one go. We tried to do that in the past, then what happened? All our leaders were imprisoned and we had to start from the beginning."'

'Merve Kavakci also said there is a bias in Turkey against those who dress up in accordance with Islam and she herself can reach out to doctors, housewives and engineers and women from different professions.'

'What is the North American Islamic Union? Dr Kavakci [Merve's father] was elected as head of its board in 1997 and which is known to be close to the government in America. At its 1998 annual meeting it gave its humanitarian award to Erbakan for his service to Islam and Turkey but he did not appear to receive it in person.'

Among the foundational goals of ISNA is to set up fully Islamic schools, to expand Islamic activities to the military and prisons, to help young people gain leadership qualities for the future and to enable Muslim communities to have a voice in the political process.

Merve talked about her 'jihad' politically.

Actually, the Islamic Association for Palestine in 1999 was what the name implies: an association of Islamic people who supported Palestine. Political Islam, or Islamism, and Islamist groups, that is groups that support political Islam, come in myriad flavours, the majority of which are not terrorist in nature. In this book we have stayed away from the terms Islamism and Islamist because of their pejorative connotations in the West and among Kemalists, and the blanket accusations that they are all looking to implement Islamic law and take over governments violently. The government looked hard for 'dirt' on Merve Kavakci and the only thing they could find was her speeches, as if advocating for the interests of Islamic people makes one a terrorist, and as if it would have any bearing whatsoever on Merve's election to the Parliament. The *Milliyet* article and all its descendants not only mislabel such organizations as the IAP, they take the 'guilty by association' approach to extraordinary lengths, using also the 'testimony' and 'reports' of anti-Islamic groups in the US and Israel. Thus Merve is guilty of everything the IAP is guilty of because she gave a speech to the organization. As noted earlier, Merve travelled overseas, first working for the Welfare Party, then the Virtue Party, giving speeches to Islamic organizations in support of her role as head of the Women's Commission of the party. But neither Merve nor her father had or have any connections to HAMAS. His mosque was not dependent on the IAP nor did it have an 'organic bond'. Her father, in fact, was so respected by the community that later on he opened the Texas legislature with a Muslim prayer. Her ex-husband had no political affiliations whatsoever. As for Ishak al-Farhan, he had also met with President Demirel as part of the Jordanian delegation (and later with President Clinton), as noted in the previous chapter. Steven Emerson labels Merve as an 'Islamic fundamentalist' with all the connotations that depiction comes with. He also blamed Muslims for the bombing of the federal building in Oklahoma City in 1995, for which Timothy McVeigh was executed, and for the crash of TWA 800 the following year, which was caused by a fuel tank problem with 747s. Finally, *jihad* in the Qur'an means 'struggle' and that is how the vast majority of Muslim people use the term, which does not generally mean holy war or violent struggle.[21]

Of course, all of these false accusations detracted from the fact that Merve was elected to office, by people who voted for her, pursuant to the Turkish Constitution.

Regarding Yasemin Congar, who worked for *Milliyet* after 28 February, a pro-Kemalist paper, Dr Arsan told me that her editor likely called the Washington Bureau and asked them to find something against Merve Kavakci so a story could be written against her, and 'Congar simply created a story based on what she found, her association with a 'fundamentalist' group. Actually it's a misperception because Hamas is mainly a political and not illegal organization that has a good reputation with Muslims in the Middle East.' Such was the state of journalism in Turkey that a reporter would fly all the way to Dallas, question Islamic community members in search of negative material, seek denigrating information from Merve's ex-husband and divulge private family matters to *Milliyet*.

Three days later *Milliyet* published another article under the headline: 'Kavakci's Every Word A Scandal'. 'Kavakci's speech which she delivered at the Islamic Society of North America's meeting in Ohio in 1996 was full of anger just like the one she delivered at Islamic Association of Palestine's (IAP) meeting in 1997.'

Congar's original article was quoted widely throughout the mainstream press and referenced by the foreign press as well. Later, Merve's speeches were repeatedly broadcast on television. *Hurriyet* joined in the fray the next day:

Caught Red Handed

Merve Kavakci has been caught red handed when it was learnt that she said, 'I chose to serve for Jihad in political field,' at the Islamic Association for Palestine's (IAP) meeting in 1997. The IAP is HAMAS' biggest supporter in the US. Kavakci, who has recently stated that she was 'a child of the Republic,' had talked like an enemy of the Turkish Republic at the IAP's meeting. Steven Emerson, an expert from the US on radical Islamist terrorism, said Kavakci 'was a typical fundamentalist militant' when he briefed her speech to *Hurriyet*. 'We are fighting with a so-called Muslim government in Turkey. We hope that all the Muslims of the world will gather under a single flag in the twenty-first century. As Muslims of Turkey, we started doing our part for the materialization of this cause,' she also had stated in the IAP's meeting.

And under the headline, 'Kavakci, VP Woman Deputy, Calls for Jihad,' *Cumhuriyet* published this the same day:

It was revealed that Merve Kavakci, the woman deputy of the Virtue Party (VP) from Istanbul, whom President Suleyman Demirel defined as 'agent provocateur,' called for Jihad in the speech she made to the Islamic Association of Palestine (IAP) conference.

While Merve was trying to bring her children to school, President Demirel reiterated his comments about her, saying, 'Yes, I defined Merve Kavakci as an agent provocateur and I used that expression purposely … There is an attempt to bring the headscarf into the Parliament after schools. If the headscarf is the symbol of fundamentalism, then the issue gains a different character in essence.'[22]

Except for the Islamic-friendly press, little was done to counter these allegations other than a few appearances by Merve on television. When she did well on television, the government stopped their repeated broadcasts. Her party did little to defend her, and Merve was overwhelmed with harassment by the press and, later, the government, this accelerating almost out of control in the weeks after 2 May. With each reiteration by the press, the news about Merve got worse, the misperceptions were amplified, and their regular repetition transformed questionable claims into accepted facts.

The *New York Times* did publish six balanced articles by Stephen Kinzer, who was assigned to, and living in, Turkey, from the day before Merve entered the Parliament until 16 May. In his interview Kinzer also noted the following:

> Critics of Ms Kavakci and her party assert that their long-term goal is to impose a radical form of religious rule that will ultimately destroy freedom in Turkey. They consider her embrace of the language of democracy deeply cynical and mendacious. A professor of social psychology at Koc University in Istanbul, Cigdem Kagitcibasi, said the wearing of headscarves created social pressure on women who did not wear them, and warned that this pressure could ultimately lead to the imposition of 'religious terror' in Turkey. 'At every point in the development of society,' she asserted, 'religion has been used as a cover to block and roll back progress.'

Professor Kagitcibasi has a distinguished background: published and educated in the US, taught at Harvard University. I questioned her about these statements, given that Merve was a college graduate and later earned her doctorate. How could her religion be a 'cover to block and roll back progress'? Professor Kagitcibasi replied that she was referring to the 'reactionary uprisings and movements that occurred repeatedly during the last period of the Ottoman Empire in reaction to and in order to stall the attempts toward modernization'. That reference was not found in the Kinzer article and of course has nothing to do with Merve Kavakci a century later. As to her other comments, she questioned the headscarf movement that began in the 1970s with Sule Yuksel and the pressures that have been placed on girls from ages eight to nine onwards to cover. She noted that 'the issues you are interested in are highly complex and require a thorough understanding of the events, trends, and influences of the recent past, if not the last two hundred years'. Professor Kagitcibasi is correct. The historical context is indeed powerful, complex and runs deep within the fabric of Turkish society, but in my opinion her characterization of religion rolling back progress did not apply to Turkey in 1999, nor did it apply to Merve Kavakci, which is what Mr Kinzer's articles were about. The 'religious terror' comment related to the long-standing argument by Turkish secularists that uncovered women will be forced to cover if covered women were given their rights. The notion of a 'modern Islamic women' as an oxymoron runs deep in Turkish secularism, especially in the halls of academia in Turkey, perpetuated almost like a religious belief.

By the time Merve Kavakci returned from her children's elementary school, twenty lawyers of the Istanbul Bar Association held a press conference to lodge their own attack against her. To loud applause, lawyer Musur Kaya Canpolat characterized her actions as rebellion against the Republic and her headscarf as a leftover from the middle ages. He also criticized the speaker of the Parliament [Septioglu] and other members of the Parliament for their silence when she entered the Parliament. And another women's group, the Women's Politicians' Association (KASIDE) also issued a statement against Kavakci, noting, 'We have nothing to do with headscarved women.'[23]

Internationally it does not appear that any non-Muslim countries were very concerned about the Turkish election. In a statement on 5 May to a joint Turkey–US Relations' conference organized by the American-Turkish Council (ATC) and American Friends of Turkey Association, President Clinton did not mention the recent Turkish election. The day before, James Rubin, State Department Spokesperson, said that the US had faith in Turkish democracy and was waiting to see the results of attempts to found the government. He added, 'This is Turkey's internal affair.'[24] Turkey at this time was a close and key strategic partner of the US. The Turkish air force logged more than one thousand hours of air strikes in Yugoslavia as part of NATO, and the US used Turkish bases to launch operations against Iraq during the first Gulf war, something that would not be allowed in 2003 for the second Gulf war.

On the run
The press surrounded Merve wherever she went, followed her relatives and friends after they visited her to find out where they lived, then proceeded to hound them, in Ankara and Istanbul. Her phones continued

to be tapped, and transcripts of calls were shared with the press. Each successive day was worse than the previous one, while sleep was the only respite and nightmare-free. Upon awakening, the real nightmare would once again emerge, one that presented insurmountable problems and frustrations. She had always been an indefatigable worker, excelling in schools in Turkey and college in the US, and enjoying friendly competition with her male cousins when they gained their degrees and became successful. When her medical school blocked covered women, she went to the US to continue her education, regardless of the difficulties in adjusting to another country. She had a problem-solving attitude about everything, which supported her positive outlook when she returned to her country to ensure that her children were raised in the country that her grandfather fought for, that was as much hers as any other person's in Turkey. Her goals were noble after being nominated: to represent people and to foster democracy, which she had become accustomed to in America. Now, regardless of her efforts, in spite of her consistently hard work, her intelligence and quick-wittedness, the evidence was all around her that the battles were being lost. Four days after her walk into the Parliament, the ruling powers in Turkey continued to mobilize against her and her fears increased.

The not-so-silent majority of religious Muslims, and their communication networks, supported her, of course. But they could do little to help, except talk. The obvious need to marshal political power on her behalf was hopeless, given the split within her party, its poor performance in the elections, the disregard by those who would normally form a coalition with Virtue, and the entrenched bureaucracy, courts, and military who opposed her – the secular bloc.

By 6 May the events were becoming unbearable for Merve. Her house was under constant surveillance and the tension was affecting her children. The only thing that seemed to help matters was leaving the house for a while. She accepted the invitation of Zeki Unal to stay in his house at the Parliamentary Residences. She hoped that when the journalists realized she was not coming home they would stop harassing her family. Unfortunately that did not happen. Every guest who came by was followed all the way home, no matter how far away they went; when they stopped, the reporters asked them questions. Meanwhile, the majority of her party remained silent. A few of them spoke out on television but the leadership simply stayed in the background. A few people from the party tried to accompany Osman, her bodyguard, who slept in his car. Otherwise, no one asked her if she needed anything.

Fortunately, the press members who followed her to the Parliamentary Residences were stopped by security personnel and could not enter the main gate. Later, however, with the help of a DSP member, they managed to get in with a guest permit and came all the way to Zeki Unal's residence, her place of refuge.

That first night at Zeki Unal's, Kutan was invited to visit and evaluate the situation. After changing the venue twice, a meeting was held at the home of Oguzhan Asilturk, VP deputy and closely aligned with Erbakan, who was out of the country. Present were also Abdullah Gul, Salih Kapusuz, Zeki Unal, Merve Kavakci and her parents. Asilturk led this meeting and Kutan rarely spoke. Oguzhan talked mostly about spirituality, prescribing patience and conveyed his own memories and experiences, but no solid course of action was discussed.

After a few days of staying in these residences, Merve decided that, until Parliament was opened, it was not beneficial to stay in Ankara. She wanted to relieve relatives of being hounded by the media. The journalists were following her uncle, aunt and even the person who cleaned her house. Four to five cars belonging to press members were waiting day and night in front of her door and immediately followed those who left the house. In the Cankaya district of Ankara, the press had situated themselves in the garden of her uncle's neighbours and harassed every passer-by. Her relatives stopped coming by.

The night she was to leave, Zeki and his wife invited Merve and Temel Karamollaolgu and his family to Hacibaba Restaurant in Ankara to provide a change of scenery, but Merve wanted to leave as soon as possible. Her mother and father went to the dinner instead. Mukadder, Zeki's wife, stayed with Merve and they devised a plan to leave undetected for Istanbul, with Ravza's collaboration, who was also under surveillance by the press. Merve's assistant, named Hulya, wearing one of Merve's dresses and headscarves, left the residences driven by Osman. The press army followed her. After touring the Ankara streets for a while, the car arrived at Hulya's residence in the Cebeci district giving Merve just enough time to leave the Parliament Residences and switch cars with Mehmet Aksay in a predetermined place, then start out for Istanbul. Once Hulya got out of Osman's car the press contingent realized they had been tricked.

Merve and her children escaped Ankara for Istanbul, a six-hour journey that for her was dark, anguished and seemed endless. Ahmet, her cousin, and Mehmet Aksay, a family friend, were in the front while Merve was in the back, her children sleeping against her, one on each side. The darkness of that night had a chilling effect after a harrowing week of being chased and disparaged. The toll on her was immense. She listened to those in the front talk about how they thought the escape was successful, while in the back she silently cried. Once in a while, Fatima and Mariam would lift their heads from her shoulders, content to see Merve beside them smiling, then close their eyes again, snuggling even closer.

They took precautions not to expose where they went in Istanbul. Ravza's house certainly was not acceptable – it was probably already under surveillance or it would be the first house they'd check once they realized Merve had left town. Instead they went to Ahmet's house in the Moda district of Istanbul, which is on the Asian side, arriving well past midnight. Zeynep, his wife, opened the door and was shocked at Merve's appearance. On television she had looked vibrant but here in her living room she seemed completely exhausted. Merve asked for some tea. The windows and curtains were drawn, even though the house had stunning views of the Marmara.

The next morning she awoke to the first light of the sun heating her room. She smiled at the sight of her children sleeping next to her, but then the nightmare began once again and she felt the weight of the world on her shoulders. She arose and saw Ahmet and immediately could read the gloom in his face. He had glanced at the newspapers and seen the morning news. The cartel newspapers' full-page headlines read: 'Kavakci's Speech 1996 America's Ohio State!' 'Another of Kavakci's Speeches made in Chicago 1997!' Now Ecevit's screaming in the Parliament made more sense to her: 'Put this woman in her place.' She remembered Abdurrahaman Dilipak's warnings to her during the campaign about how investigators were looking for dirt on Merve, even in the USA, how the party was being threatened, and she could see now that all the resources of the state were being used to collect information on her. She felt she had nothing to hide but she underestimated the dark side of Turkish politics.

Like most Turks Merve read the newspapers at the breakfast table. On this morning her jaw dropped at the headlines. She thought, 'What? My God, what are they talking about?' The papers mentioned her speech at the thirty-third ISNA Conference on behalf of the Welfare Party where she described the strategy that carried the party to the top in 1994 and mentioned the support that was needed among Islamic countries. She had been a young mother speaking in front of 20,000 people, sent there by her party as a 'relief soldier' being a 'modern, Western-like' high-level female party member in a party that was on its way to ruling the country and playing an important role in the women's political movement. The newspapers, on the other hand, accused her of being backward.

Merve:

> At a time when leaders of other parties were encouraging their female members to work like the Welfare Party female members, I was invited there to enlighten them on our inner-workings. However, the Turkish journalists were given the task of showing Merve Kavakci as a traitor of the people, breaking down the respect she may have earned from her struggle for human rights and women's rights. It seems that they were compelled to lie, make accusations, or whatever was needed to achieve this end.

She turned on the television in time to see Aydin Menderes threatening to quit the party if no explanation were provided for what was happening. Merve wondered what explanations could be given. He quit the party that afternoon. Several stations were broadcasting her ISNA speech as the headline news with special effects in a continuous loop. Merve and her cousins in the apartment in Moda were trying to keep up with what was happening in the media and assess the situation. Despite her pleas going back to the campaign, no one in the party was addressing the media.

Merve felt that things could not go on like this any longer. There was a lawful need to respond to all the accusations and lies appearing in the media. She immediately contacted the law firm that Abdullah Gul had recommended, resulting later in a group gathering at the home of Abdurrahman Dilipak – lawyers, writers, businessmen and leaders of several associations – to set a strategy and tactics to handle what was happening. But Merve remained in shock from the morning news, devastated by the horrible and unbelievable comments of the reporters about her speeches as if she had committed a crime. They had to be stopped, but it was like an avalanche – too wide, too deep and too overwhelming to be halted. It was no use. The campaign against her was going too fast. Some law professionals were calling to lend their support, declaring that there was no crime in her speeches and that they would sign a petition accordingly. She thought, however, that a petition would have no impact and she was probably right.

Dual citizenship

The next day Abdullah Gul arranged for an interview with the main news section of TGRT, the Turkish national network. Merve borrowed a dress from Zeynep and arrived at the station to crowds of cheering people who had heard about the programme; they also cheered her when she left. It was an emotional outpouring of support that moved Merve Kavakci as well.

That same night she was interviewed by phone with Hulki Cevizoglu on another television programme. He asked her if she was an American citizen and she answered yes. Several newspapers would soon report inaccurately that she had hidden this information. She had become naturalized in the USA on 5 March 1999, less than six weeks before the elections. She explained that she had gone to America with her family, then returned to Turkey to ensure that her children spoke Turkish and because they missed their country.

Meanwhile, Parliament was to open on 12 May to elect a new Speaker, and Merve was still in Istanbul. She found out that, for various reasons, some Parliament members had not taken their oath during the initial session, and could still take it at the beginning of this second session. She saw this as a new chance for her. However, her party did not. In fact, Kapusuz and Gul met with her, Ahmet and Mehmet Aksay, and passed along a warning for her not to come to Ankara. Even worse, others in the party were asking her to sign a document to give up being a Member of Parliament altogether. Merve thought this was impossible and refused. She could not even think of doing this to the very people who had voted for her.

Then things got even worse. Prime Minister Ecevit and Husamettin Ozkan had approached Virtue Party officials to suggest that they should all encourage Merve Kavakci to get out of the country, which they would facilitate. They argued that the revocation of her citizenship would invalidate her Parliament membership, which would end her 'untouchable' status (which came with her being a Member of

Parliament). The possible loss of her citizenship and untouchable status were being reported in the press. They said it was extremely dangerous for her to remain in Turkey. Ending her untouchable status would open the road to prosecuting her for entering the Parliament wearing a headscarf and giving that speech in the US in 1996. As noted above, there were lots of laws concerning repressing dissent with which to prosecute her. Given these impending threats, the party agreed not only that she should avoid coming to Ankara but that she should leave the country, as suggested by Ecevit's warnings. However, they were so reluctant to present this offer directly to Merve that they instead asked Ahmet Hakan, a television journalist who had met with Kapusuz and Gul, to speak to her on their behalf. Ahmet called her with the message. Merve had to sit down and could barely speak. She believed that the party leadership's intentions were good because they thought her life was in danger. Given Turkey's reputation for 'non-judicial executions', the disappearance of people, arrest of journalists critical of the regime, and murders on the part of the deep state, their fears were understandable. Yet she was once again disappointed by their complying with the DSP and the government.

Ahmet Hakan rushed back from Ankara after speaking with her. He wanted to conduct an interview with her on the *Iskele Sancak* programme on Channel 7. He wanted to record it at a private location to prevent the government or deep state from staging a sensational attack on her during normal live programming on Friday night.

Meanwhile, the police visited her home in Ankara at least three times. The first two times they asked for the relinquishment of her green passport so that they could give her a red one instead, the passport given to all Parliament members. Her family told them she would bring her green passport back herself when she returned. The last time the two police officers visited, they said they had 'sensed things', that she was in danger and that they wanted to protect her. They offered to have a woman police officer escort her at all times but neither Merve nor her family was ready to trust them.

Another cause of stress in Merve's family was the continuing tapping of her phones. Once, a conversation her mother had with one of her relatives about a serious matter was published word for word by a newspaper the following day. Although Merve was eventually able to send the children back to Ankara to start school, she could not even make a phone call to find out how they were or simply to hear their voices. The tension was also affecting the children. Mariam, her seven-year-old, after seeing the police clashing with a group of covered women on television, ran to her aunt in fear, asking if her mother were among them.

In the midst of all these difficulties, she met Ali Bayramoglu, the head of MUSIAD, who lent the use of his home. It was in his home in the Bebek district of Istanbul that they found refuge for holding meetings. She and Ravza met in Ali's rooftop study with her cousin Ahmet, Ahmet Hakan, Mehmet Aksay, Abdurrahman Dilipak and Ahmet Tasgetiren to strategize. But the big unknown was what her party was doing and how to deal with the constant stream of news about the crisis, actions by the state, statements by various people and accusations that emerged on a daily basis. They called Numan Kurtulmus, the Istanbul city head of the Virtue Party, and he joined them later for one meeting, but after sitting quietly all night, he left and was never heard from again by Merve.

The interview with Ahmet Hakan was to be recorded in Ali's rooftop study. Merve, along with her father, waited for Ahmet Hakan and Besir Atalay (currently the Minister of Internal Affairs) to land on the midnight flight from Ankara after their meeting with party officials. She was completely miserable that night. The warning to leave her country or be incarcerated hung over her. She missed her children, whose presence and innocence always comforted her; and an agonizing wave of sadness took hold of her. Wherever she looked she saw them, and the idea of prison added to her misery: the idea of being away from them for years, of their seeing their mother in prison. Why should she be punished? For running for office? Getting elected? It seemed bizarre, unreal to her. The television crew did not complete their work until 2.30 a.m. She threw water on her face to stay awake. The goal was to respond to everything written in the mainstream media so as to help convey who Merve Kavakci really was.

She spoke as frankly as possible and tried to address each matter, including personal and private areas. Hakan suddenly brought up the fact that she had become a *hafiz*, one who had memorized the entire Holy Qur'an. This accomplishment was a source of pride for Merve and made her happy no matter how down she felt. Noting that one has to be passionate about it, she told him, 'If you don't love the Qur'an, then you can't memorize it.' She recommended the Qur'an to anyone who felt a void in their spirituality, in their life. She viewed it as a miracle, and felt it was another miracle for a person to begin memorizing it at only twenty-six despite the extreme difficulty of doing so (the Qur'an is in Arabic). When her mother had arrived from the USA to take care of her children, Merve had been given a leave of absence from the party and went to Dallas, Texas for more intense study with her teacher. Of course, this was all before her candidacy, and prior to accusations that her headscarf was but a political symbol.

While they were shooting the programme, Ahmet Hakan and Atalay, who had been in such a hurry coming from Ankara that he had grabbed someone else's briefcase by accident, were talking to her father about the offer from Husamettin Ozkan to help her leave the country.

In the early hours of the morning, they were able to deliver what Merve and her family thought was a useful, enlightening programme. Its broadcast was well received, so Channel 7 was on the verge of broadcasting it again the next day until an ultimatum came to the TV station from the 'deep state' warning that if they did so their station would be shut down.

Now the issue of her citizenship turned into a major issue with her young lawyers: should she formerly inform the state of her dual citizenship or not? Meanwhile Abdullah Gul called her cousin Ahmet recommending that she should go and get her deputy salary immediately. Merve initially objected to the idea, thinking people in the media would criticize her as money-hungry; then she realized it would validate her election. So she immediately set out for the bank. Of course, for Merve Kavakci the process was not so simple. While everyone was receiving their salary relatively easily, when her turn came suddenly barricades began to appear. The bank claimed that Parliament had not yet approved it, while the Parliament's General Secretary's Office responded that her money had already been placed in the bank for her. After three attempts, she finally received her first salary instalment. This news resulted in a media attack on the new Speaker of the Parliament, Yildirim Akbulut, for paying her. As a result he suspended any further payments and fired the General Secretary of the Parliament, who had fulfilled this obligation at her relentless insistence. This was obviously unfair because other Parliament members who did not take their oaths, five auxiliary deputies, received their salaries. In fact, the wife of a deceased deputy was still receiving her husband's salary! This list of Parliamentarians was printed in the *Akit* newspaper: M. Sancar, U. Bayulken, B. Cenkci, C. Mentes and F. Melen all received their salaries from the day they were selected but had never taken their oaths.

Before Merve returned to Ankara, she met a few more times with the volunteer group that had tried to help her, including Mehmet Aksay and his friends, her cousin Ahmet, Ahmet Hakan, and Ali Bayramoglu. One of these meetings took place on a boat cruising on the Bosphorus. They kept scanning the primary newscasts for any new developments.

For Mother's Day, a large gathering from the Capital City Women's Platform and National Youth Foundation hung a banner at the entry of her apartment building in Ankara. All day various groups came to her house to congratulate her on Mother's Day. Unfortunately for security reasons, her family could not accept them into the house but were happy to receive their messages. The door to the building of her house had turned into a flower garden. Seeing this, and wanting to show opposition to this sincere act of goodwill, others had obtained a black banner and hung it on her door. Her apartment door was adorned with Ataturk pictures hung by her neighbours in protest against Merve Kavakci.

That Sunday a short interview that her mother had given to Channel 7 was broadcasted. Merve watched in sadness. Her mother's normally lively and energetic tone was missing. She was talking about her daughter – her daughter and her shattered dreams.

On another TV channel that night, an interview with Merve's ex-husband was broadcasted. The interview was given in English with Turkish subtitles provided by Yasemin Congar. However, the Turkish subtitles did not at all match the original English. It was just another example of media bias.

With the worry that legal action might be starting, Merve sought to replace the young and inexperienced lawyers that Gul had recommended. She objected to their insistence on doing things their own way. Professor Cemal Sanli had told her that in order to have her dual citizenship not cause any problems, all she had to do was submit an application fulfilling the formality of informing the Turkish government. However, her lawyers failed to submit such an application despite her directives, and the opportunity to maintain her Turkish citizenship was slipping away. She immediately had to find a lawyer she could trust. Based on the recommendation of Nazli Ilicak, she contacted Salim Ozdemir, who handled Nazli's court cases against the Ecevit government. Later, another law firm hired by her party took on the responsibility of prosecuting the newspapers for the baseless and fabricated news they were publishing.

The government now started digging into her American citizenship. When Merve heard this, she and Ravza met with Emine Erodogan at her home – her husband was still in prison – Emine having called to see how things were going. Just as she sat down, a reporter called her on her cell phone wanting to know what she thought about her American citizenship being taken away. She also got the news that the Turkish media were trying to persuade the American government to take away her US citizenship. The shock was immense. It was not enough that they were after her Turkish citizenship; now they wanted to take away her recently acquired American citizenship too!

Merve felt that not being well represented early on by competent attorneys was hurting her. Perhaps she and the Virtue Party did not anticipate the depth and breadth of the firestorms that enflamed the country from all quarters after the incident in Parliament, nor the degree to which the state had marshalled its forces. She had fled from the press to Istanbul and had thus been handicapped in responding effectively. Perhaps decisions weren't made quickly, the right lawyers weren't hired, a strategy was not determined early on. However, as noted earlier, it is highly unlikely that any legal manoeuvres would have mattered in Turkey in 1999, even if she had managed to take her oath of office. The wheels of the state were operating against her without regard to judicial processes anyway.

She returned to Ankara. Parliament had opened without her. She heard a rumour that if she had attempted to enter the Parliamentary Hall when it opened the second time, the DSP Parliamentarians would have attacked her as she walked to the pulpit and ripped up her clothes.

She found refuge again in the home of Zeki and Mukadder Unal in the Parliamentary Residences because her house was still under constant monitoring by the press. Her relatives visited her at the Parliamentary Residences, which alerted the press to her being back in Ankara, but security at the gates kept the press out. But the press was the least of her problems.

Notes

1 M. Hakan Yavuz, *Islamic Political Identity in Turkey*, Oxford University Press, 2003, p. 249.
2 Human Rights Foundation of Turkey, Report of 1999, p. 7, available at: http://www.tihv.org.tr/index.php?english-1.
3 *Ibid.*
4 Human Rights Foundation of Turkey Report, of 1999.
5 *Sabah*, 5 May 1999.
6 *Hurriyet*, 5 May 1999.
7 *Radikal*, 5 May 1999.
8 Akbar S. Ahmed, *Islam Today: A Short Introduction to the Muslim World*, IB Tauris, New York, 2002, pp. 9–10.
9 *Hurriyet*, 5 May 1999.
10 *Milliyet*, 5 May 1999.
11 Jenny B. White, *Islamic Mobilization in Turkey: A Study in Vernacular Politics*, University of Washington Press, 2002, p. 240.
12 Interview in offices of ESAM, Ankara, 21 April 1999.
13 'DSP Lone Voice in Parliament', *Turkish Daily News*, 4 May 1999.
14 'Merve Kavakci: "I'm a Child of the Republic"', *Turkish Daily News*, 4 May 1999.
15 'Bare your Head', *The Economist*, 13 May 1999.
16 See 'FP Deputy Malkoc Files Complaint against Savas' and 'Savas Responds to Criticism: Integrity and Secular Establishment are Under Threat', *Turkish Daily News*, 12 May 1989.
17 'Headscarf, the Emblem of Political Islam, Stirs Turkish Parliament', *Turkish Daily News*, Kemal Balci, 4 May 1999.
18 'Bare your Head', *The Economist*, 13 May 1999.
19 *Hurriyet*, 6 May 1999, translated by Umit Cizre.
20 *Washington Post*, 5 May 1999.
21 'The concept in Western literature and usage has come to mean the idea of holy war, of Muslim fanaticism. In fact, *jihad* means struggle, and there are various forms of it; physical confrontation is one. The holy Prophet identified the greatest *jihad* as the struggle to master our passions and instincts. It is therefore a much more complex and sophisticated concept than that bandied about in the media', Ahmed, p. 8.
22 *Milliyet*, 5 May 1999.
23 *Turkish Daily News*, 6 May 1999.
24 *Anadolu News Agency*, 5 May 1999.

8

Persecuted and Prosecuted

Irony of ironies, there is a modern mosque on the grounds of the Turkish Parliament, just behind the main building, constructed in 1985. It was built during a time 'when elements of Islam were incorporated into public discourse to provide a moral basis, ideological unity, and some certainty in the face of global capitalism ...'[1] It provides a convenient place for Parliamentarians to pray without much interruption to their work. To the casual uninformed observer, it appears to be in stark contrast to the vociferous battles that took place against Merve Kavakci's Islamic headscarf just 100 metres away.

But everything changed on 28 February 1997. In Turkey the military had always played a guardianship role protecting Turkey from 'internal threats' that it defined, although this role is not specified in any Turkish Constitution. That role was expanded significantly in 1997. The demands it issued on that date in the National Security Council to the Erbakan-led government launched a 'process' that altered the political environment, targeted political Islam as separatists that threatened the Kemalist doctrine at the heart of Turkey's secular democracy, and expanded the power of the military to areas normally run by civilians. There was no more room for democratic debate. Laws were changed to ensure that security concerns were prominent when it came to 'anti-terrorism, media, public order, political parties, education, civil rights, and liberties'.[2] Moreover, what was defined as a military internal threat was up to the military.

> Especially after the 1995 elections, the TAF [Turkish Armed Forces] has been involved in making and breaking governments, initiating crucial policy decisions, becoming directly involved in political intrigue, issuing public demands and warnings to civilians, structuring new bills through its own research units and departments, launching campaigns to inform the public about the possibility that political Islam might be acting as cover for reactionary intentions ... and continually impinging on the daily operations of elected governments.[3]

The expanded role of the military was assuaged just a bit after the Helsinki Summit at the end of 1999 when Turkey would have to meet numerous criteria relating to democratization for EU membership.

The military intervention that began on 28 February aimed at preserving Kemalism in the face of 'creeping Islamization' was supported by President Demirel and the secular establishment. Political parties at the time provided little opposition, with the exception of Mesut Yilmaz of the ANAP party, Prime Minister from July 1997 to January 1999, who did not think that *irtica* (separatism) was the biggest problem in Turkey. But his tenure was cut short by allegations of corruption and, like others, he retreated in the face of the military, turning his focus to supporting the state and implementing the coup's directives, rather than listening to his own constituents.[4]

As noted earlier, the Virtue Party retreated after the reaction to Merve Kavakci. From the beginning it had been insecure because its predecessor party, Welfare, had been shut down. In addition, the military never believed Virtue's pro-democracy rhetoric and viewed this as self-serving, aimed at preventing its closure. On the other side, the Virtue Party's traditional leadership (mainly Erbakan) did not seem to abandon its religion-based values but let Merve Kavakci herself defend the concept of religious freedom. After the Virtue Party was shut down in 2001, both Kutan and Erbakan eventually joined and supported the traditional Saadet (Felicity) Party, which has not been much of a factor in Turkish politics.

At the other end of this ideological/political spectrum was the rare figure of Merve Kavakci, whose six years in the United States, after she and her family suffered from the headscarf ban, inculcated in her a wholly different view of democracy and religious freedom than typically expressed in Turkey. Living without restrictions in Richardson, Texas, she grew accustomed to America's hands-off view of religious freedom: 'Congress shall make no law respecting an establishment of religion, or prohibiting the free exercise thereof.' Turkish secularism went far beyond the separation of religion from politics and included its control and restrictions in support of what it viewed as a modern and Western identity and lifestyle, one that promoted a belief in Turkey's singular, uniform culture and unity. Moreover, 'because the Kemalist Westernization project has relied more on symbols than substance, it has associated publicly visible instances of Islamic identity with reactionism'.[5] The Virtue Party talked about its democratic values and religious freedom but was lacking in support for this American version, because of its own patriarchy and desire to avoid being closed down. Other than Nazli Ilicak, Zeki Unal and some other non-leadership members of the Virtue Party, along with the Islamic press and people, Merve had virtually no political support behind her. One could see early on that the military, government and Kemalist establishment would easily win their battle against her, using whatever resources were necessary. Despite her eloquence, innocence and legal representation, nothing would get in the way of the secular bloc.

President Demirel's references to Merve Kavakci as an agent for outside forces, particularly Iran, prompted a response from Turkey's neighbour. The Iranian Foreign Ministry summoned Turkey's ambassador to Tehran, Sencar Ozsoy, to ask him what exactly the President said. At around the same time there were well-publicized demonstrations in support of Merve by headscarved and black-chador-wearing students at Tehran University. A Tehran deputy spoke to the crowd, implying that Turkey was an enemy due to its 'stopping the spread of the ideas generated by the revolution and Islam from outside the country'. Ecevit then criticized the demonstrations and told Iran not to interfere in Turkey, as the protests were viewed as sanctioned by the Iranian government and thus interference in Turkish politics. Women in Palestine also demonstrated in support of Merve around the same time.

None of this was good public relations for Merve Kavakci, connecting her to Iran and confirming in some people's minds their negative perceptions of her. *Sabah* wrote that the demonstrations 'revealed the forces guiding Merve'. The *Star* exclaimed that the 'Merve crisis spills into Iran'. The ties with Iran also put Merve Kavakci and PKK chief Abdullah Ocalan – who had recently been captured and was going on trial on an island in the Sea of Marmara – in the same paragraph. Turkey's conflict with the outlawed Kurdistan Workers' Party had brought about tens of thousands of deaths and Ocalan was widely hated. The press kept writing of Merve's so-called ties to Islamic movements, and accused Iran of broadcasting videos towards Turkey that linked Erbakan and Ocalan using satellite stations. On 22 May Ayatollah Jenneti accused Turkey of being an opponent of religious freedom during his sermon at Tehran University, continuing the association.

Merve Kavakci appreciated the support of Islamic women in Iran, but did not agree with the Iranian government's mandating the wearing of a headscarf and publicly criticized Iran years later in an interview in Paris.

Apart from the Iran connection, the government's actions against her were continuing to mount and develop. They sought to take away her citizenship and then use that to officially end her Parliamentary status. The Ankara State Security Court wanted to prosecute her for inciting hatred and supporting terrorism, but was discouraged by her 'untouchability' status as a Member of Parliament. And, as noted above, there was a renewed effort to shut down the Virtue Party.

'Unlawfully stripped of her Parliamentary mandate'

Merve soon learned through the newspapers and from reporters that there was an effort to strip her of Turkish citizenship because she had failed to inform the Turkish authorities of her American citizenship. As noted earlier, she was asked in an interview about her dual citizenship and responded affirmatively without trying to cover it up. On hearing the rumours, she promptly contacted Cemal Sanli, an Istanbul University professor, who explained dual citizenship and its technicalities, adding that it only required informing the Turkish government as a formality. There were tens of thousands of Turkish-American dual citizens, although the exact number is unclear. According to the 2000 census more than 117,000 Americans were of Turkish descent in the USA. This figure, of course, does not include the number of dual citizens in Turkey. Like thousands of other Turkish citizens living in the US, Merve was hearing about this for the first time, so she told Cemal Sanli that she would take the appropriate action. The clause in the law concerning informing the authorities, which was initially included in the law in 1981 by the military regime, was not enforced for Turkish citizens living in America who had acquired American citizenship. Only Turks living in Germany had been informing the government because Germany did not accept dual citizenship. The Turkish government would drop the Turkish citizenship of Turks who wanted to acquire German citizenship; only after the German citizenship process was complete could the citizens apply for reinstatement of their Turkish citizenship. However, due to the different laws of the American government, the thousands of Turkish citizens living in the US could take on American citizenship and comfortably carry both countries' passports without feeling a need to inform the Turkish government. The government now selectively decided to enforce the law at the expense of Merve Kavakci.

In a statement to the press, Professor Bakir Caglar, who represented Turkey for five years in the European Court of Human Rights in Strasbourg, and who was a well-known professor and expert on constitutional law at Istanbul University, stated that the government's going after Merve Kavakci was unlawful. Mustafa Kamalak, a deputy and well-known constitutional lawyer, as noted above, also stated, and told me, that it was an obvious excuse to prosecute her and only her.

On 12 May, Prime Minister Ecevit answered reporters' questions about the rumours in the press. He said that the government had gained information from the Turkish Consulate in Houston, via the US Immigration and Naturalization Service in Dallas, that Merve Kavakci had received a green card on 2 March and became a US citizen on 5 March. Ecevit stated the government's position:

> We are facing a totally illegal situation. Even if she takes off her headscarf, it would be impossible for her to take the oath of office and legally become an official deputy ... Candidates for deputy submitted their applications to the Supreme Electoral Board [YSK] on 24 February. After filing her application to become a Turkish deputy, Kavakci became a US citizen on 5 March. While she was preparing to take an oath as a deputy of Parliament, she had already taken a US oath of allegiance.

Kavakci, he said, was supposed to inform authorities when she assumed a second citizenship but the Interior Ministry had not received any such notification from her.

This all seemed logical. How could she be a Turkish Member of Parliament while swearing allegiance to another country? It made for good press for the government and put Merve Kavakci even more on the defensive. In the public relations war, the battle for the hearts and minds in the media, this appeared to be a stunning victory for the government. An example is how the news was covered by *The Observer* in the UK:

Turkish PM Hits Back at Scarf Rebel

The female deputy who caused uproar by wearing an Islamic-style headscarf while sitting in Turkey's secularist Parliament should not be allowed to keep her seat because she is a US citizen, the prime minister, Bulent Ecevit, said yesterday.

Merve Kavakci, portrayed as a dangerous fundamentalist for wearing the headscarf – banned in many Turkish offices as a symbol of the movement to introduce strict Islamic law – took out dual nationality on 5 March, a month before her election.

'This is a completely illegal situation,' Mr Ecevit said. 'Her Parliamentary mandate is no longer valid even if she uncovers her head.' The issue has stirred deep passions in Turkey. Ankara issued a warning to Iran to stop interfering in its affairs after students in Tehran protested in support of the MP.

Officials at Turkey's election board said they were still investigating but Ms Kavakci, a member of the Islamist Virtue party, might lose her seat. Last week Turkey's chief prosecutor launched a case to ban Virtue for aiming to overthrow the secular regime and warned that Ms Kavakci could face charges of provoking religious hatred.[6]

To this day the Kemalist opposition in Turkey has adopted the catchphrase 'US citizen Merve Kavakci' when referring to her. More importantly, and unfortunately, her dual citizenship is often used as the legitimate explanation for her losing her seat in Parliament. Everything else seems to have been forgotten, from her legitimate election, to the military's threats, the lies fed to and espoused by the press, the government's campaign against her, the differential treatment of her when enforcing laws, prejudicial comments from the Prime Minister and President, and moves by prosecutors to charge her with crimes punishable by prison sentences. Decisions by the Inter-Parliamentary Union and the European Court of Human Rights ruling in her favour also seemed to have been forgotten. Too many publications that cover the history of modern Turkey are dismissive and misleading on the topic of Merve Kavakci, her treatment by the government of Turkey and the outcome of her election. *The Cambridge History of Turkey*, a monumental four-volume work, is typical in this regard and is cited here only for that reason. It views Merve Kavakci as an example of Erbakan's 'badly timed confrontational tactics' and explains the loss of her citizenship this way:

> For instance, in 1999, the female deputy Merve Kavakci, newly elected on the VP ticket, tried to take her seat in Parliament while wearing her headscarf, causing pandemonium in the chamber. When she refused to unveil, she was not allowed to take the oath of office and was escorted out. She was later stripped of her Turkish citizenship when it was discovered that she had taken out United States citizenship without informing the Turkish authorities.[7]

As we have seen, however, her candidacy was legitimate and not a confrontational tactic of Erbakan. (And she did actually take her 'seat' in Parliament; nor was she 'escorted out'.) But those departures from what really happened are minor compared to the last sentence, which has an unfortunate air of validity, and which can be found in most books and articles about this period of time in Turkey, many of which reference each other. Actually, the government misused knowledge of her dual citizenship status – which she did not hide – to selectively prosecute her, specifically to take away her citizenship, and eventually her seat in Parliament, without regard to Turkish law or its equal application, as we shall see.

The next day, 13 May 1999, with a decision that the President quickly signed, Merve Kavakci was stripped of her Turkish citizenship based on Section 25(a), on the grounds that she acquired US nationality without the prior agreement of Turkish authorities. The removal of her citizenship was one of the first decisions of Ecevit's new Cabinet, the Council of Ministers, hardly a normal administrative process for a minor regulation that was not enforced for Turkish–US dual citizens up until that time, and hardly a matter for the Prime Minister of Turkey and his ministers. The matter was referred to the Supreme Election Board in the hope that they would thus invalidate her seat in Parliament.

However, they did not.

The *Hurriyet* and *Radikal* newspapers claimed that there were other legislators in addition to Kavakci who had dual citizenship.[8] One article said that Oya Akgonenc of the Virtue Party, Tayyibe Gulek, and Ziya Aktas of the DSP were US citizens, among others. It also mentioned that two former prime ministers, Tansu Ciller and Mesut Yilmaz, were also accused of being dual citizens with the US. And Kutan complained that there were twenty other members of Parliament who held foreign passports and wanted to know why the others had not been investigated.[9] Moreover, tens of thousands of Turkish–American dual citizens similarly did not have their citizenship taken away from them for not informing the Interior Ministry.

In fact, Tansu Ciller was indeed a US citizen while Prime Minister. She became a naturalized US citizen in 1970.[10] Oya Akgonenc admitted on 20 May to being a US citizen when she was elected to Parliament for the Virtue Party at the same time as Merve Kavakci and offered to give up her seat to VP leaders.[11] It's not known exactly how many other elected officials also 'swore allegiance to America' without informing the government. No one seemed to care that Merve was being singled out, or perhaps they were afraid to object. The *Turkish Daily News* wrote a long article called 'The Kavakci Debacle' after Yuksel's bungled midnight raid on Merve's apartment (see later):

> Of course there are other known and suspected dual nationals inside the Turkish Parliament in addition to Kavakci. No one to date has been able to determine exactly how many and who these people are, nor whether each, or indeed any of them, had followed the proper administrative procedures.[12]

Interestingly, there were reports at this time of seventeen elected headscarved female municipal assembly members, mostly from the Virtue Party but also from the MHP, DYP and ANAP, who attended assemblies without uncovering. The women said they wore their scarves for religious not political reasons, to the consternation of local governors and other members. In some cases, protests broke out.[13] Newspaper articles and comments by politicos could not point to how their headscarves were unlawful.

One of the ministers who signed the document removing Merve's citizenship was Ismail Cem. One day later, when Zeki Unal ran into Cem at the Parliament elevator and commented on how surprised everybody was by his signing of that document, he replied: 'My hands were tied.' Over the course of several days, Zeki Unal took every opportunity as a member of the Budget Commission to express how this decision was against the law in their meetings, but to no avail. It only made for tense moments in the Parliament.

On 17 May, while the Supreme Election Board (YSK) met to decide whether the Cabinet's ruling about her loss of citizenship affected her election, Merve had guests at her house, including Kristeen Wood from the American Embassy, who followed the Virtue Party and knew Merve when she had headed the Foreign Relations Committee. While they were waiting, Merve received a call from her party suggesting, yet again, that she leave the country. And again she refused. They were discussing to what extent the US could intervene if Merve were in legal difficulty in Turkey; the answer appeared to be little. Then Salih Kapusuz called to tell her that the YSK was not ruling against her.

On 18 May the YSK announced that it had refused to change Merve's Parliamentary status. Sabri Coskun, Deputy Chairman of the YSK, explained the reason:

> The YSK has the authority to investigate situations that would negatively affect a person's eligibility to stand for election, and we have done that in this case, preparing a report on the matter. However, since the person in question lost her eligibility after the elections, Parliament will have to make the final decision about removing her from office. Parliament will make that decision according to Article 84 of the Constitution, which stipulates the procedures for removing a deputy from his or her seat in the legislature.[14]

The YSK thus referred the matter to Parliament, for a decision based on the following section of the Turkish Constitution:

Article 84 Loss of Membership

(1) The loss of membership of a deputy who has resigned shall be decided upon by the plenary [the entire body] of the Turkish Grand National Assembly after the Bureau of the Turkish Grand National Assembly attests to the validity of the resignation.

(2) The loss of membership, through a final judicial sentence or deprivation of legal capacity, shall take effect after the final court decision in the matter has been communicated to the plenary of the Turkish Grand National Assembly.

(3) The loss of membership of a deputy who insists on holding a position or continues an activity incompatible with membership according to Article 82 [working for the state or Ministry], shall be decided by a secret plenary vote, upon the submission of a report drawn up by the authorized commission setting out the factual situation.

(4) Loss of membership by a deputy who fails to attend, without excuse or permission, five meetings in a period of one month shall be decided by an absolute majority of the total number of members after the Bureau of the Turkish Grand National Assembly determines the situation.

(5) The membership of a deputy whose statements and acts are cited in a final judgement by the Constitutional Court as

having caused the permanent dissolution of his party shall terminate on the date when the decision in question and its justifications are published in the Official Gazette. The speaker of the Turkish Grand National Assembly shall immediately take the necessary action concerning such decision and shall inform the plenary of the Turkish Grand National Assembly accordingly.

On the surface, it appears that Parliament did not have grounds for voting to remove Merve Kavakci. She had not resigned; nor had there been a court decision against her; she didn't work for the State or Ministry; a month had not yet passed, so she had no attendance problem; and the Constitutional Court had not closed her party because of her. On 24 May lawyer deputies from the Virtue Party stated that it was impossible to deny her a seat in Parliament based on the 84th Article of the Turkish Constitution.[15]

According to Merve, the discussion in the YSK meeting regarding her was heated. Several committee members wanted to take away her seat in Parliament. Tufan Algan, the head of the committee, suggested that Merve Kavakci be called in to testify in her defence. To this suggestion, some members replied that if she came wearing a headscarf they would leave. Algan is reported to have said, 'Then leave. I will take responsibility for getting her testimony myself. Even a criminal's testimony should be taken before being judged.' Regardless of the reasons, the ball was, rightfully, passed to Parliament.

Regarding the Cabinet's decision to strip her of Turkish citizenship, Merve filed an appeal to the Council of State on 11 June 1999. She had spent weeks in preparation with Seref Malkoc, Mustafa Kamalak, her uncle, and her lawyer Salim Ozdemir.

The fourteen-page petition claimed that 'the report sent by the US State Department which caused Merve Kavakci to lose her citizenship is not an official one' and that it is not possible for the deputy to lose her citizenship according to the Citizenship Law.[16]

Section 14.2.5 of the Citizenship Law, entitled 'Loss through a decision of the authorites', states:

The *third* method is the withdrawal of Turkish citizenship from individuals because of specific actions, such as working against the interests of Turkey in a foreign country despite warnings, acquiring another citizenship without informing the Turkish authorities, working for a foreign state which is at war with Turkey, not responding to a call to military service for three months and residing abroad for more than seven years and not showing any interest in maintaining ties with Turkey.[17]

Most of the people who lost their citizenship in 2000 were those who did not return to do their military service (1,868 of 1,920); only forty-two lost it for not informing the authorities about their acquiring other citizenship. But that was after the 'Merve Kavakci affair'. The data for the years 1997 to 1999 was missing. Zeynep Kadirbeyoglu, an Assistant Professor from Bogazici University in Istanbul, did the analysis above and wrote the following to explain an increase in numbers for the years 2000 to 2005 for people who did not inform the authorities:

> The application of this rule is random at best since there are many people in this situation who have maintained their Turkish citizenship for many years. The increase in the numbers in this category cannot really be explained with the available data or information. The only possibility is the sensitization of the authorities as a result of events that led to the withdrawal of the Turkish citizenship of a Member of Parliament who had sworn allegiance to the US by becoming a citizen there prior to the elections in Turkey.[18]

I think we know at this point who this 'Member of Parliament' was. It appears that Merve Kavakci was singled out in enforcing the regulation regarding not informing the authorities. We do not have the data for 1999, but it may have been just one person. There were other members of Parliament in the same position and thousands of Turkish–US dual nationals.

On 20 September 1999, Merve's appeal was rejected: 'In upholding the government's decision, the appeals court rejected Kavakci's contention that other Turks obtained foreign citizenship without permission. Previous "improperly conducted procedures cannot be an example," the court said, according to the Anatolia news agency.'[19] Two days later the Parliament Speaker's Office, in view of the appeals court rejection, indicated it would be asking the YSK to once again decide on her status, believing that she did not fulfil one of the main prerequisites of Turkish citizenship. 'Coalition parties also reportedly believe that the debate should be settled by the YSK, so as to prevent Parliament from being involved in the controversy.'[20]

In response, Bulent Arinc, Deputy Group Chairman of the Virtue Party, stated in a press conference that only Parliament can decide to strip Kavakci of her deputy status. "'Legally, Kavakci is a deputy. [Although] she is unable to participate in the Parliamentary assembly as she has not yet taken her oath, she carries Parliamentary immunity," Arinc insisted, adding: "The attitude demonstrated by [Parliament Speaker] Akbulut is unjustified, as the speaker has no authority to decide on his own if the Parliamentary status of a deputy is valid or not.'"

Then, on 25 September, it was reported by *Anadolu News Agency* that Yildirim Akbulut, the Speaker of the Parliament, had said the following in response to rumours in the media that Merve Kavakci could be a Member of Parliament after becoming a Turkish citizen again by marrying with a Turkish national: 'Merve Kavakci will, of course, again be a deputy if the Interior Ministry sends us an official document stating that she is a Turkish citizen.' He added, 'For the time being, Kavakci is not a deputy because she is not a Turkish citizen. In accordance with the Constitution and Election Law, a person should be a Turkish citizen to be elected as a deputy,' he said. Had the Speaker forgotten that the Supreme Election Board has referred the matter to Parliament? The Parliament had not decided on her citizenship. Akbulut did not have the authority to make any of the statements he did, and he changed his position frequently. However, the statement he made about her reobtaining her citizenship seemed to provide a clear opportunity for Merve, who was in fact planning on marrying a Turkish man. But when she later petitioned Akbulut to take her oath, she received no response.

On 30 September 1999, in a speech to the Federation of American-Turkish Associations in New York, Eceivit said, 'I wish you to remain as our citizens, but at the same time the citizens of this friendly country. There is no obstacle for that in our Constitution and laws. Those who want to benefit from dual citizenship or who want to leave Turkish citizenship, have to inform the state about it and get permission. But Merve Kavakci didn't abide with that.'[21] Apparently, the worried dual citizens in the audience, and the ones who contacted the Turkish Consulate in New York and Embassy in Washington after hearing about Merve Kavakci, did not have to worry, even though they had not secured permission from Turkey. Dual citizenship seemed to be welcomed and accepted. They could apparently ask for permission after the fact; there is no evidence that anyone other than Merve Kavakci was prosecuted in 1999.

Ilnur Cevik, the independent owner of the *Turkish Daily News*, perhaps the only mainstream newspaper that tried to maintain objectivity in its reporting during this period, wrote the following about the reason given for Merve Kavakci's loss of citizenship:

> Of course this created quite a bit of furor among tens of thousands of Turks who live abroad and who have become citizens of their host countries while preserving their Turkish citizenship. None of these people had secured permission, just like Merve, but the government put them at ease, saying that Merve's case was an exception, which means, 'She misbehaved and we penalized her.' Even this explanation shows the depths of the crooked situation in our country.
>
> If the authorities feel Kavakci has done something wrong and deserves to be punished, then they should prosecute her in the proper manner and penalize her. But when we start twisting the laws and try to create special rules for individuals, then the system starts cracking ...[22]

Meanwhile, Merve Kavakci optimistically prepared for her appearance in Parliament, believing that the legal process would be followed. Merve:

> In order to take away my membership in the Parliament, this issue was to be discussed by the combined committee composed of the Justice Committee and Supreme Law Committee members regarding the 84th item of the Supreme Law and 135th through 138th items of the Parliament Internal Regulations. My defence would then be heard, and, if approved, it had to be passed on to the General Assembly. Upon coming to the General Assembly, they would be required to give me the right to defend myself, and only after that could voting take place, whereupon they could strip me of my Parliamentary membership.

Merve did not feel that Parliament would actually give her the chance to speak before them. She was correct. Since the Cabinet's decision, the Parliament's speaker steadfastly refused to follow the procedure set out by the Turkish Constitution. For example, in October, Deputy Parliament Speaker Murat Sokmenoglu said 'This issue is very clearly under the YSK's authority, and it cannot just hand it over to Parliament', which resulted in the YSK reiterating that no, since she lost her citizenship after they determined she was eligible to run and after the election, it was not in the YSK's jurisdiction.[23] Kutan and the Virtue Party agreed. Why? It will be recalled that only the DSP protested against Merve's entrance into Parliament and that a majority of Turks are practising Muslims. The MHP had claimed in their campaign during the election that they would resolve the headscarf issue 'once and for all'. Many Islamic people had voted for them on this premise and now demonstrated against them for their pressuring Nesrin Unal to remove her headscarf before entering Parliament and doing nothing to change the repressive policies of the YOK (the Education Directorate), which gave rise to demonstrations around the country at universities. In summary, the government likely did not have sufficient votes in Parliament to take away her seat, especially after Merve's reobtaining her citizenship through marriage. The True Path Party (DYP) and Motherland Party (ANAP) also had conservatives in their party. 'It is no wonder that Parliament – with the exception of the FP [VP] – is avoiding the issue like the plague.'[24]

Meanwhile, Merve prepared in September and October for her marriage to a US and Turkish citizen which would automatically result in her regaining her Turkish citizenship. He had been living in the US for twenty-five years and also had to inform the Turkish authorities that he had acquired US citizenship, which he did.

Zeki Unal went to the Ministry of Foreign Affairs for required documents for the marriage and was surprised to be told by a high-level official, 'Although we were insistent in asking for these papers many times from the American Embassy, we were not able to acquire any documents from them indicating that Merve is an American citizen.' He was confessing to the invalidity of the document that had been used as proof to strip Merve of her Turkish citizenship, which was claimed by her in her unsuccessful appeal. But it did not matter for the outcome of her appeal.

On 27 October, one day before her marriage, she got a call from a reporter. He said, 'Miss Kavakci, I thought that you should know … Today the Prime Minister submitted a document suggesting a legislative change with a note asking Parliament to "pay attention right away" which he had written and signed in his own handwriting.' She asked what kind of change in the law and he responded, 'It is about the citizenship law. Currently, when a woman of foreign origin marries a Turkish citizen, if she desires, she can then become a Turkish citizen. With this proposal, this procedure of acquiring citizenship would be postponed by three years.'

The three-year waiting period is now the law in Turkey, but it was not in 1999. It is obvious that the Prime Minister was rushing this new law through just to stop Merve from reacquiring her Turkish citizenship. Her marriage took place the following day, performed by Virtue Party Mayor of Istanbul Ali Mufit Gurtana, who also made the announcement to the press. On the morning of 29 October, Prime Minister Ecevit, unable to get the new law passed so quickly, withdrew his proposal after it was leaked to the press as 'Merve's Law'.

News of her wedding created the normal confusion. How would her newly gained Turkish citizenship affect her seat in Parliament? Parliament Speaker Yildirim Akbulut said that he had no idea, in spite of all the pronouncements he had made earlier, including how she would regain her seat, and he refused to comment further. Mustafa Kamalak, FP Deputy and constitutional lawyer, said that there should now be no obstacles to prevent her from 'assuming her legislative duties'. However, Omer Izgi, deputy chairman of the MHP, claimed that it changed nothing and would not help her. Prime Minister Bulent Ecevit incredibly said, 'Do not involve me in that issue; I am not interested.' But the press knew that the opposite was true, that in fact, 'Once word of Kavakci's imminent marriage appeared last week in Turkish newspaper headlines, Ecevit immediately submitted a proposal to Parliament requesting an amendment of the Turkish Citizenship Law.' Meanwhile, a new dress code proposal that would prevent women from wearing headscarves in Parliament was withdrawn from the agenda due to objections from the Virtue and True Path parties.[25] Parliament was reluctant to add the headscarf prohibition to the dress code. Ecevit's DSP presented the amendment three different times at the Constitutional Committee, but failed.

Merve and her husband left for a trip to Paris. The papers again presented a confusing picture of what would happen when she returned:

> Some authorities likewise maintain that Kavakci retained her status as a duly elected official despite losing her Turkish citizenship, and that only a majority vote in Parliament or a decision by the Supreme Election Board (YSK) could deprive her of her right to be a deputy. Neither of these institutions cared to deal with the issue of Kavakci's deputy status prior to her marriage, each saying that the decision to remove her deputy status was the responsibility of the other. Neither body is likely to care to tackle the issue now,

either. Therefore, it is suspected that Merve may again enter the halls of Parliament and attempt to take her oath of office, once again wearing an Islamic headscarf, once she returns from overseas.

Kavakci's attorney Salim Ozdemir applied on behalf of his client earlier this week for her to regain her employee rights with Parliament. Those rights include back wages, state lodging and a red diplomatic passport. But despite the attorney's claim that he delivered the application to the Office of the Parliamentary Speaker in person, officials from that office claim that no such application has yet reached them.

Answering press questions on the subject, Virtue Party leader Recai Kutan stated that although he knew that Kavakci had intentions of applying to regain her personnel rights with Parliament, he had no news of what action had been taken. 'I don't know anything about it. This has nothing to do with our party,' Kutan said. However, FP deputies Zeki Unal, Abdullah Gul and Seref Malkoc are said to be assisting Kavakci in her endeavours.

A lively debate can be expected in Ankara once Kavakci returns.[26]

Kutan's comment, that 'this has nothing to do with our party', represents a complete 'hands-off' attitude after six months of the controversy, and probably a reactive posture to the closure case then in process against the Virtue Party.

On 8 February 2000, the Council of State rejected an appeal against the decision of the appeals court on 20 September 1999 to expel her from Turkish citizenship 'and thus effectively closed the door permanently for her to take her seat as a Parliamentarian'.[27] That assumption, linking her loss of citizenship to her seat in Parliament, was made by the press, and perhaps was in everybody's head, but the original decision of the Cabinet referred it to the Parliament (see earlier), which has criteria to follow when removing a deputy as set by the Turkish Constitution. The Cabinet did not rule on her seat in Parliament, nor did members have a right to make that decision. Salih Ozdemir argued that the decision was purely political, that there was no dress code in the Parliamentary bylaws which Merve supposedly violated, and that their ruling against her was unjust and unprecedented. Altan Akkaya, representing the Ministry of the Interior, stated:

Kavakci took an oath in the US that she would protect the national interests of that country. Moreover, the headscarf is used as a political symbol for those who wish to replace the democratic and the secular system with Shariah law. Kavakci was also motivated by similar feelings and therefore her appeal should be rejected.[28]

Of course, all of the above arguments have no basis in fact or law, as has been discussed above.

The next day, Parliament Speaker Yildirim Akbulut said he would wait for final appeals before making a statement. He also said that the government decision to take away Merve's citizenship meant she had lost her rights as a deputy, another erroneous conclusion. Interestingly, Administrative Supreme Court Chief Justice Erol Cirakman was asked if Merve could reclaim her seat subsequent to regaining her citizenship through marriage.

> Cirakman said there are conflicting views on this issue. He said there are those who say if you marry a Turk, you automatically become a citizen, while some say you only become a citizen if this is approved by the government. However, he said in the case of Kavakci, even if her citizenship is restored by marriage, she will have to enter new elections to get into Parliament.[29]

Cirakman's comment, 'those who say if you marry a Turk', is interesting. It is very clear that up until 2003 marrying a Turk gained you Turkish citizenship automatically.[30]

The 8 February decision revoking Merve's citizenship and denying her appeal was upheld in June 2000. Two months later Merve Kavakci announced while attending a UN summit in New York that she would be applying to the European Court of Human Rights 'to win back the rights the government took from me. I am still a citizen of Turkey and a deputy in Parliament.'[31] She could only appeal for a 'correction of decision' after that.

On 15 March 2001 it was reported that 'Parliament Speaker Omer Izgi sent a note to the Parliament General Assembly pointing out that after a drawn-out trial at the Council of State, the Cabinet decision to revoke Kavakci's nationality had been legally upheld. The note stated that, as such, Kavakci was no longer entitled to be a Parliamentary deputy in Turkey.' It also noted the following: 'As her status as Parliamentary deputy has been revoked, she is no longer immune from prosecution.'[32]

Actually, Merve Kavakci was the plaintiff in the case against the Parliament seeking her seat. As noted above, there was nothing in the law regarding her citizenship decision by the Cabinet that related to her seat in Parliament. It was referred to the Election Commission, which stated that it was up to the Parliament, based on the Constitution, to make a decision. This was never done. The Parliament Speaker, without authority to do so, made his own decision contrary to Turkish law.

After his decision, all information concerning the election of Merve Kavakci was deleted from the Parliament's Data Systems and archived, as if it had never occurred.

However, Merve Kavakci found vindication outside of Turkey.

In November 2000 she met Lord Eric Avebury, a long-time advocate for human rights and member of the British Parliament. He invited her to speak in the House of Lords about her experience in Turkey. After consulting with the Queen, Lord Avebury requested that the Inter-Parliamentary Union (IPU), headquartered in Geneva, Switzerland, take up her case. The IPU is an international organization of Parliaments with 155 member countries today, including Turkey. It was established in 1889. The IPU 'is the focal point for worldwide Parliamentary dialogue and works for peace and cooperation among peoples and for the firm establishment of representative democracy'.[33]

After examining materials from both sides, the IPU held a hearing on the matter at its 105th meeting in Havana, Cuba, in March 2001. Merve was able to get a visa with short notice to attend. When she arrived she saw Turhan Alcelik and Bahri Zengin of the Virtue Party and the three had tea; however, Cavit Kavak was surprised to see her and became indignant. Apparently the Turkish delegation, led by Cavit Kavak of the ANAP and Ziya Aktas from the DSP Party, had counted on 'American Merve Kavakci' not being able to make the trip. They contacted the Turkish Embassy in the US to find out how it was possible. Later, Kavak allegedly told Zengin, 'We called the Embassy. They will inform the American government. She will see what is going to happen to her and understand. How dare she come here.'

The Virtue Party attendees were not given assignments from the head of the delegation and were kept from attending commission meetings and workshops during the IPU conference. The next day Merve testified to the human rights commission of the IPU for one and a half hours about her case against Turkey. The commission was made up of representatives from Sri Lanka, Britain, Chile, Nigeria and the Czech Republic. The Turkish delegation led by Ziya Aktas presented its defence the next day.

On 28 May 2001 Merve filed an application with the European Court of Human Rights (ECHR). The IPU ruled in her favour on 27 September 2002 and tried unsuccessfully to get redress for her from Turkey for the next five years, even after one Turkish delegation expressed their regret and criticized their predecessors, who were long gone from power in the Parliament. The IPU found that 'in no way can loss of eligibility after the election invalidate an election'; she was 'arbitrarily prevented from taking her oath'; nothing in Turkish law supports her loss of membership in the Parliament or for the President of the Parliament to make such a declaration; according to the Supreme Election Council only Parliament can revoke her seat. The IPU cited Article 84 of the Turkish Constitution, which was not followed, and noted that Article 76 of the Constitution regarding eligibility 'neither excludes persons with dual nationality from standing for election nor requires that dual nationality be disclosed'. The IPU failed to understand 'on what legal basis the President of the Turkish Grand National Assembly declared that Ms Kavakci was no longer a member of the Assembly without the latter having taken a decision to that effect'. Nor did they understand how the Council of State declared in December 2000 that she had lost her Turkish nationality when she regained it in October 1999. They concluded that she was arbitrarily prevented from being an elected representative 'without any valid legal basis ...'

As noted earlier, the IPU kept trying to settle Merve's case with Turkey. Because the AK Party, led by Tayyip Erdogan and Abdullah Gul, had come to power after the 2002 elections, the IPU assumed that Turkey would be amenable to a settlement, but the AK Party provided the same rhetoric as the original delegation and was not responsive to any settlement initiatives. Merve tried contacting Abdullah Gul, who was then Secretary of State, about this but he did not respond to her. Instead, his wife returned the call and said she would pass the information on to him. The head of the Turkish delegation to the IPU was Remzi Cetin. Merve called him also, and pleaded with him about her case. He simply told her, 'Look sister, what are you going to gain by winning this?' Bulent Arinc, who was the Speaker of the Parliament at this time, told her he had received no information about it. When she found out that Arinc was coming to Washington, where she now lived, she called him at his home in Ankara and asked to meet him when he arrived. He said no, that the media would pick it up. The IPU could also not understand Turkey's unwillingness to admit to what had happened.

Merve Kavakci was once again terribly disappointed in her former party members but should have realized that after 2 May she was a big political liability. Now that Erdogan and Gul were in power, it was obvious that there was no way they would jeopardize that by associating with her. And to this day, publicly, they do not.

The European Court of Human Rights held a hearing on her case against Turkey, along with those of Mehmet Silay and Nazli Ilicak, on 13 October 2005 in Strasbourg and concluded unanimously on 5 April 2007 that there had been a violation of Article 3 of Protocol No. 1 (right to free elections) in all three cases, awarding Merve Kavakci 4,000 euros. 'At the hearing … Merve Kavakçı asserted that the decision to close the Virtue Party was anti-democratic and the political ban imposed on her targeted all headscarf-wearing women in Turkey.'[34]

The IPU had submitted a third-party intervention to the ECHR on 4 October 2005. On 4 May 2007, the IPU made two final statements on the case:

(1) *Notes with satisfaction* the decision of the European Court of Human Rights and *decides* to close it.
(2) *Deeply regrets*, however, that Mrs Kavakci was unlawfully stripped of her Parliamentary mandate and hence her electorate deprived of representation by a person of its choice.

Yuksel and the State Security Court

Three days after Merve Kavakci's walk into the Parliament, at the height of the hysteria that swept the Kemalist establishment, Nuh Mete Yuksel of the State Security Court called for an investigation to determine if she was a member of an illegal organization. Nuh Mete Yuksel was the prosecutorial guardian for the coup process, with a history of prosecutions of those who threatened the secular state. He had a notorious reputation. For example, he sought the death penalty against three Welfare Party deputies – Ahmet Tekdal, Hasan Huseyin

Ceylan and Sevki Yilmaz – for their membership in an 'Islamic Group' [the Welfare Party] which he claimed aimed at 'overthrowing the secular order'. He brought a case against Mehmet Kutlular for articles published by an Islamic-friendly newspaper that he owned. He tried in vain to prosecute Fethullah Gulen, and leaked information to the press about one of his investigations into Tayyip Erdogan for 'subverting the secular state' for a speech he had made ten years ago.[35]

Initial reports were that Yuksel wanted a copy of Merve's 1997 speech to the Islamic Committee for Palestine in which she allegedly called for a holy war, or jihad, and claimed she had incited racial hatred on religious grounds by attempting to take her oath of office wearing a headscarf. Merve Kavakci was alleged to have said, 'Our activities constitute the jihad's political side. This is the path I have chosen for my own jihad, but my brother or sister can actively contribute to the jihad.' Yuksel also wanted the videotapes and newspaper reports as 'proof'. As noted earlier, *jihad* generally means 'struggle' and not 'holy war'. Yuksel also appealed to the court to ban Kavakci from travelling abroad.

He filed charges against her under Articles 312 and 169 of the Turkish Criminal Law, charging her with 'inciting the public to hatred or enmity based on ethnic, regional, class, or religious difference' by entering into the Parliament Hall and 'for supporting terrorism' based on what she said in a speech in a meeting set up by the Islamic Society of North America in Ohio. With these allegations, he was demanding her imprisonment for up to twelve years.

Yuksel had a problem, however, and that was Merve Kavakci's untouchable status as a Member of Parliament, which would prevent any prosecutions against her while she had this status. He stewed and waited while the Cabinet, YSK and Speaker Akbulut tossed her case back and forth without a firm conclusion. The only bright spot for him was an occasional, inconsistent statement by Akbulut that she was no longer a deputy, which motivated him to continue working on the case, but which would be contradicted a week later when Akbulut made statements that if she won her appeal she would be a deputy again. Her citizenship status also created issues. Back in May he asked the Court for Kavakci to be banned from going abroad. Finally in October he was successful. As Ilnur Cevik wrote, 'People are asking us why the authorities are not allowing a person to leave the country, especially after that person has lost the citizenship of that country simply because she was also the citizen of another country ... If we want to persecute Merve Kavakci, we should do it in a more subtle fashion.'[36]

Yuksel had often not followed judicial norms when detaining people for questioning. Staunch supporters of the coup process commended him for his actions. Now he apparently wanted to question Merve Kavakci. Towards the end of October Yildirim Akbulut stated that Merve was not currently a deputy because she had lost her citizenship, even though appeals were still being made in her case.

Yuksel sent a petition to Akbulut seeking clarification and got back a letter saying that she was not a deputy and thus was not immune from prosecution. With this 'green light', Yuksel decided to take her deposition ... at night. According to *Milliyet* he said, 'I decided to take a deposition from Kavakci after receiving a letter from Parliament Speaker Yildirim Akbulut stating that Kavakci is not a Member of Parliament. We proceed on the path we deem to be the correct one. Our path is the illuminated path of Ataturk.'[37] According to Turgut Kazan of the Istanbul Bar Association, such 'night raids' had been happening for years without any objection.[38] Perhaps for this reason Yuksel thought it was okay to not only seek her deposition at 10 p.m. but to do so with fifty or more armed security personnel from the Anti-terrorism Department. However, Yuksel made the mistake of leaking the operation to the media ahead of time.

On 13 October Yuksel succeeded in getting a ban on Merve leaving the country because of news reports two days earlier that she was supposed to be attending the general assembly meeting of the National View Party in Koln, Germany. Someone may have actually added Merve's name to the programme, however she had no knowledge of it and was thus not planning on going there. Several people called her about it, including her mother from Dallas – that's how far the news travelled. It also reached the attention of Yuksel. That seems to be why he decided to act now. Regardless, Merve was not planning on 'fleeing' Turkey, something offered to her on many occasions which she consistently refused. She spoke at similar events. Yuksel was unnecessarily rattled by the rumours, however.

Tired of hiding from the press, Merve returned to her apartment the weekend of 16 October. On 18 October, Zeki Unal stopped by because he was in the area and wanted to know how she was doing.

He was worried about the news of her travel ban. Zeki, Ravza, Merve and her grandmother were in the living room when a reporter called to inform her that the Anatolian News Agency had just reported that Nuh Mete Yuksel will be arresting her. 'What?' she said. Merve looked out of the window and saw that the street was filling with hundreds of people plus television vans topped with satellite dishes. She turned on the TV and saw that every channel had a text message scrolling across the bottom of the screen, 'Flash News! Merve Kavakci Has Been Arrested!' At that point there was a knock on the door. Merve went into the kitchen while Zeki Unal answered it. Five anti-terror policemen wanted to know if she were home. Unal said no she wasn't. They said that they would return tomorrow and left. Downstairs the crowds continued to build to more than one thousand people and many more television trucks.

By 10 p.m. Merve and her uncle remained in the house while Zeki Unal, Ravza and her daughter, Merve's daughters, her ninety-two-year-old grandmother, and Latife, one of Merve's closest friends, left the apartment. This was all recorded by the camera crews in front of the apartment house. After they left, Latife called her and whispered, 'Don't think that we came back because we forgot something' just as the doorbell rang. She added, 'Because Nuh Mete Yuksel is coming upstairs.' Merve and her uncle did not answer the bell. Yuksel banged on their heavy steel door repeatedly and screamed: 'I KNOW YOU ARE INSIDE. OPEN THE DOOR!!! OPEN UP, I KNOW YOU ARE INSIDE!!! I WILL BREAK THE DOOR, IF YOU DON'T OPEN IT!!! I AM TELLING YOU TO OPEN THIS DOOR, I KNOW YOU ARE INSIDE!!!'

The sound reverberated throughout the apartment as she and her uncle sat in the back room terrified. In Turkey, unlike America, apartment doors are not easily breached. They are usually made of thick reinforced steel with several heavy bolts on both sides making them almost impossible to knock down. Spotlights from the camera crews now shone on all the windows as Yuksel continued to bang and scream. Merve and her uncle recited the Qur'an in quivering whispers. After several minutes of his banging and yelling, she called Gul, who could not believe that Yuksel was there, and said he would come over immediately. Downstairs in Latife's car Ravza's young daughter, Erva, was telling her young cousin Mariam, 'Let's get out and beat up those police so that they won't take away my Auntie Merve.'

Meanwhile, Zeki Unal was in the hallway and he was pointed out by one of Yuksel's men. Yuksel was furious, breathing heavily, and screamed at Unal, 'I know Merve Kavakci is inside this apartment, and if you guys do not open this door, I will break it and will take her away!' He asked M. Emin Aydinbas, a former deputy who was with him, who Zeki was; then, without waiting for an answer, he ordered the policemen to throw him out of the building. Zeki Unal informed him that he was a Member of Parliament and told him, 'Mr Yuksel, you are making a mistake. You are a lawman. Merve Kavakci is still a Parliamentarian. She holds untouchable status. You cannot enter her house.' With a demeaning voice, Yuksel asked if Unal was trying to give him law lessons. Unal then blocked the door himself and said, 'You cannot open this door. You are making a big mistake.' Yuksel and the police hesitated. Yuksel calmed down a little, then said he would dictate a report. He immediately called an officer over and started dictating it. He told him to write down that he had come to Merve Kavakci's home, but he was not allowed to do his job by Parliamentarian Zeki Unal. He stated that if the door did not open in the next half an hour then he would have it opened by a locksmith. Unal insisted that it should be one hour instead of half an hour. Yuksel did not say anything. The policeman who was keeping the records made a nice gesture and changed half an hour to one hour without waiting for a response from the prosecutor. It was now 10.45 p.m. Zeki figured that he had until 11.45 p.m. to resolve the matter. Merve heard some of this from inside the door and was comforted by it. The voices stopped. She sat at the edge of the bed and thought that everything was over and the end had come. These events had worn her out, mentally and physically. She called Ravza, who was downstairs. Back in Texas her mother thought that Merve was in jail, and was crying and praying for her daughter. According to Ravza, several people were now standing in front of the door. One of her father's friends, Saim Altunbas, was among them, as were many deputies from the Virtue Party, as well as from the ANAP Party, and a thousand other people, mostly her supporters, so many that street vendors also arrived to sell snacks.

Zeki called Recai Kutan but his cell phone died, so he rushed to a pay phone and told him, 'If we don't stop this bullying in an hour, they will take Merve away.' Kutan then called Prime Minister Ecevit as well as the Minister of the Interior. The police would not let anyone in but then Aslan Polat, another deputy, showed up, out of breath, and told them that he and Zeki could go in, so the two went up the stairs, running into Yuksel on his way down. Yuksel lashed out at Polat until he found out he was a deputy, then let him continue upstairs. Bulent Arinc, Ismail Kahraman, one of Kutan's assistants, Abdullah Gul, Nazli Ilicak and all the other Virtue Party deputies that could be reached came to the apartment, a rare show of VP force and togetherness, finally.

Yuksel left but did not return as promised. Not knowing this, Merve was up all night and did not fall asleep until light came. In the morning Ravza said that the party administration had reached the Minister of Interior Affairs, Saadettin Tantan, and that he had told the police to have Merve go to the Police Station the next morning to give her testimony. Merve did not want to go and felt that it would indicate that she had no untouchable status. Nonetheless, she prepared by collecting together her toothbrush, personal copy of the Holy Qur'an, and prayer beads left to her by her grandfather. She felt the ominous prospect of a Turkish prison bearing down on her once again. The rumours of prison that had circulated in the days after she lost her citizenship in May now seemed about to be realized, with the road opening for a trial. She walked into the next room and could see that her uncle had been up all night. He told her, 'Everything is under control. It looks like Nuh Mete is not coming back.' Her uncle said that as soon as a document is received from Yildirim Akbulut confirming her 'untouchable' status, God willing, she would then be able to leave home safely. Members of the Virtue Party had angrily stormed Akbulut's office and insisted that he generate a document confirming the untouchable status of Kavakci. Although Akbulut did not want to comply with this request he eventually gave in and provided them with this document by noon that day.

Meanwhile, around 11 a.m., Murat Mercan, VP Deputy, called Merve and said that there was a high-level officer next to him from the American Embassy who said if she wished they could get her out of the country safely and fly her to Washington. She responded, 'I thank you for thinking of me, but to accept your offer is as impossible as opening my head cover in public.' Despite the previous night's raid and the possibility of jail, which she feared, she would not run away. As she waited for the document coming from the Parliament, her house began to fill up with party members, relatives, friends and other Parliamentarians. Congratulations notes were also pouring in. She called her children. Her youngest daughter, Mariam, said, 'Where are you mom? Please don't hide it from us. Mom, are you in jail?'

With the help of Bulent Arinc, Ismail Kahraman, and Vecdi Gonul, who had taken on this responsibility, the document was obtained. It specified that the case was in the hands of the Ministers of State, and even if it resulted in a decision by the Supreme Election Commission against Merve, the authority to drop Merve's Parliament membership rested with the Grand National Assembly, which required the matter be taken to the General Commission. With this document finally in hand at 1.45 p.m. a record was prepared, and Yuksel's siege was officially over, with Merve's rights to leave the country restored even though Parliament Speaker Akbulut was contradicting his previous ruling with this letter. The letter likely saved her from being arrested.

Recai Kutan called her when she arrived again at the Parliament Residences. In a joyful voice, he said that she had suffered a lot, but it had turned out very well. Merve thought that if the party had displayed the same diligent unity on the day she had entered the Parliament floor as they did in response to Yuksel's raid, then things might have turned out differently. Abdullah Gul attended some TV programmes regarding Yuksel's actions.

For Yuksel, the next day was a bad one. The 'midnight raid' had been televised and members of Parliament from all parties condemned his actions, even, surprisingly, the President and Prime Minister. Demirel said, 'This is a country which upholds the rule of law. And law-enforcers must be careful. I have duly warned them.' Ecevit said, 'Why take a step at night and not during the daytime? We had already solved the [Merve Kavakci] problem in Parliament. She will reportedly settle in the United States. Let her do that.' Deputy Prime Minister Devlet Bahceli said, 'That was an incident bound to increase tension.' The Justice Ministry opened an investigation into the matter. The papers also confirmed that Kutan's call had prompted Deputy Prime Minister Husamettin Ozkan of the DSP to ask Interior Minister Sadettin Tantan to intervene, who then ordered the Governor of Ankara to withdraw the police. It was also reported that President Demirel called Kutan twice to express his sorrow and concern about what had happened. *Yeni Safak*, the Islamic-friendly paper, said, 'Even the state became ashamed and the "attack" has been repulsed.' Kutan observed, 'They are acting in a manner to ensure that

Turkey will not be admitted into the European Union',[39] which referred to the upcoming attendance by Turkey at an EU conference. Yuksel, as noted earlier, claimed he just wanted to take her deposition and that Akbulut had told him in writing that Merve was not a Member of Parliament.

And yet, Yuksel still had his supporters. The head of the Turkish Bar Association and former Chief Justice of the Constitutional Court, Yekta Gungor Ozden, said that no one has the right to 'warn' the judiciary, referring to the comments of President Demirel. The deputy leader of the Republican People's Party (CHP) accused Interior Minister Tantan of interfering with the judiciary. And the Head of the Association of Republican Women called on 'all prosecutors and those who want to protect secularism to do their duties now. Otherwise, we will all be called to apologize to Merve Kavakci and carry her into Parliament on our shoulders.'[40] In December, the Supreme Board of Judges and Prosecutors (HSYK) issued a warning to Yuksel over the method he used to try and take the testimony of Merve Kavakci, but then reversed their recommendation based on his excellent record as a prosecutor.[41] It was not until three years later that the HSYK demoted Yuksel after a videotape was discovered showing him with a woman in a hotel room.[42]

'Our daughter Merve'

The rumour spread by Prime Minister Ecevit after the Yuksel raid that Merve wanted to live in America anyway was correct. Although by November of 1999 Merve had regained, for the moment, her Parliamentary immunity and her Turkish citizenship through marriage, she was still in a tenuous situation.

Her seat remained vacant and there was no hope that Parliament would vote on the matter as directed by the Electoral Commission. The fact that she had regained her citizenship and was a citizen when elected were ignored, as was the fact that she was not found to have violated any laws related to her election, including any provisions in the Constitution, nor the regulations of the Parliament regarding dress. At some point it seemed obvious that she would lose all appeals to the Cabinet's decision, eventually lose her seat and immunity, and be prosecuted by Yuksel – all this despite the fact that there was no legal relationship between the Cabinet's decision and her Parliament seat.

Although the Virtue Party has come to her rescue with courage and conviction during the midnight raid, their support of her generally was lacking, except for a few staunch supporters. They had passed on to her several recommendations to leave the country. Now she was not invited to Virtue Party activities except for ones with its leadership and in the Parliament complex. Even though group meetings were open to the public, she was not allowed to attend them, and she was not given any assignments or duties. And in yet another example of patriarchy or simple discrimination, Kutan met with US Ambassador Robert Seiple, head of the International Religious Freedoms Committee of the US State Department, discussing her but not inviting her to the meeting. When she told Kutan she wanted to speak to the Ambassador directly, Kutan told her, 'We've already talked to him in the Parliament.' Only after moving to America would she have her meeting with Ambassador Seiple.

The press continued to badger her. Unable to go to her home, she was still not able to secure a special Parliamentary residence for her privacy and relied on the help of Zeki Unal and his wife for living accommodation in his residence. In Turkey there were simply too many insurmountable barriers for her to live in peace.

Thus Merve Kavakci decided to return to the one country that had provided her with educational opportunities and religious freedom. She would continue her education in America, at Harvard University, receiving her MA, and at Howard University, earning her doctorate; she would teach, speak, and write for the political and religious freedoms of headscarved women.

After a bureaucratic struggle to get passports for her children, Osman Ulusoy drove Merve and their children to Anakara Esenboga Airport, a one-hour drive north of the city. Osman talked about all that had happened and mentioned some job opportunities that he had lost simply because of his association with Merve Kavakci. He told me that he did not care and would do it all over again. They knew the press would be waiting for them at the airport. She was leaving Turkey again and stared out the window at the rolling hills that ten years later would be covered with apartment blocks, but now looked barren and isolated. She thought of the campaign and the crowds, the thousands of covered women who had shouted, 'We are women, we are strong and we exist.' She had touched the sky so often when she was among her constituents before the descent into hell began, for months now. Holding back the tears was no longer possible for her.

When they reached the Departing Flights area Osman escorted them into the airport, all the way to Passport Control, where they said their goodbyes. Zeki Unal and his wife had also made the trip to the airport to offer their prayers and best wishes to Merve, Ravza and the three children, who then made their way to the gate area.

It was unusually quiet as they waited. For once, no one seemed to notice the two headscarved women and their three children in the waiting area, not an uncommon sight in Turkey. However, a bearded elderly man kept looking at them. Merve thought she had seen him at the departing area when they had entered as well. Finally, he walked over and stood before her. 'It's you, isn't it? I was looking and looking and looking, trying to figure it out. But it is you, it's our daughter Merve.' She looked back at him and her heart swelled. To feel that strong and sincere connection with this stranger was almost too much for her, this bond of faith and love, as with the people of Umraniye who had openly showed their love for her. It all came back to her, what her struggle was about, which was about their struggle. She looked at him and could barely speak. A rush of warm memories enveloped her, and the eyes of this bearded man carried her as she walked with her children through the door and up the stairs to the waiting jet. As she walked, she rejoiced to herself, 'Praise be to Allah.'

Notes

1   Umit Cizre and Menderes Cinar, 'Turkey 2002: Kemalism, Islamism, and Politics in the Light of the February 28 Process', *The South Atlantic Quarterly*, 102:2/3 Spring/Summer, 2003: 9312, p. 320.

2   Cizre and Cinar, p. 321.

3   *Ibid.*

4   'Throughout 1998 both Yilmaz and Ecevit gave vent to their irritation at the continued interference of the army in politics. Each time this happened, however, the Chief of the General Staff, General Karadayi, rebuked them and they were forced to express their support for the army publicly', Zurcher, p. 301.

5   Erik Zurcher, *Turkey: A Modern History*, IB Tauris, London, 1997, p. 310.

6   Chris Morris, *The Observer*, 13 May 1999.

7   *Turkey (Volume 4): Turkey in the Modern World*, Cambridge University Press, ed. Resat Kasaba, Cambridge, UK, 2008, p. 373.

8   'Cabinet to Discuss Fate of US Citizen Deputy Kavakci', 13 May 1999.

9 'Turkish President Strips a Muslim Parliamentarian of Citizenship', *NY Times*, 16 May 1999.
10 http://www.nndb.com/people/484/000161998.
11 *Sabah*, 21 May 1999.
12 'The Kavakci Debacle,' *Turkish Daily News*, 24 October 1999.
13 'Headscarf Issue Heats Up in Municipal and Provincial Assemblies', *Turkish Daily News*, 12 May 1999.
14 'YSK's View about Merve Kavakci', *Turkish Daily News*, 19 May 1999.
15 *Sabah*, 24 May 1999.
16 *Turkish Daily News*, 11 June 1999.
17 Zeynep Kadirbeyoglu, 'Changing Conceptions of Citizenship in Turkey', in Rainer Baubock (ed.), *Acquisition and Loss of Nationality (Volume 2): Policies and Trends in 15 European Countries*, Amsterdam University Press, 2006, p. 248.
18 Kadirbeyoglu, pp. 430–431.
19 'Council of State Refuses to Reverse Ruling to Revoke Kavakci's Turkish Citizenship', *Turkish Daily News*, 21 September 1999.
20 'YSK Expected to Decide on Kavakci's Status', *Turkish Daily News*, 22 September 1999.
21 *Anadolu News Agency*, 1 October 1999, item no. 6.
22 Editorial, *Turkish Daily News*, 16 October 1999.
23 *Ibid.*
24 *Ibid.*
25 'A New Episode in Ongoing Kavakci Crisis', *Turkish Daily News*, 30 October 1999.
26 'Merve Saga Begins Anew', *Turkish Daily News*, 12 November 1999.
27 'Supreme Court Rejects Kavakci', *Turkish Dialy News*, 9 February 2000.
28 *Ibid.*
29 'Akbulut: We'll Wait for the Appeals Process to be Completed for Kavakci', *Turkish Daily News*, 10 February 2000.
30 http://www.mymerhaba.com/Turkish-Nationality-in-Turkey-202.html.
31 'Kavakci to Appeal to European Court', *Turkish Daily News*, 31 August 2000.
32 'Merve Kavakci Loses Deputy Status', *Turkish Daily News*, 15 March 2001.
33 www.ipu.org.
34 'European Court Condems Turkey for Violating Kavakci's Rights', *Today's Zaman*, 6 April 2007.
35 'Sex Scandal Hits Staunch Prosecutor of Feb 28 Process', *Turkish Daily News*, 23 October 2002.
36 *Turkish Daily News*, 16 October 1999.
37 *Milliyet*, 20 October 1999.
38 *Turkish Daily News*, 20 October 1999.
39 All quotes are from *Milliyet*, 20 October 1999.
40 All qotes are from 'The Kavakci Debacle', *Turkish Daily News*, 24 October 1999.
41 *Turkish Daily News*, 18 December 1999.
42 'Sex Scandal Hits Staunch Prosecutor of Feb 28 Process', *Hurriyet*, 23 October 2002.

Afterword

On a warm night in July 2010 an elegantly dressed assembly of two hundred friends and relatives gathered at a restaurant in Beykoz Korusu, a park overlooking the Bosphorus on the Asian side of Istanbul. Most guests arrived by taxi and, as often happens in Istanbul, passengers and the driver got to talking. A guest asked the driver to hurry because she was going to a wedding reception. 'Whose is it?' asked the driver. He seemed like a devout man with pictures of his children in the cab, so the passenger told him. He looked in the rear-view mirror in shock. 'Really?' he said. 'My wife named our daughter after Merve Kavakci.' The passenger, who was the groom's aunt, told him that if he and his daughter wanted to meet her, they were welcome to the party. Two hours later, an eight-year-old girl walked over to Merve Kavakci Islam, dressed in an elegant purple embroidered coat specially designed by Merve's fashion designer sister in Manhattan, Elif Kavakci, and a dark blue and black headscarf. 'My name is Merve too,' said the girl. For Merve Kavakci Islam it was the greatest gift of all. She had received thousands of letters over the years, from Turkey and other countries, from parents who named their daughter after her. Each letter was an honour, each meeting of another Merve she took to heart. She tried to compose herself as she met yet another little Merve: 'I am so happy to meet you,' said the elder Merve, 'this is my husband, Nazir Cihangir Islam.'

Cihangir and Merve graduated from the same high school in Ankara and studied in the same medical school, at different times, and only met recently. Cihangir is an orthopaedic and spine surgeon also experienced in the world of politics. The son of a former Member of Parliament, he was a Virtue Party nominee in 1999. After the closure of the Virtue Party, he became a founding member of Erbakan's Felicity Party and later Numan Kurtulmus' People's Voice Party.

It seemed a lifetime since that September morning in 1994 when Merve shyly walked into the Welfare Party Headquarters building in the Balgat district of Ankara and entered a meeting of the Women's Commission, holding the hands of Fatima, four, and Mariam, three.

Her experience with the party was transformative. Throughout it all she found her voice representing the interests of women. Despite a horrific event in which half a nation attacked her, she kept that voice, her faith and her mission. Instead of representing the First Electoral District of Istanbul, she represented the interests of headscarved women and those who suffer from religious persecution and repression.

After leaving Turkey she returned briefly in June 2000 to vote for Abdullah Gul's election as the head of the Virtue Party at its convention. Gul lost, but the significant opposition to Kutan and the conservative wing of the party was a bad sign. Gul, Erdogan and others would go on to form the AK Party, which came to power in 2002. She also asked Erbakan, in a meeting with others, for monetary support for her case in the European Court of Human Rights, but almost no monies would be sent. Back in the states she was interviewed by CNN about the issue of religious freedoms around the world, including the impact of Turkish secularism on covered women in Turkey. Shortly thereafter the Prosecutor of the Sisli District of Istanbul applied to the court to open a case against her for insulting the state by claiming that covered women could not attend universities in Turkey, which was of course true at the time. Finally, notification of the loss of her Parliament seat came to her in a letter.

In 2001 she argued her case in Havana (noted in the previous chapter) at the IPU conference. Later that year while at a meeting with Karl Rove at the White House, she got a call informing her that the Virtue Party had been shut down by the Constitutional Court for 'being the source of all activities against secularism' and five people, including Merve and Nazli Ilicak, hardly members who determined policies, were banned from politics for the next five years. Interestingly, no one in the party's leadership was banned. How had Gul and Kutan escaped the wrath of the court? One theory is that they lobbied against being banned; another is that the court wanted to see the party split and therefore be weakened. Certainly, if the latter, the strategy backfired, given how the AK Party rose to power in 2002. The Court's vote was eight to three, but it ruled six to five against Virtue being an illegal continuation of Welfare, which would have resulted in sixty-nine Virtue members who were previously part of Welfare losing their seat and brought about new elections.

Then came 11 September 2001. Merve's father had lived in Richardson, Texas since 1988 as a religious leader of an Islamic Centre and had a good reputation in the area, evidenced by the fact that the police called and offered assistance and protection if necessary. There were some incidents in Fatima's school, where her teenage daughter had problems with one assistant principal who would not let Muslim students pray on school premises so she, Fatima, contacted the Justice Department on her own. The matter was settled before the students went to court. However, the media picked up the story and Fatima appeared on several TV stations, including Fox News. Both Fatima and Mariam later played for the girl's basketball team in their school wearing headscarves and long pants.

In March 2002 Merve was invited to a State Department banquet honouring women's day. After Colin Powell spoke about the US involvement in Afghanistan and the need for Afghan women to regain their rights from the Taliban regime, she cornered him to make her case for the needs of Turkish women, calling America's stance 'callous'. Uncomfortable with her comments, he responded, in a frustrated tone: 'This is Turkey's internal affair. You can't imagine the President of the US picking up the phone and calling the President of Turkey on this matter.' Merve responded, 'Why not? Sure he can. Isn't that what he does for other countries?' The result was a meeting with April Palmerlee, head of the International Women's Issues Department that Powell had built. It was the start of many similar meetings after she had settled in Washington.

In 2004 Merve's grandmother passed away. She had cared for Merve and then her daughters for so many years, right up until Nuh Yuksel Mete's raid in 1999. By happenstance, her grandmother ended up in GATA military hospital, made famous three years later when Prime Minister Erdogan's wife was not allowed entrance to visit a patient, due to her headscarf. Merve and her mother had a difficult time visiting her. Doors were often slammed in their faces. They were allowed, when at all, only a few minutes per day with her. It is an Islamic tradition to soothe a dying patient by reading verses from the Qur'an to them during their final hours. Merve was doing this in a low voice when a doctor entered with a shocked look on his face and told her to stop, that she was scaring other patients. She never got to complete her verses and her grandmother died alone the next day. The same morning of her grandmother's passing, Merve had to appear at the Ankara Criminal Court about a case opened against her, for which she would be exonerated.

In October 2005, the headscarf Merve wore when she walked into the Parliament on 2 May 1999 was exhibited in the lobby of the US Senate as part of an exhibit on religious freedom.

In 2007 Merve returned to Istanbul to speak at the International Conference on Islamophobia. In Turkey, information on hotel guests is automatically reported to the police, who came to arrest her in the middle of the night at her hotel for no apparent reason. Once again, she refused to let them in. She tried reaching Gul and Erdogan, who were out of the country. Eventually her contacts in the Justice Ministry called off the police. That same year the AK Party was re-elected with an enhanced majority of 47 per cent of the vote. The military tried but failed to block Abdullah Gul's election to President because of his headscarved wife via a threatening internet memo.

In 2008 the Parliament passed an amendment to allow headscarved women to attend universities, only to see the Constitutional Court overturn it. Then, on 30 July, the Constitutional Court voted six to five to shut down the AK Party for supporting such a law but lacked a seventh vote to make the closure stick.

Over the years Merve spoke at dozens of universities across the US and at conferences in Europe and the Middle East, as well as at the United Nations. Students at New York University, the University of Milan and elsewhere wrote master's thesis and dissertations on the 'Kavakci Affair' and she became a popular speaker on issues regarding the headscarf and religious freedom. She chose to be the voice of the headscarved girls who had no chance of being heard in America's capital. In 2010 she was named among the 500 Most Influential Muslims in the World by Georgetown University.

In autumn 2010 a memo from the YOK, the Directorate of Education, seemed to lift the headscarf ban at universities, including prohibitions on taking university entrance exams, a practice that was still banned by many university rectors. The headscarf once again dominated the media. Merve Kavakci Islam was thus interviewed on CNN Turk, the mainstream media, and treated with respect; however, she called in to another television show in which two well-known women Kemalists from the Ataturk Thought Association could not contain their sarcasm and insults. I had often asked *Today's Zaman*, for whom I was a part-time writer, if there was any interest in an article about Merve. Now there was an interest, so I interviewed her. The paper ran the interview on the front page on 31 October 2010. During that interview I asked her the inevitable question: What are your plans for running for office? Would you consider doing it again? Her reply:

> Women must be represented in higher numbers in all facets of the political machinery. Therefore I believe that more women including women with headscarves must run for office in the next election. After all, all concur that Turkey must democratize itself, and this is one way of doing it. As far as my case is concerned, I have a court decree in hand, that of the European Court of Human Rights, that states that Turkey violated free elections in the Kavakci Affair. I was ready to do my job but was never permitted to complete it. Not only was I precluded from carrying the responsibility of representing people of Istanbul but they were also stripped of their right to representation. Because the due process never took place, my seat remained vacant, leaving the constituents deprived of their representation. There is a suspended duty that needs completion.[1]

In spring 2011 the AK Party presented its list of nominees for the upcoming 12 June elections. Despite the lobbying efforts of the AK Party's headscarved women, much discussion in the media (including debate about democracy for headscarved women), and a feeble threat by a group of covered women not to take part in the elections without headscarved AK Party candidates, there were ultimately none on the AKP's candidate list.

Merve Kavakci's supporters adamantly pressed her to run as an independent candidate, but she declined. Her disappointment in the party of Erdogan and Gul ran deep, especially as she had watched secular women with few qualifications receive AK Party nominations. She seemed unable to resign herself to her 'untouchable' status in Turkey. When I initially sought out Turkish publishers for my book, from Islamic, secular and left-liberal presses, the response received was always that the Kavakci incident was a bad memory that Turkey wanted to forget. A second candidacy was thus out of the question.

However, the real reasons were much more political. Erdogan and Gul did not support her candidacy in 1999 and the reaction to her entrance into Parliament validated their position that this was a line that could not be crossed with the secular bloc. Despite their rise to power in 2002, continuing to the present, and the public's strong support for democratic reforms as evidenced by the results of the 2010 referendum for constitutional reforms, their experience in power reaffirmed the political correctness of their position. On the one hand their rise to power demonstrates the success of a party that is socially conservative, Islamic-friendly yet moderate and not Islamic-based, while being liberal economically. Turkey's economic turnaround that they led after the global recessions of 2001 has sustained them. On the other hand, they have had to endure threats over Gul's becoming President related to his headscarved wife, a threatening e-memo from the military in 2007, the revelation of Ergenekon and Sledgehammer coup plots, political murders by the deep state, the near-closure of the AK Party in 2008 because of its support for lifting the headscarf ban, and the military's boycott of President Gul's Republic Day celebrations in 2011 because his wife was present, among other threats. They were not about to jeopardize everything by crossing an obvious line.

Before Erbakan's passing in 2011 he had briefly engineered a takeover of the conservative Saadet Party. After Erbakan's passing, its new leader was Mustafa Kamalak, the person who argued with Gul in the Parliament in support of Merve Kavakci. Not surprisingly, as noted earlier, Mr Kamalak nominated headscarved candidates for the 2011 elections, without success.

Turkish democracy

I recently wrote in *Turkish Review*, 'The headscarf issue in Turkey is emblematic of fault lines that run as deep and dangerously as the geologic ones beneath the Marmara Sea, with similar, possibly cataclysmic results for Turkish Society.'[2] This line still encapsulates for me what *Headscarf: The Day Turkey Stood Still* is about. The Merve Kavakci affair exposed those fault lines as few other incidents have done in contemporary Turkish history.

Entering and researching this story for the first time, I was probably naive in thinking that uncovering new information about the incident would somehow fix matters and that I would perhaps no longer get those blank stares and an uncomfortable silence from all quarters when I conveyed what the book I was writing was about. Undoubtedly mistruths about Merve Kavakci will persist regardless of the myths that she violated the Constitution; that the Parliament threw her out; that she broke the law; that she lost her citizenship lawfully; that she lost her seat because of her loss of citizenship; that she was not really elected by the people but appointed; that she was thrown out of the country; that she supported Hamas and terrorist organizations; that she wanted to implement Islamic law in Turkey; that she was hiding her real motivations; that she is backward and not modern; that she was manipulated by outside forces – by men, by her political parties, by Erbakan, and by the government of Iran; that she wore her headscarf for political reasons; and that she was an 'agent provocateur'. I hope I have made at least a 'dent' in setting the record straight for those who are interested in knowing what really happened on 2 May 1999 and who Merve Kavakci really is.

The bigger problematic in Turkey goes beyond the facts of the Merve Kavakci affair to how the country will define democracy in the future. Kemalist doctrine has been taught in schools in Turkey for three-quarters of a century now and by law is not to be questioned. Ask an educated, secular Turk about whether or not Turkey is democratic, and you will often hear that in America democracy is based on individual rights while in Turkey it is more based on the rights of 'society' or the 'survival of the secular state'. Their view is that Turkey is democratic because it is 'secular'. That view is represented by just 38 per cent of the population, those who voted against the AK Party's recommended constitutional reforms in the June 2010 referendum. The underlying doctrine of Ataturk's revolution that implemented controls of religion in response to its perceived threat to modernism and progress in Turkey in the 1920s is under attack by the sheer force of globalization and the democratization of information in the twenty-first century. It's an increasingly difficult doctrine to defend. Indeed, Turkish secularism has become its own religion, based more on faith than anything else. Caught up in this different notion of democracy is the fact that, as John Esposito has written, 'Women's dress remains a contentious issue in Turkey, symbolizing an alternative moral/social order that many Muslim women seek within modern secular Turkish society.'[3] The secular bloc will instinctively accuse such women of not being modern, in spite of the obvious fact that they are modern. Intelligent and educated Islamic women particularly rile them because they knowingly intrude on the Kemalist 'modern secular Turkish society' that underscores their view of 'secular democracy'. But some Muslim women don't see it that way at all: 'The choice is not seen so much as one between Islam and modernity or

Islam and secularism as it is an effort to define an alternative Islamically informed model for being a modern Turkish woman, to build an Islamic way of life within a secular order,' as Mr Esposito has aptly noted. In this vein, Merve Kavakci represents for millions in Turkey 'a modern Turkish woman'.

A personal note on Turkey's red lines

The 'post-modern coup process' that began on 28 February 1997 with the military's demands of Prime Minister Erbakan to come down on Islamic activities lasted until the election of the AK Party government in 2002; however, the military as a player in Turkish politics did not end. The military intensified its efforts to manipulate Turkish politics by perceiving Islam-friendly political players and movements as 'fundamentalism and reactionism' and 'creeping Islamization of Turkey' that they defined as threats to the secular character of the regime. It should be noted, however, that the military acted as the self-appointed guardians of Turkish secularism as a means of sustaining their power in the face of the challenge of Islamic-friendly political movements, such as Erbakan's, to the Republic's paradigm. In the first election after the military's intervention along came Merve Kavakci. The military's reaction to Merve Kavakci stuck in the minds of the current leaders in Turkey, Tayyip Erdogan and Abdullah Gul, and just about everyone else in Turkey's political leadership. Dr Merve Kavakci Islam, who is a Lecturer on International Relations at George Washington University and Howard University today, has little hope of reclaiming her seat in Parliament, and even gaining a similar teaching job in Turkey may be difficult. But having covered women students begs the question: when will covered women teachers and academics join them?

Merve Kavakci stuck her foot across the red line and Turkey erupted. Arriving in Turkey ten years after the fact, and twelve years after the '28 February Process' started, I thought perhaps that I missed out on what had happened. The coup process had ended, I was told. Things had changed. I arrived during the eighth year of a government led by an Islamic-friendly party that seemed to me not to pose a threat to the secular order. On the contrary, the AK Party emphasized liberal economic development along with social conservatism, supporting close ties with the West and entrance into the European Union, while gaining a major leadership role in Middle Eastern politics, especially in light of the Arab Spring of 2011. Nevertheless, the AKP's moderate politics did not totally assuage the aggressiveness of the secular bloc nor the military's attempts at playing a political role. The military no longer tells the government what to do, directly, but the red line has not been crossed since. Perhaps I did not miss that much.

Merve Kavakci did not 'break the ice' so to speak, but instead defined exactly where that red line was located. In spite of the AK Party's solid support, some of which is reflected in the 58 per cent who voted 'yes' in its referendum for constitutional reforms in June 2010, and its victory in the elections on 12 June 2011 with 50 per cent of the vote, the line has been intact for eleven years. There are several reasons for this. The first revolves around the capacity of the Constitutional Court to shut down political parties. The AK Party had hoped that a reforming of the law which supports party closures by setting stricter standards would be on the referendum ballot; however, despite its power, the AK Party could not get the Parliament to approve that change. Gul and Erdogan were both members of the Welfare and Virtue Parties, both of which were shut down. The threat of party closure, although the make-up of the Constitutional Court has changed, is still a possibility unless the post-election government overhauls the Political Parties Law along with the 1982 Constitution, which they are currently planning.

Another reason for the 'line' being intact is that, despite the widespread discontent and activism of covered women, there is no broad political lobbying or demonstrations to have covered women represented in Parliament. There are some advocacy groups, of course, notably MAZLUMDER, the Association for Human Rights and Solidarity for Oppressed People, which advocates not only for the rights of covered women, but also for dozens of other human rights concerns in Turkey. Another organization called AKDER, Women's Rights Organization against Discrimination, has also been at the forefront of removing the headscarf ban in universities and ending other restrictions in public space led by courageous lawyers and writers like Fatma Benli, who cannot appear in court herself because of her headscarf. And there are a few rare secular advocates (like Nazli Ilicak), fearless, articulate and willing to argue with anyone on the many talk shows in Turkey and to risk prison through her columns. On the other hand, secular women's groups continue to ignore the concerns of Islamic women, and

Islamic men are at the very least conflicted on the subject. Covered women themselves will need to be more organized politically and perhaps promote their own independent candidates irrespective of their 'loyalties' to male-centred conservative parties to make an impact, but that does not appear likely.

After its victory in the 2011 elections, Tayyip Erdogan's government is writing a new Constitution to finally break from the one created in 1982 by a coup government. Will the new Constitution provide unfettered religious freedoms, remove employment restrictions for covered women, provide clear enunciation of civil and political rights, and ensure civilian control of the military? I have my doubts, based on the fact that candidates for election in 2011 spent hardly any time detailing and debating their positions regarding the new Constitution, and that few groups are visibly arguing for such provisions.

But by far the biggest stumbling block to Turkey's democratization and establishment of individual rights in Turkey, which prevents the line from being crossed, is the Turkish military. Yes, many issues regarding its internal management and role in Turkish politics have been put on the table in the last couple of years, but that really is the fault of the military itself, whose emails, websites, communications and disrespect for the headscarved wives of the President and Prime Minister (which could possibly be tolerated) have evolved into outrageous coup plotting and threats against the government, with hundreds of people, including generals and active officers, under arrest. Incredibly, the military also has open allies, including the Republican People's Party, which nominated, and got elected, people charged for taking part in the coup planning. The AK Party was forced to seek more civilian control over the military, not simply because of the principle of civilian control of the military and its being common in Western democracies. The other pressure on the military comes from the EU if Turkey is ever to become a member, although opposition from key founding states, like France, still stands in its way.

However, the Turkish military remains a world in itself. Its members live in isolation from the rest of the country, with their own movie theatres, schools, apartments and social life. It refuses to police or rid itself of anti-democratic forces from within; its education and promotion systems are still not subject to inspection and are barely monitored by the government (it recently stopped a prosecutor with a search warrant for Ergenekon coup-planning materials from entering the Third Army Command); and it still controls its own budget. Although gradually being dismantled, the Turkish armed forces keep a tutelary regime by maintaining a separate military judiciary and the Chief of the General Staff is still not subordinate to the Minister of Defence, something that does not align with the practices in America and European countries for many years. Many more measures need to take place for the military to truly retreat from politics.[4]

It appears likely that the position and the nature of the red line will only change when military reforms are enacted and a new Constitution is approved and implemented. Will such a Constitution be thrown out by the Constitutional Court? Will the military act in aggressive opposition to a new Constitution? Will the red line still stand or be crossed? No one knows for sure and, of course, there are strong opinions on both sides.

Also, Turkey's chronic issue regarding the treatment of its Kurdish population, 15 million citizens, continues. It presents a massive challenge to the AK Party to resolve, an issue that threatens the stability of its democracy.

On the fifteenth anniversary of the 28 February coup Merve Kavakci was again back in the headlines, informing the public that she was opening a court case to gain her reinstatement in the Parliament, lost compensation, pension and lost privileges. The Deputy General of CHP stated that his party did not oppose a headscarved deputy but seemed uninformed of the circumstances preventing Merve to take her oath of office. No major party indicated their plans to nominate a covered candidate in the future.

Finally, there are two ways to look at Turkey. One is within the context of the Middle East, where it shines with a stable and no-longer fragile democracy, a booming economy, and an increasingly respected leadership position. On the other hand, from a Western perspective, there are clear fault lines created by an aggressive secularism that takes away religious freedoms, particularly in employment, and qualified rights that continue to hover over journalists and academics. Which perspective is the most valid? Turks will have to face these and other issues in the coming years, which incidentally will determine not only if Merve Kavakci Islam or another covered woman ever walks into the Turkish Grand National Assembly and actually serves her constituents, but also if headscarved women will truly be enfranchised and be able to represent themselves in significant numbers.

Notes

1   *Today's Zaman*, 31 October 2010, p. 1.
2   Richard Peres, 'The Headscarf Conflict in Turkey: As Deep as the Marmara', *Turkish Review*, Volume 1, Spring 2011.
3   Foreword of Merve Kavakci Islam, *Headscarf Politics in Turkey: A Post Colonial Reading*, Palgrave Macmillan, New York, 2010, p. xv.
4   For a good brief discussion of this point, see an interview with Umit Cizre in *Today's Zaman*, 20 February 2011.

Glossary

AK Party (Adalet ve Kalkınma Partisi): Justice and Development Party. Led by Tayyip Erdogan, the AK Party has been in power since 2002 in Turkey.

ANAP (Anavatan Partisi): Motherland Party. Founded by Turgut Özal in 1982, merged with the Democratic Party in 2009.

Anatolia: formerly known as Asia Minor, the part of Turkey located in the East.

Atatürk, Mustafa Kemal: the founder of the Turkish Republic and its first president until his death in 1938.

Başörtüsü: the common term for 'headscarf' in Turkish.

Besir, Atalay: former Virtue Party Deputy, now Minister of Internal Affairs.

Bir, General Çevik: former Deputy Chief of the General Staff and one of the leaders of the 28 February coup.

Byzantine Empire: known as the Eastern Roman Empire, led by Emperor Constantine starting in 324 until the fall of Constantinople (now Istanbul) in 1453.

Caliphate: the government in Islam that represents all Muslim people (ummah). Caliph Abdülmecid II was the last representative of the Caliphate, which was abolished in 1924 by Atatürk. Its powers were then transferred to the Turkish Parliament, ending almost 1,300 years of its existence, the last 400 of which were under the rule of the Ottomans.

Camii: mosque in Turkish.

Çarşaf: literally meaning 'sheet' in Turkish it is also known as *chador* (Arabic), and refers to the black covering used to completely cover an Islamic woman from head to toe with an opening for the eyes and sometimes the face. It is practised by a small minority of women in Turkey.

CHP (Cumhuriyet Halk Partisi): Republican People's Party, the first political party in Turkey, which ruled with little opposition until 1950. Currently it is the main opposition party in Turkey.

Çiçek, Cemil: the current Deputy Prime Minister of Turkey and a former deputy of the Virtue Party nominated as the new Speaker of the Parliament after the June 2011 elections.

Çiller, Tansu: Turkey's first woman Prime Minister from 1993 to 1996 and Deputy Prime Minister in the Erbakan-led coalition government, 1996 to 1997.

Danıştay: the Turkish Council of State, the highest administrative court in Turkey.

Demirel, Süleyman: President of Turkey from May 1993 to May 2000. Prior to that period he had a long political career and was Prime Minister seven times.

DSP (Demokratik Sol Parti): Democratic Leftist Party, was founded in 1985 by Bülent Ecevit through his wife, Rahşan, because he was banned from politics after the 1980 coup.

Dilipak, Abdurrahaman: a conservative intellectual, writer and journalist who has had many conflicts with the courts in Turkey because of his views.

Directorate (or Presidency) of Religious Affairs (Diyanet İşleri Başkanlığı): established in 1924 after the caliphate was abolished. It sets religious policies in Turkey, including control over construction, religious instruction and the content of sermons, and has a budget of approximately one billion dollars. More information can be found at www.diyanet.gov.tr.

DP (Demokrat Parti): Democratic Party, defeated the Republican People's Party in 1950, ending one-party rule in Turkey. Its first leader, Adnan Menderes, became Prime Minister.

DYP (Doğru Yol Partisi): True Path Party, founded in 1983 by Süleyman Demirel. It merged with the ANAP in 2009.

Ecevit, Bülent: Prime Minister of Turkey four times, first as a leader of the CHP and later of the DSP.

Eraslan, Sibel: a lifelong advocate of women's and human rights, writer, and graduate of Istanbul Law School.

Erbakan, Ecmettin: Prime Minister of Turkey from 1996 to 1997, founder of the *Millî Görüş* (National View) organization and manifesto, the National Salvation Party, and Welfare Party (*Refah Partisi*). He was the foremost Islamic political leader in modern Turkey. He died on 27 February 2011.

Erdoğan, Recep Tayyip: currently in his third term as Turkey's Prime Minister, he has been the leader of the AK Party since 2001. He was elected mayor of Istanbul in 1994 as a member of the Welfare Party.

Ezan (Arabic): the Islamic call to prayer issued five times a day from minarets, most often from loudspeakers today.

Fez: is a cylindrical, red felt hat common in the Ottoman Empire in the nineteenth century as a symbol of modernity. It was legally banned in Turkey in 1925, viewed by Atatürk as Greek and anti-modern.

Fundamentalism: originally a movement by Presbyterians in the United States more than one hundred years ago. Today it is often used with negative connotations to describe strict belief in a religion which goes back to its root principles.

Gül, Abdullah: the current President of Turkey and its first devout Muslim President. His wife, Hayrünnisa Gül, wears a headscarf. His initial election was held up by the Constitutional Court in 2007. He was previously elected to Parliament with the Welfare and Virtue parties.

Gurtuna, Ali Mufit: appointed mayor of Istanbul in 1998 with Tayyip Erdoğan's imprisonment and was elected mayor in 1999, serving until 2004.

Hafiz (Arabic): a person who has completely memorized the Qur'an. Memorization was the main way in which the Qur'an was originally conveyed, since Arabic writing was not completely developed in the seventh century. A *hafiz* is highly respected in the Islamic community.

Hijab: means curtain or cover in Arabic and 'refers to both the head covering traditionally worn by Muslim women and modest Muslim styles of dress in general' (wikipedia.org/wiki/Hijab). It has been used to refer to Islamic headscarves, although that is not its direct meaning.

Holy Qur'an: the main religious text of Islam and considered by Muslims to be the word of God.

HSYK (Hâkimler ve Havcılar Yüksek Kurulu): the Supreme Board of Judges and Prosecutors responsible for the administration of the judicial branch in Turkey.

Ilicak, Nazli: a well-known writer and journalist who has consistently advocated for human rights and freedoms in Turkey.

İmam: the person who leads a mosque or Islamic community in worship.

İmam Hatip Lisesi: vocational schools originally created to educate imams, although they have a similar curriculum as regular high schools. They were popular with preacher students and parents until restrictions were placed on their graduates. Prime Minister Tayyip Erdoğan is an Imam Hatip graduate.

Islamic: describes a person who believes in Islam or anything that is associated with belief in Islam.

Islamist: adherents of political Islam (Islamism), or a diverse set of ideologies that view Islam as also a political system uniting all Muslims around certain goals and political beliefs and, to varying degrees, the enforcement of shariah or Islamic law. There is little agreement on the definition of Islamism as described by Islamic intellectuals and leaders from various countries, cultures and eras.

Kamalak, Mustafa: constitutional law professor, past deputy of the Virtue Party and now leader of the Saadet (Felicity) Party.

Karamollaoglu, Temel: a leader in the Welfare and Virtue Party.

Kavakci, Ravza Kan: the sister of Merve Kavakci.

Kemalism: a loosely defined ideology based on the reforms and policies of Mustafa Kemal, whose six tenets are republicanism, populism, secularism, revolutionism, nationalism and statism. Its current interpretation and application is subject to considerable debate in Turkey.

Kurdistan Workers' Party (Parti Karkerani Kurdista): (PKK) a militant organization that has been fighting in Turkey for an independent Kurdistan and more political and cultural rights for Kurds.

Kutan, Recai: the head of the Virtue Party and after its closure the head of the Felicity Party until 2008.

Laicism (laiklik in Turkish): coming from the French *laïcité*, means secularism. Kemalist secularism opposes Islam on the grounds that it is anti-modern and bans the presence of religious symbols in the public sphere. Turkish secularism should not be compared to America's advocacy of separation of 'church and state' combined with religious freedom of expression.

Menderes, Adnan: Turkish Prime Minister 1950–1960, hanged by the military after the 1960 coup.

MGK (Milli Güvenlik Kurulu): National Security Council, which sets security policies. Today civilians are in the majority within the

MGK, which consists of the Chief of Staff and four force commanders from the military, and the President and Prime Minister, plus several other ministers of the government. As a result of reforms approved by Parliament beginning in 2003, the military's political role and authority over civilian institutions has been lessened.

MHP (Milliyetçi Hareket Partisi): Nationalist Movement Party, which was founded by Alparslan Türkeş in 1965. Its political views are ultra-right-wing. Türkeş was one of the officers who staged the 1960 coup.

MÜSİAD (Müstakil Sanayici ve İşadamları Derneği): Independent Industrialists and Businessmen's Association; an Islamic-friendly NGO representing 15,000 companies and more than 17 billion dollars in export revenue for Turkey.

National Order Party (Milli Nizam Partisi): founded by Necmettin Erbakan in 1970 and adopted his National View (Milli Görüş) Ideology.

Ocalan, Abdullah: leader of the militant Kurdistan Workers Party (PKK), captured in 1999, tried and sentenced to life.

Ottoman Empire: also known as the Sublime Ottoman State, lasted more than 600 years, and at one time included a vast territory from the Eastern edge of the Arabian Peninsula to the walls of Vienna. Its capital was Constantinople, now Istanbul. It was dissolved with the rise of the Turkish Republic, and officially ended on 24 July 1923 with the Treaty of Lausanne.

Özal, Turgut: a highly popular Prime Minister of Turkey from 1983 to 1989, and President, from 1989 until his death in 1993. He is widely credited with liberalizing Turkey's economy.

Özkan, Hüsamettin: Deputy Prime Minister during the last Ecevit administration.

Shariah: the religious law of Islam, coming from the Qur'an, examples set by the Prophet Muhammad and other sources, but also refers to how those who believe in Islam should conduct themselves. There is considerable disagreement among Islamic people on the interpretation of Shariah and how it should be implemented in contemporary societies at the governmental level, if at all.

Turban: headscarf in Turkish but with negative connotations, as compared to *başörtüsü*.

Turkish Grand National Assembly (Türkiye Büyük Millet Meclisi): often referred to simply as the *Meclis* (Parliament), it is the central hall where discussions and voting takes place, and where Merve Kavakci entered to take her oath of office.

TÜSİAD: Turkish Industry and Business Association; this is the largest business association in Turkey, founded in 1971. It now represents 2,500 companies and about 65 per cent of Turkey's industrial production. While it advocates neo-liberal economic policies and democratization, its membership companies are generally not Islamic-friendly.

Ummah: an Arabic word referring to the diaspora or global community of Islamic people.

Ünal, Nesrin: an MHP deputy who removed her headscarf before taking her oath in Parliament on 2 May 1999.

Ünal, Zeki: a Virtue Party deputy and supporter of Merve Kavakci.

VP (Fazilet Partesi): Virtue Party. Founded in December of 1998 as a successor to the closed-down Welfare Party. It too was closed by the Constitutional Court in June 2001.

WP (Refah Partisi): Welfare Party. Founded by Necmettin Erbakan in 1983 as a successor to the National Order party and National Salvation Party. It was closed by the Constitutional Court in 1998.

Wuda (Arabic): refers to washing of parts of the body in water before prayer. Mosques in Turkey, and other public places, including restaurants and universities, have rooms set aside for this purpose.

Yılmaz, Ahmet Mesut: leader of the ANAP party and Prime Minister in Turkey three times during the 1990s.

YOK (Yüksek Seçim Kurulu): Higher Education Board (or Council); this was established in 1981, after the 1980 military intervention, to control higher education, including all 140 Turkish universities, public and private.

YSK: Turkey's Supreme Election Board, which is responsible for administering and certifying all elections.

Index

courses on, 18
Hafız al-Qur'an, 22, 93, 149,
   208–9
prayers recited by Merve Kavakci,
   125, 128, 157
use by Merve Kavakci, 37

racist nationalism, 23
Radikal (newspaper), 76, 86, 108,
   186, 219
radio broadcasts, religious, 18
radio stations, seen as reactionary, 45
Ramazanoglu, Yildiz, 72
religion
   control of in Turkey, 3, 4, 6, 14,
      15, 18, 19
   popular, 16
   religious education in schools, 17
   religious Islamic women, 1, 10
   religious people, 7–8
   religious radio broadcasts, 18
   state attitude towards, 21
religious courts, abolition of, 16
religious freedom
   American view of, 3
   Merve Kavakci on, 214, 244
   Turkish view of, 3, 215
   and the Virtue Party, 214–15
   and the Welfare Party, 37
religious orders (*tarikats*), suppression
   of, 16
religious schools
   abolition of, 15, 16
   opening of, 18
   see also İmam Hatip Lisesi
Rove, Karl, 244
Rubin, James, 201
Rumeli-Hasari, Castle of, 12

Saadet (Felicity) Party, 57, 103, 133
Sabah (newspaper)
   on 1999 election results, 98
   attitude towards Merve Kavakci,
      151, 185, 186, 215

bias towards the military, 75–6
criticism of Erbakan, 186–7
criticism of Septioglu, 186
on Erbakan meeting with
   el-Qaddafi, 41
on headscarves in Parliament, 99,
   108
Nazli Ilicak column, 74
on the Virtue Party, 104
Sahin, Helin, 153
Sahin, Leyla, 21
Sahin, Mehmet Ali, 157, 163
Sanli, Professor Cemal, 210, 216
Savas, Vural, 91, 154, 189
schools
   banning of headscarves in, 28
   changes to curricula, 45
   religious education in, 17
   see also İmam Hatip Lisesi
script, use of Latin, 15
Second World War, 153
secular bloc, 5–6, 118, 202, 247,
   249, 251
secular Turks, 6, 11, 43, 135, 249
secularism
   aggressive, 6, 19, 21, 28, 30, 43,
      90–1, 253
   embedded in the Turkish
      Constitution, 3, 46
   intensification of issue in 1950s,
      18
   as its own religion, 201, 249
   Merve Kavakci on, 84
   military as protector, 110, 250
   NSC directive, 161
   violations of, 4, 45, 87, 110, 129,
      244
secularists
   attitude towards the headscarf, 20,
      21, 63
   current attitude towards Kavakci,
      10
secularization
   of education, 15

[274]